# THEMES AND TRANSFORMATIONS IN OLD TESTAMENT PROPHECY

## SAMUEL A. MEIER

IVP Academic

An imprint of InterVarsity Press
Downers Grove, Illinois

InterVarsity Press
P.O. Box 1400, Downers Grove, IL 60515-1426
World Wide Web: www.ivpress.com
E-mail: email@ivpress.com

InterVarsity Press® is the book-publishing division of InterVarsity Christian Fellowship/USA®, a student movement active on campus at hundreds of universities, colleges and schools of nursing in the United States of America, and a member movement of the International Fellowship of Evangelical Students. For information about local and regional activities, write Public Relations Dept., InterVarsity Christian Fellowship/USA, 6400 Schroeder Rd., P.O. Box 7895, Madison, WI 53707-7895, or visit the IVCF website at <www.intervarsity.org>.

All Scripture quotations, unless otherwise indicated, are the author's own.

Design: Cindy Kiple

Images: the prophet Isaiah, Sistine Chapel: Erich Lessing/Art Resource, NY
the prophet Jeremiah, Sistine Chapel: Erich Lessing/Art Resource, NY
lines from the Dead Sea scroll: Erich Lessing/Art Resource, NY

ISBN 978-0-8308-1768-9

Printed in the United States of America ∞

Library of Congress Cataloging-in-Publication Data

Meier, Samuel A.
   Themes and transformations in Old Testament prophecy / Samuel A.
   Meier.
       p. cm.
   Includes bibliographical references and index.
   ISBN 978-0-8308-1768-9 (pbk.: alk. paper)
   1. Prophecy. 2. Prophets. 3. Bible. O.T.—Criticism,
interpretation, etc. I. Title.
   BS1198.M45 2009
   224'.06—dc22

                                                                    2009000468

| P | 21 | 20 | 19 | 18 | 17 | 16 | 15 | 14 | 13 | 12 | 11 | 10 | 9 | 8 | 7 | 6 | 5 | 4 | 3 | 2 | 1 |
| Y | 27 | 26 | 25 | 24 | 23 | 22 | 21 | 20 | 19 | 18 | 17 | 16 | 15 | 14 | 13 | 12 | 11 | 10 | 09 | | | |

For my wife,

*ʾēšet ḥayil māṣāʾtî*

# CONTENTS

# ABBREVIATIONS

| | |
|---|---|
| AB | Anchor Bible |
| AOAT | Alter Orient und Altes Testament |
| BZAW | Beihefte zur Zeitschrift für die alttestamentliche Wissenschaft |
| CBQMS | Catholic Biblical Quarterly Monograph Series |
| CEV | Contemporary English Version |
| *COS* | W. W. Hallo & K. L. Younger, *Context of Scripture.* Leiden: Brill, 2000 |
| Dtr | Deuteronomistic |
| FAT | Forschungen zum Alten Testament |
| GKC | Gesenius, Kautsch, Cowley |
| HKAT | Handkommentar zum Alten Testament |
| *HTR* | *Harvard Theological Review* |
| *JBL* | *Journal of Biblical Literature* |
| JPS | Jewish Publication Society |
| *JSOT* | *Journal for the Study of the Old Testament* |
| JSOTSS | Journal for the Study of the Old Testament, Supplement Series |
| KJV | King James Version |
| LBH/OTS | Library of Hebrew Bible/Old Testament Studies |
| LXX | Septuagint |
| MT | Masoretic Text |
| MVAG | Mitteilungen der Vorderasiatisch-ägyptischen Gesellschaft |
| NAB | New American Bible |
| NASB | New American Standard Bible |
| NEB | New English Bible |
| NCV | New Century Version |

| | |
|---|---|
| NIV | New International Version |
| NJB | New Jerusalem Bible |
| NJPS | New Jewish Publication Society translation |
| NLT (se) | New Living Translation (second edition) |
| NRSV | New Revised Standard Version |
| OBO | Orbis Biblicus et Orientalis |
| OTL | Old Testament Library |
| REB | Revised English Bible |
| RSV | Revised Standard Version |
| SAA | State Archives of Assyria |
| SBL | Society of Biblical Literature |
| SBLMS | Society of Biblical Literature Monograph Series |
| STDJ | Studies on the Texts of the Desert of Judah |
| TNIV | Today's New International Version |
| *VT* | *Vetus Testamentum* |
| VTS | Vetus Testamentum Supplements |

# 1

# INTRODUCTION

AN OLD AND INSIGHTFUL RABBINIC OBSERVATION compares the accounts of two prophets, Isaiah and Ezekiel, who wrote that they had seen God. The observation centers upon the fact that the written records of Isaiah's and Ezekiel's encounters with God could hardly be more different. Isaiah in four brief verses succinctly describes God seated on his throne with an entourage of winged seraphim thundering the majesty of God (Is 6:1-4). A far more verbose Ezekiel spills out twenty-five verses (Ezek 1:4-28) that elaborate details far beyond the brief schematization that Isaiah provides. One account is six times as long as the other, and yet Rabba, a fourth-century Babylonian rabbi, observed that each prophet saw the same panorama. Why the difference, he asked? Rabba explained that Ezekiel was like a fellow from the country who had seen the king and had to confirm that fact with appropriate detail to his rustic companions. Isaiah, on the other hand, behaved more like a seasoned urbanite who had seen the king, relating to more savvy fellow city-dwellers for whom the details were not necessary.[1]

The prophets are not uniform in their language, their concerns, their

---

[1] *b. Hagiga* 13b.

personalities, their remedies or their visions of the future. It is too easy to gain a cursory acquaintance with the prophetic books of the Old Testament and assume a continuity that is not really there. Although the prophets as a whole share much, each prophet makes a distinctive contribution. In many ways, Rabba's observation and attempt to explain the contrast between Isaiah and Ezekiel is the starting point for the chapters that follow. The pages below are an attempt to explore further why some prophets behave in ways that differ from others.

In particular, this study will scrutinize certain features of the prophets that run throughout the prophetic books like leitmotifs. Because the prophets were not static icons but humans whose personalities and concerns adapted to the changing centuries, these themes undergo a variety of permutations. The themes that we will investigate are at the core of the prophetic world, and consequently their changes reflect fundamental shifts in the very nature of the prophet's mission. These issues are so fundamental that they are often overlooked as essential in traditional introductions to the prophets. It is a short step from the essential to what is taken for granted, and this study aims to retrieve the vision of the former in prophetic studies.[2]

As a result, although this book is intended for experienced readers of the Bible, it is also appropriate for those reading the prophets for the first time. On the other hand, if you read the following pages in order to find out more about the time in which Isaiah lived, you will be disappointed. If you hope to discover more about Jeremiah and how scholars view the composition of his book, you are advised to go elsewhere.[3] These concerns are not the focus of these pages. Rather, if you find of interest how the books of Isaiah or Jeremiah are situated among other prophetic texts with respect to

---

[2]The fact that there are changes in the prophetic institution over time is well-documented (e.g., William M. Schniedewind, *The Word of God in Transition: From Prophet to Exegete in the Second Temple Period,* JSOTSS 197 (Sheffield, U.K.: Sheffield Academic, 1995). Jewish tradition long ago affirmed that prophecy even came to an end after Malachi (e.g., *b. Sanhedrin* 11a; cf. *b. Bava Batra* 12a). The stress in the pages that follow, however, will be upon transformations within common themes that are found in the biblical corpus.

[3]Helpful resources for general perspectives on the prophets include Robert P. Gordon, ed., *"The Place Is Too Small for Us": The Israelite Prophets in Recent Scholarship,* Sources for Biblical and Theological Study 5 (Winona Lake, Ind.: Eisenbrauns, 1995), for a collection of central and defining articles.

certain crucial, overarching themes that pervade the prophets and what variations or unique perspectives are contributed by each, then the following chapters will encourage you in a direction you want to go.

Over the last century, biblical scholarship has commonly focused part of its prophetic research upon identifying successive strata within the prophetic books, from the original words of a prophet to scribal modifications, from explanatory expansions by subsequent disciples to interpolations from dissonant perspectives. There is no question that the prophetic literature has developed in this way, as the texts themselves indicate (e.g., Jer 36:32; 51:64 with Jer 52 appended from 2 Kings 24:18–25:30). But ferreting out all levels with confidence is by definition a task that tapers off into speculation. When two scholars such as Hans Walter Wolff and Shalom Paul affirm contrary positions on the book of Amos in this regard,[4] the former seeing extensive editing throughout and the latter seeing an essentially unitary whole, one is cautioned against any undue confidence at this stage in prophetic research. Although such questions have their place, they have little place for the most part in the following pages where the quest is for the continuity of prominent prophetic themes.

As a result, in the pages that ensue we will follow the broadest consensus with respect to the activities of the various prophets.[5] Thus, we will assume that in the eighth century B.C. Amos and Hosea addressed primarily the northern kingdom of Israel before it was destroyed by Assyria in 722 B.C., much as Isaiah[6] and Micah addressed the southern kingdom of Judah. A handy acronym to remember these four approximate contemporaries is the name "Micah" itself: M for Micah, I for Isaiah, A for

---

[4]Hans Walter Wolff, *Joel and Amos* (Philadelphia: Fortress, 1977) and Shalom Paul, *Amos* (Philadelphia: Fortress, 1991), both appearing in the same series (Hermeneia) and both simultaneously in print as of this writing (the former being a translation from a German volume published in 1975).

[5]Among less idiosyncratic recent Old Testament Introductions that one can consult for the following generalizations, see Michael D. Coogan, *The Old Testament: A Historical and Literary Introduction to the Hebrew Scriptures* (Oxford: Oxford University Press, 2005).

[6]The vacillating fortunes of the book of Isaiah at the hands of scholars have of late focused upon its unity, in particular the final form of the text, without denying the many layers that have gone into its production, but simply recognizing a new priority in investigating the text (cf. Rolf Rendtorff, "The Book of Isaiah—A Complex Unity: Synchronic and Diachronic Reading," pp. 109-28 in *Prophecy and Prophets: The Diversity of Contemporary Issues in Scholarship*, ed. Yehoshua Gitay, SBL Semeia Studies [Atlanta: Scholars, 1997]). We will assume a distinction between Isaiah 40–66 and the chapters that precede them.

**Table 1.1**

| 800 B.C. | 700 B.C. | 600 B.C. | 500 B.C. | |
|---|---|---|---|---|
| Amos | Habakkuk | Haggai | Malachi | |
| Hosea | Zephaniah | Zechariah | | |
| Micah | Jeremiah | | | |
| Isaiah | Ezekiel | | | |

Amos and H for Hosea (one can posit the intervening C as the Country that divides the pairs, the first two addressing their messages to the southern kingdom of Judah and the last pair addressing the northern kingdom of Israel).

Similarly, we follow a general consensus in this book that Habakkuk, Zephaniah and Jeremiah are active a century later in the southern kingdom of Judah at the end of the seventh century B.C. At the beginning of the sixth century B.C. Jeremiah continues to function as a prophet in Jerusalem at the same time that Ezekiel is at work in Babylon, both prophets continuing their activity even after the Babylonians destroy Jerusalem and the kingdom of Judah in 586 B.C.

When the Persians dominate the Near East in the latter half of the sixth century, the prophets Haggai and Zechariah[7] are active in a reviving Jerusalem. The book that bears the name Malachi represents a time subsequent to Haggai and Zechariah, and is generally placed in the fifth century (or very late sixth century). The matter of dating the oracles in Joel and Obadiah is slippery, and as a result no stance will be assumed on that subject.

These prophets who have just been listed all have discrete books associated with their names. It will be customary in the following pages to refer to such prophets and their books as the "literary prophets." This is a convenient epithet by which to identify what is known in Hebrew Bibles as the "Latter Prophets." These prophetic books are sometimes further refined into the categories "Major Prophets" and "Minor Prophets," "major" because they are large in size (i.e., the 66 chapters of Isaiah, the 52 chap-

---

[7]The relationship of the oracles in Zechariah 9–14 to the first eight chapters of the book is problematic. For a concise summary of the issues, see David Petersen, *Zechariah 9–14 and Malachi* (Louisville, Ky.: Westminster John Knox, 1995), pp. 3-6; for a more detailed treatment, see Mike Butterworth, *Structure and the Book of Zechariah*, JSOTSS 130 (Sheffield, U.K.: Sheffield Academic, 1992). Consequently, these chapters will be treated distinctly below.

ters of Jeremiah and Ezekiel's 48 chapters), while the minor prophets are so named not because they are insignificant but because they are by comparison smaller in size (the largest of these twelve books, i.e., Hosea and Zechariah, contain fourteen chapters). Because the arrangement of material by size is a frequent template in antiquity for ordering material in book form, one can not expect the literary prophets to appear in a chronological sequence. This principle of arrangement by size appears, for example, in the ordering of Paul's letters in the New Testament, the Suras of the Qur'an and tractates within the six orders of the Mishnah and Talmud, where the largest appear first and the smallest appear last (with exceptions, of course), regardless of content or date of composition. Consistent with such ordering, the three largest literary prophets (Isaiah, Jeremiah and Ezekiel) are grouped together before the smaller twelve Minor Prophets, even though many of the Minor Prophets contain material that is prior to Jeremiah and Ezekiel.

In contrast to the literary prophets, there are a number of prophets about whom we have stories but whose names are not associated with any discrete collection of oracles as is true with the literary prophets.[8] Many of these stories appear in the collection of books that stretches from Joshua through Judges and into 1–2 Samuel and 1–2 Kings, a collection that will be for the sake of convenience referred to in its entirety as the Deuteronomistic (Dtr) History. This is a term that has come into use and has been vindicated in the last century as a usable moniker for this unified, extended composition that now appears divided into separate entities only because it was once written on scrolls that had a practical limit to what they could efficiently contain. Although the Dtr History reached its present shape for the most part in the sixth century B.C., it contains material

---

[8]The book of Jonah shares a number of features with these stories, even though it presently appears among the literary prophets. The book of Jonah stands apart as a book primarily about the prophet himself, a narrative that pays only secondary attention to the public he addresses, and non-Israelites at that. In contrast to the literary prophets whose books are composed primarily of their oracles, Jonah's message is known in this book only from the five Hebrew words of Jonah 3:4 (in English, "Forty more days and Nineveh will be overthrown!"). His name appears in an isolated verse (2 Kings 14:25) that connects him with the first half of the 8th century B.C., but present investigative tools permit no confidence in narrowing the composition of the book to any of the succeeding five centuries that follow this reference. For a succinct and informed overview of the issues with appropriate bibliography, see Jack M. Sasson, *Jonah*, AB (New York: Doubleday, 1990), pp. 20-28.

from a variety of sources, many of which go back centuries before its final editing. The stories about prophets in the Dtr History include names associated with contexts that often antedate the literary prophets. Thus, in the latter half of the ninth century B.C., stories in the Dtr History cluster around the prophets Elijah (1 Kings 17–2 Kings 2), Elisha (1 Kings 19; 2 Kings 2–13) and Micaiah (1 Kings 22; not the literary prophet Micah). Even earlier from the preceding 10th century, figures like Samuel (1 Sam 9–19; 25:1; 28:8-25), Nathan (2 Sam 7; 12; 1 Kings 1) and Gad (2 Sam 24) dominate the prophetic horizon.

Materials from all these texts will find their way into the discussion that follows. Our concern in sifting through these texts remains focused upon a few bedrock perspectives that permit comparison and contrast among all these figures. Other texts that are relevant for prophetic activity will on occasion be mentioned for the broader perspectives that they can provide, from Genesis to the New Testament, and from apocalyptic literature to the Talmud.

We have not included the book of Daniel in our discussion of prophets above precisely because the Old Testament makes no effort to present him as a prophet. The distinction was early recognized, as Africanus wrote to Origen in the third century, "It is always in some other way that Daniel prophesies—by visions, and dreams, and an angel appearing to him, never by prophetic inspiration."[9] Daniel is never called a prophet in the Hebrew Bible, and he never hears God speak to him. Indeed, the voice of God is never heard in the book of Daniel. Never does Daniel say, "Thus says the Lord!" nor does he claim a special gift. He is not connected in any way to any special power associated with a gift from God or the spirit of God. It is with good reason that the book of Daniel is not placed among the prophetic books in the Jewish sequence of biblical books, taking its position instead as the fourth book from the end of the entire biblical collection: Daniel, Ezra, Nehemiah and, finally, 1–2 Chronicles appear as the last books of the Hebrew Bible.[10] The present placement of Daniel in Chris-

---

[9]"A Letter to Origen from Africanus about the History of Susanna," *The Ante-Nicene Fathers* volume 4 (Buffalo, N.Y.: Christian Literature Publishing Company, 1885) p. 385.

[10]Cf. the observation in the Babylonian Talmud that Haggai, Zechariah, and Malachi were greater than Daniel since they were prophets while he was not (*b. Sanhedrin* 94a). Individuals who were not originally prophets were able in the eyes of later generations to gain prophetic status by a re-

tian Bibles between Ezekiel and Hosea is a result of the principle of size[11] in conjunction with an ordering that groups together all visionary books (thus mixing prophetic with apocalyptic).[12]

The visionary material in Daniel is also quite distinct from the literary prophets, for it belongs in the category of apocalyptic. How is apocalyptic literature distinguished from the classical literary prophets? Certain features will be developed in the pages that follow as an important part of the changes that prophecy itself experienced. A connection between apocalyptic and prophecy is difficult to deny[13] and thus it will be appropriate at times to note important connections between the two. For now it is sufficient to note that apocalyptic literature is material that focuses upon a dramatic revelation (Gk *apokalypsis*) to an outstanding religious figure from history, a revelation that typically anticipates the climax of history for a deteriorating world with the destruction of the forces of evil and the victory of God. This revelation is characteristically coded with striking images and mediated through angelic revelators. None of these features characterize the classical prophets.[14]

We will discover as we progress that a variety of motifs, themes, characterizations and activities in prophetic literature converge to depict a common fund of general perspectives in the prophets associated with the period before 586 B.C., otherwise known as the preexilic prophets. The shared prophetic culture undergoes serious modification in the context of the exile and into the postexilic prophets, those associated with the period after the decree of the Persian King Cyrus in 539–538 B.C. that permitted

---

definition of what a prophet was. Neither Daniel nor David qualifies as a prophet in his lifetime, yet each is called a prophet at a much later time. See the discussion in James Kugel, "David the Prophet," in *Pottery and Prophecy: The Beginnings of a Literary Tradition*, ed. James Kugel (Ithaca, N.Y.: Cornell University Press, 1990), pp. 45-55, that traces the process in the case of David and makes reference to Daniel in this regard.

[11]Noted above. Daniel is almost twice as long as Hosea which follows it, but significantly shorter than the preceding Ezekiel.

[12]For an articulate defense of Daniel as a prophet, see Klaus Koch, "Is Daniel Also Among the Prophets?" in *Interpreting the Prophets*, ed. James Luther Mays and Paul Achtemeier (Philadelphia: Fortress, 1987), pp. 237-48, but his argument is compromised by Kugel's observations noted above in note 9.

[13]Horst Dietrich Preuss, *Old Testament Theology*, trans. Leo G. Perdue (Edinburgh: T & T Clark, 1992), 2:277-79.

[14]For a survey of apocalyptic, see Christopher C. Rowland, *The Open Heaven: A Study of Apocalyptic in Judaism and Early Christianity* (New York: Crossroad, 1982).

Jews to return and rebuild their temple. At the same time, we will also point to a number of features in prophetic material that provide a sustained unity in spite of an ever unfolding diversity in the middle of the first millennium B.C.

Translations of the Bible will be my own unless otherwise specified. We will not follow the tradition that began at the end of the first millennium B.C. of replacing the divine name with the translation "Lord" (Heb *ădōnāy*, Gk *kyrios*). Thus what often appears in Bible translations as "Lord" will appear here as "Yahweh," the personal name of Israel's God, which does not mean "lord, master, sovereign." When "Lord" does appear in translations that appear here as a reference to God, it translates Hebrew *ădōnāy*, which does mean "my master" or "my lord."

# 2

# THE PROPHET AND
# THE DIVINE COUNCIL

A NUMBER OF CRITERIA ARE EMPLOYED by researchers in trying to define the prophet and his role in ancient Israel. If prophecy as an institution was in a process of change in the first millennium B.C., as we will argue, it is not surprising that finding agreement upon these criteria is a difficult enterprise.

However, there is one feature found explicitly in some prophets that is unique, predicated of no other individual or group in the Hebrew Bible. Only the prophet ever made the claim that he stood in the presence of God and those creatures who composed God's deliberating council.[1] Various aspects of this advisory council are described in a number of places in the Bible. God's council was composed of numerous supernatural creatures associated with the stars and planets and the rule of the cosmos: "all the host of heaven" (1 Kings 22:19), the "sons of God" (Job 1:6; 2:1), and "seraphs were in attendance above him" (Is 6:2). The

---

[1]For detailed study of God's council, see E. Theodore Mullen, *The Assembly of the Gods: The Divine Council in Canaanite and Early Hebrew Literature* (Chico, Calif.: Scholars, 1980). Walter Brueggemann, *Theology of the Old Testament: Testimony, Dispute, Advocacy* (Minneapolis: Fortress, 1997), p. 628, highlights the divine council as the "dominant rubric for authority" for the prophet.

council is not always in session but meets at particular times:

> The day arrived that the sons of God came to present themselves before
> Yahweh, and the Adversary also came among them. (Job 1:6; 2:1)

God is typically depicted as one who poses questions to the members of
the council, seeking a response or advice on the administration of the
cosmos. These are generally not rhetorical questions, for most of them are
answered by members of the council:

> Yahweh said to the Adversary, "Where have you come from?" (Job 1:7; 2:2)

> Yahweh said to the Adversary, "Have you considered my servant Job?" (Job
> 1:8; 2:3)

> Yahweh said, "Who will entice Ahab, so that he may go up and fall at
> Ramoth-Gilead?" (1 Kings 22:20)

> Yahweh said to him, "How?" (1 Kings 22:22)
> I heard the voice of my Lord saying, "Whom shall I send, and who will go
> for us?" (Is 6:8)

> How long will you judge perversely and play favorites with the wicked? (Ps
> 82:2)

Other occasions where God solicits input from supernatural beings reflect this same point of view, as in the case of the deliberative question
posed by Yahweh to his accompanying angels after they had visited
Abraham in his tent: "Shall I hide from Abraham what I am about to
do?" (Gen 18:17).

A common misperception of the God of the Bible is that he is an auto-
crat who insists on his own way, one who behaves imperiously toward his
creatures without compromise, dispensing commands only. But passages
such as the above undercut this selective reading of the text. Throughout
the Hebrew Bible, God addresses angelic beings with stunning deference.
Because God often approaches even men in this same fashion, his behavior in the divine council should come as no surprise. The first words from
God's mouth after Adam and Eve have eaten the fruit of the forbidden
tree are the following:

> "Where are you?" (Gen 3:9)

"Who told you that you are naked? Did you eat from the tree that I ordered you not to eat from?" (Gen 3:11)

"What is this that you have done?" (Gen 3:13)

Similarly, God's response to Cain's murder of Abel are questions: "Where is your brother Abel?" (Gen 4:9), and "What have you done?" (Gen 4:10). A fleeing Hagar is accosted by Yahweh with this inquiry: "Hagar, maid of Sarai, where have you come from and where will you go?" (Gen 16:8), in the same way that God may query a fleeing Elijah, "What are you doing here, Elijah?" (1 Kings 19:9) or a recalcitrant Jonah, "Is it good for you to be angry? (Jon 4:4; cf. Jon 4:9). God does not always confront men with such deference, but it is a pattern too prominent to overlook (cf. Gen 18:9; Num 22:9).

No human being apart from the prophet is ever described in the Bible as being allowed to attend God's council meeting. The unique status of the prophet in this regard is captured with Amos's words, "My Lord Yahweh will do nothing unless he has revealed his secret *(sôd)* to his servants the prophets" (Amos 3:7). So important to a prophet is a place at the divine council that it becomes for Jeremiah the distinguishing criterion for separating genuine prophets from their counterfeits (Jer 23:16-22):

Do not listen to the words of the prophets who prophesy to you. . . .
A vision from their own hearts they speak, not from the mouth of Yahweh. . . .
For who has stood in the council *(sôd)* of Yahweh
That he might see and hear his word? . . .
I did not send the prophets, yet they ran;
I did not speak to them, yet they prophesied.
But if they had stood in my council *(sôd)*,
Then they would have proclaimed my words to my people.

Some prophets simply record what they see in the council, without actively participating (e.g., Micaiah in 1 Kings 22:19-23). Isaiah is the only prophet who ever volunteers for a commission, and he does this by responding to God's question addressed to the council in session:

I heard the voice of my Lord saying, "Whom shall I send, and who will go for us?" I said, "Here am I; send me!" (Is 6:8)

Other prophets go even further and actually offer God advice that prompts God to consider alternate plans. This is comparable to Abraham's reasoning with God about the destruction of Sodom, a dialogue in which God expressed a willingness to spare the city should the number of righteous equal or exceed the number that Abraham proposed (Gen 18:22-33). The prophet Amos behaves like Abraham in this fashion twice in Amos 7:

> My Lord Yahweh showed the following to me. He was fashioning a swarm of locusts. . . .
>
> I said, "O my Lord Yahweh, please forgive! How can Jacob stand, for he is so small?"
>
> Yahweh changed his mind *(nhm)* about this. "This will not come to pass," said Yahweh. (Amos 7:1-3)

> My Lord Yahweh showed the following to me. My Lord Yahweh was calling for a judgment by fire. . . .
>
> I said, "O my Lord Yahweh, please stop! How can Jacob stand, for he is so small?"
>
> Yahweh changed his mind *(nhm)* about this. "This, too, will not come to pass," said my Lord Yahweh. (Amos 7:4-6)

This is a remarkably bold individual who feels comfortable in using an imperative ("stop!") to tell God what to do. Even more remarkable is the fact that God obligingly retracts the plan when his prophet objects. As in the case of Abraham and Sodom, God defers to the counsel of the one with whom he dialogues. God went to the trouble of showing Amos various possibilities about the future in order to receive input from his prophet as to the appropriateness of these plans. And when Amos objected with good reason, the proposed plan was shelved.

When the prophets speak of seeing God in council, God is typically seated on his throne, an emphatic reminder that the cosmos is not a democracy and that God is in control.[2]

> I saw Yahweh sitting on his throne, and all the host of heaven standing beside him on his right and his left. (1 Kings 22:19)

---

[2]The prophet could see God less frequently in other poses: "I saw the Lord standing by the altar, and he said, 'Strike the capital'" (Amos 9:1). When Elijah refers to Yahweh as one "before whom I stand" (1 Kings 17:1; 18:15), this language also reflects the image of a prophet as one who stands in the presence of a king who is surrounded by courtiers prepared to do his bidding.

> I saw my Lord sitting on a throne, high and lifted up, and the hem of his robe was filling the temple. Seraphs stood above him. (Is 6:1-2)

> What looked like a throne with the appearance of sapphire was above the expanse that was over their [i.e., the cherubim] heads, and above the semblance of the throne was a semblance like an appearance of a man. (Ezek 1:26)[3]

Some prophets are even asked to approach God, and in so doing they brush against God's hand. The prophet who physically comes closest to God himself is Jeremiah in a breathtaking scene:

> For thus Yahweh, the God of Israel, said to me: "Take this wine-cup of wrath from my hand and make all the nations to whom I send you drink it. . . ." I took the cup from Yahweh's hand and made all the nations to whom Yahweh sent me drink it." (Jer 25:15-17)

It is quite possible that the picture assumed here is one where Jeremiah approaches God's throne and takes the cup from God's hand, walking from member to member of the divine council so that the appropriate members may drink from this cup. What may be metaphor in Habakkuk 2:16 becomes in Jeremiah a prophetic activity: "The cup of Yahweh's right hand will come around to you." After all, each nation was perceived as having a representative supernatural being responsible for its people,[4] and the members of the council could be punished for the proliferation of evil within their areas of responsibility (Ps 82).

The prophet Habakkuk's dialogue is most comfortably explained as a part of the prophetic participation in the divine council. Habakkuk initially expresses some frustration as he asks God why chaos continues unabated for so long in Judaean society (Hab 1:2-4). Curiously, God's response is addressed to a group, and not just Habakkuk, for the opening verbs in Habakkuk 1:5 are plural imperatives: "Look! Observe! Be aston-

---

[3]Cf. Dan 7:9-10: "I was watching until thrones were set up, and one ancient of days sat down. His clothing was white like snow and the hair of his head like clean wool. His throne was flames of fire, its wheels were burning fire. . . . A thousand thousands served him." This scene is to be distinguished from the experience of the prophets, for Daniel can not interact with these events, which are pictured as taking place at the end of time, a vision of the future.

[4]Dan 10:13, 20-21; 12:1. "When the Most High assigned the nations their heritage, when he parceled out the descendants of Adam, he set up the boundaries of the peoples after the number of the sons of God" (Deut 32:8 NAB).

ished! Wonder!" Who is this group that is addressed, for only Habakkuk has spoken in the preceding verses? The divine council is the body to whom God characteristically reveals his plans, and it is probably presupposed here as well, particularly as Habakkuk continues to dialogue with God (Hab 1:12-17; 2:1-2).

A transformation in the depiction of the prophet in his relationship to the divine council surfaces in the exile when Ezekiel encounters God. At this time, God is pictured as departing from his Temple (Ezek 10–11), his "house" where he had resided for several centuries after it was built by Solomon. For the first time since its construction, God is not in his temple, and for the first time a literary prophet is not in Israel or Judah when he receives his revelation: Ezekiel is a captive in Babylonia. These new circumstances correspond to a new depiction of the prophet's relationship to the divine council, for no longer does Ezekiel stand among the hosts of the heavens. Instead, in the first chapter of the book of Ezekiel, God's guards and throne bearers (the cherubim[5]) bring God's portable throne on wheels from the divine realm in the north (Is 14:13) to Ezekiel in exile. Unlike the deliberations of the council depicted in the earlier prophets, there is no give-and-take between prophet and God in this encounter. "Listen!" says God (Ezek 2:8), as he presents to Ezekiel his plan of action as a *fait accompli*. All that Ezekiel can do is to accept and swallow the scroll of doom that has been prescribed as God's plan for his people (Ezek 2:8–3:4). God is still on his throne, and the angelic retinue is present, but the prophet no longer sees nor participates in the deliberations of the council. The council comes to him, so to speak, with a decree that is not negotiable.

After the exile, a further transformation—indeed, deterioration—of the prophet's relationship to the divine council occurs: no prophet is explicitly depicted as taking part in God's council.[6] Although one may sug-

---

[5]Their role as guards appears in Gen 3:24; Ezek 28:14, 16, while their function as throne-bearers is clear from 1 Sam 4:4; 2 Sam 22:11 (=Ps 18:10); Ps 80:1; 99:1; Is 37:16 (cf. Ex 25:22; Num 7:89).

[6]Although the Masoretic text in Zech 3:5 represents Zechariah speaking in the midst of a group of angels that bear some resemblance to God's council, there are two problems. "Then I said" in many textual witnesses appears as, "Then he said," referring not to Zechariah but to an angel. Second, the high priest Joshua is also present, a feature otherwise unknown to occur in the divine council. This is one of many symbolic visions in Zechariah and does not represent the council in action.

gest that this is a weak argument from silence, in the light of the significance that the concept bears in the earlier prophets, its total omission is noteworthy. It is not entirely an argument from silence, as we will see below, for other developments occur which replace the function of the divine council. It will become clear that the change that occurred in the book of Ezekiel was a harbinger of the later complete exclusion of the prophet from the divine council.

A word remains to be said about the book of Daniel, for the peculiar developments of apocalyptic deserve special attention in this regard. The precise origins of apocalyptic literature remain a contested matter, but this visionary literature becomes a pronounced feature in Jewish culture in the latter part of the first millennium B.C. There is a vigorous tradition in extra-biblical apocalyptic texts that the heavens are accessible to the visionary to whom God grants revelation (cf. *1 Enoch*, *2 Enoch*, *Apocalypse of Zephaniah*, *3 Baruch*).[7] One biblical apocalypse records such an experience:

> After these things I saw, and behold a door open in heaven, and the first voice that I heard was like a trumpet speaking with me, saying, "Come up here, and I will show you the things that must take place after these things." Immediately I was in the spirit, and behold a throne was set in heaven and there was someone seated upon the throne, . . . and around the throne were twenty-four thrones, . . . and before the throne was something like a sea of glass resembling crystal, and in the middle of the throne and around the throne were four living beings full of eyes in front and behind. (Rev 4:1-6)

Paul also refers to such a journey that he experienced when speaking of himself as one who was "a man . . . caught up as far as the third heaven . . . into Paradise and he heard inexpressible words that a man is not permitted to speak" (2 Cor 12:2-4).[8] On a number of points, however, the divine

---

[7]The ascent to heaven becomes in literature after the Old Testament a widely productive topos in a variety of genres and religious traditions from Dante's *Paradiso* to Greek magical texts (e.g., the so-called Mithras Liturgy, in Hans Dieter Betz, *The Greek Magical Papyri in Translation*, 2nd ed. (Chicago: University of Chicago Press, 1992), pp. 48-49. See Jeffrey Burton Russell, *A History of Heaven: The Singing Silence* (Princeton, N.J.: Princeton University Press, 1997), and Sarah Johnson, "Rising to the Occasion: Theurgic Ascent in its Cultured Milieu," in *Envisioning Magic: A Princeton Seminar and Symposium*, ed. Peter Schäfer and Hans G. Kippenberg (Leiden: Brill, 1997), pp. 169-95.

[8]Words to which the privileged human alone has access reappear on other occasions (e.g., "When the seven thunders spoke, I was about to write, and I heard a voice from heaven saying, 'Seal up

council experiences of the early prophets are quite unlike those of the later apocalyptic visionaries. The latter (1) devote considerable attention to describing their heavenly journeys and what they see, and (2) they do not appear in heaven in order to assist, or even observe, the decision-making process.[9] However, the book of Daniel displays none of the apocalyptic interest in cosmological observations and descriptions, nor does Daniel ascend to heaven for any of his revelations. Furthermore, although he describes God's throne room at one point (Dan 7:9-14), Daniel is not present in the throne room since he is describing a vision of something that will take place in the distant future. The book of Daniel, then corresponds to the trajectory already plotted for biblical literature, namely, the declining role of the prophet in the divine council. The visionary aspects of the book of Daniel do not correspond with the peculiar development in apocalyptic of the visionary who becomes the heavenly traveler, in contrast to the prophetic counselor.

In sum, we have observed that prophetic texts associated with the preexilic period have a decided stress upon the unique status of the prophet as one of God's advisors on his council.[10] Indeed, there are some statements that affirm this experience as an essential component of what constitutes a prophet.[11] Although echoes of this privileged status continue in modi-

---

[9]what the seven thunders spoke and do not write them'" (Rev 10:4). This is simply an extension of the notion that the prophet has access to the divine council where God frankly discusses his options with the prophet and no other human.

[9]John's extended and detailed experience that begins in Revelation 4 is noteworthy for the absence of the voice of God despite substantial angelic discourse. Even the questions that one expects God to pose from the throne, on the basis of the prophetic experience of the Old Testament, are instead voiced by angels: "Who is worthy to open the scroll and to break its seals?" (Rev 5:2).

[10]It may be that the voices that speak in an exilic context in Is 40:1-6 also reflect the prophet's presence in the divine council (e.g., Edwin C. Kingsbury, "The Prophets and the Council of Yahweh," *JBL* 83 [1964]: 279-86). Even if this is so, it does not compromise the exilic period as the general period in which a change takes place with respect to the prophet's relationship to the divine council.

[11]When Alexander Rofé, *The Prophetical Stories: The Narratives About the Prophets in the Hebrew Bible, Their Literary Types, and History* (Jerusalem: Magnes, 1988), pp. 146-52, drives a chronological and phenomenological wedge between two grades of prophecy, the reliable classical prophets who participated in the divine council in contrast to both earlier and later occasionally misleading prophets who stressed the spirit—indeed frenzy—as their channel of revelation, he may be tapping into an important development for, as he notes, the classical prophets hardly stress the role of the spirit in their activity. Nevertheless, the basic insight, elaborated by Sigmund Mowinckel "The 'Spirit' and the 'Word' in the Pre-exilic Reforming Prophets," *JBL* 53 (1934): 199-227, has serious problems (see H. H. Rowley, "The Nature of Prophecy in the Light of Recent Study," *HTR* 38 [1945]: 1-38).

fied form in apocalyptic texts, the experience of the prophet Ezekiel points to a possible metamorphosis of the prophet's role as a member of this divine council. Are there reasons to see this shift as a significant part of a larger picture? To answer this question, we will turn in succeeding chapters to other transmutations of the prophet's role that are related to his position as one of God's counselors.

# 3

# Is the Future Determined?

THE PRECEDING DISCUSSION FOCUSED upon God's willingness to entrust the fate of the cosmos to the deliberations of his creatures. God was not pictured as running the universe like a tyrant, for he freely accepted the input of select individuals, even adjusting his plans according to their insights. If God waits for temporally-bound creatures to make decisions that affect the destiny of humans, this raises the perennially perplexing question as to the contingency of the future: has the fate of humanity already been decreed, or is the future yet an unwritten chapter whose outcome is—at least in some details, if not in its entirety—open to negotiation?[1]

The very notion of a council to which the prophet is privy seems to imply that the future is negotiable and open to manipulation by choices that are unfolding in the present. God does not approach the council with

---

[1]Josephus used this issue two thousand years ago as a feature useful in demarcating Pharisees, Sadducees and Essenes within the Jewish community of the Second Temple period (*Antiquities* 13.171-73 [13.5.9]). Clark H. Pinnock, *Most Moved Mover* (Grand Rapids: Baker Academic, 2001), presents a case from within traditional Protestant theology for God's openness with respect to the future, while Abraham J. Heschel, *The Prophets, Part II* (New York: Harper & Row, 1962), makes similar overtures from a Jewish perspective: "The ultimate power is not an inscrutable, blind, and hostile power, to which man must submit in resignation, but a God of justice and mercy, to Whom man is called upon to return, and by returning he may effect a change in what is decreed" (p. 20-21).

a plan for which he merely solicits the council's perfunctory approval. If God is not playing games and acting out a masquerade of false condescension—and there is no hint that he is—then the drama portrays the future as contingent upon the decisions that the council recommends and God approves. The preceding discussion confirms this whenever the prophet or council asked God to change his mind or when they proposed a plan for God to consider. These images are so persistent in the prophets that one can not dismiss them as mere metaphor (metaphor for what?) or as marginal detritus of little consequence.[2]

In addition to the relevance of the preceding discussion, there is a changing facet of prophecy that underscores this contingency: the early prophets are not always sure how the future will unfold. The word "perhaps" appears prominently among the early prophets:

> Seek righteousness, seek humility. Perhaps *(ʾûlay)* you will be hidden in the day of Yahweh's anger. (Zeph 2:3)[3]

It would have been more comforting for this late seventh-century prophet's listeners had he omitted that single word and instead proclaimed with confidence, "You will be hidden." But Zephaniah can provide here no guarantee about the future when it comes to the results of repentance. Could the people's repentance reverse the coming judgment? Or could repentance only temper the extent of disaster? Or was repentance, in fact, too late to avoid disaster? Zephaniah can say no more than that "perhaps" some may avoid the judgment.

Amos provides a similar perspective on this same issue when he likewise counsels the people to reform:

> Hate evil, and love good, and establish justice in the gate. Perhaps *(ʾûlay)* Yahweh, the God of hosts, will be gracious to the remnant of Joseph. (Amos 5:15)

Again, the prophet cannot say what will happen. This stance is consistent

---

[2]The options are subject to considerable nuancing and span a continuum from the extreme of taking the drama at face value as real events to the other extreme of seeing all as figurative (e.g., Maimonides *Guide for the Perplexed* 2.45-48; cf. 1.45-60).

[3]See Terence Fretheim, *The Suffering God: An Old Testament Perspective* (Philadelphia: Fortress, 1984) pp. 45-59, for a convenient discussion that links deliberations of the divine council with the prominence of the divine "perhaps."

with the mechanism of the divine council, for presumably a new state of affairs resulting from repentance will mean that new celestial deliberations will need to take place between God and the council: "Back to the drawing board!"

The most surprising aspect of this presentation of the future as conditional is that it is not only the prophet who uses the word "perhaps." Jeremiah, like Zephaniah and Amos, may say "perhaps" with respect to the future (ʾûlay, Jer 36:7), but most stunning is that occasion when God himself refuses to commit himself to prognosticating what will happen:

> This word came to Jeremiah from Yahweh, saying, "Take a scrolled document for yourself and write on it all the words I have spoken to you. . . . Perhaps (ʾûlay) the house of Judah will hear about all the evil I intend to do to them, so that every man will turn from his evil way. (Jer 36:1-3)

> Thus said[4] Yahweh, "Stand . . . and speak . . . all the words that I have commanded you to speak to them. Do not omit a word! Perhaps (ʾûlay) they will listen and each person will turn from his evil way, so that I may relent of the evil that I intend to do to them because of the evil of their deeds." (Jer 26:2-3)

Now, it is possible that God is to be pictured here as really knowing what the people will do. If God really does know the outcome, however, his approach to the prophet is disingenuous, unwilling for whatever reason to give the future away and so spoil the appearance of human freedom. At the least, God is reluctant to tell his prophet what the final effect will be. But such an understanding does justice neither to God nor to the intent of the passage. According to Jeremiah, God is doing all he can through his prophet to prompt his people to repent, but God is unsure that the effort will be successful.[5] In the book of Ezekiel, God assumes a similar posture:

---

[4]Although one often finds this phrase translated as, "Thus says the LORD," the prophet is citing a message that God had earlier articulated. The past tense significance of this citation formula must not be overlooked and will be so translated throughout (Sam Meier, *Speaking of Speaking: Marking Direct Discourse in the Hebrew Bible*, VTS 46 [Leiden: Brill, 1992], pp. 277-91).

[5]Similarly, God himself admits that his anticipation of Israel's future behavior was not vindicated: "I said, 'After she has done all these things, she will return to me,' but she did not return" (Jer 3:7).

> The word of Yahweh came to me saying, 'Son of man, . . . make for yourself
> baggage for exile, and before their eyes go into exile by day. . . . Perhaps
> (*ûlay*) they will see even though they are a rebellious house. (Ezek 12:1-3)

Once again, the future is open to negotiation, even from God's perspective.

One may come to the Bible with the impression that the prophets are confident vaticinators who speak with assurance about things yet to come. Nevertheless, there is an undeniable haziness about certain features of the future. This vagueness appears in particular with respect to one question addressed to the future: what are the results of repentance? The prophet characteristically runs into a dead-end in venturing beyond the possibility of repentance. Whether blessing follows repentance, or whether calamity comes after all, is not something open to prophetic scrutiny, and, as just seen, even God does not speculate about it. The book of Joel, whose date is not entirely certain, captures this dimension with a different turn of phrase:

> Tear your heart and not your garments. Return to Yahweh your God. . . .
> Who knows whether he may return and relent, and leave a blessing in his
> wake? (Joel 2:13-14)

It is a curious commentary on the prophetic insight into the future that this same question appears on the lips of untutored Ninevites when they hear Jonah's preaching: "Who knows whether God may turn and relent, and turn from his burning anger?" (Jon 3:9). The prophet Joel knows no more than the most ignorant Gentile when it comes to the consequences of repentance.

An open future in the writing prophets echoes in narrative texts throughout the Bible where divine pronouncements can be reversed if new factors emerge. God is prepared at Abraham's request to reverse the destruction of Sodom and Gomorrah if a few righteous can be found there (Gen 18:16-33). Although David with full awareness and deliberation chooses three days of pestilence from among the three consequences God proposes to him through the prophet Gad, David's prayers for mercy and God's compassionate change of mind prevent the full devastation from occurring (2 Sam 24:14-17, 25). God himself selects Saul as Israel's first king (1 Sam 9:15-17), but Saul's poor performance prompts God to rescind his mandate and to appoint David in his place: "I regret[6] that I have made Saul king" (1 Sam 15:11). When King Hezekiah is deathly ill, Isaiah provides an unconditional oracle of demise: "Thus said Yahweh, 'Set your house in order, for you shall die; you shall not recover'" (2 Kings 20:1). The emphatic double statement of the positive ("you shall die") and the negative ("you shall not live") does not prevent Hezekiah from asking God for restored health based on the king's early piety, nor does God feel bound to the death sentence already delivered by Isaiah:

> It happened that Isaiah had not gone out from the middle court when the word of Yahweh came to him: "Return and say to Hezekiah, leader of my people, 'Thus said Yahweh, the God of your father David, "I have heard your prayer. I have seen your tears. I am about to heal you."'" (2 Kings 20:4-5)[7]

The reversal of an earlier oracle is an embarrassment neither to God nor his prophet. Isaiah certainly is not branded as a false prophet because he delivers an oracle that decrees the exact opposite of one he relayed earlier. God has simply changed his mind.

A reliable prophet's oracle is reversed elsewhere in the Dtr history when God tells Elijah to pronounce doom both upon Ahab and his dynasty:

> Yahweh's word came to Elijah the Tishbite, saying, "Get up, go down to meet Ahab, . . . and speak to him, saying, 'Thus said Yahweh, "Have you murdered and as a result come into an inheritance?"'" And speak to him, saying, 'Thus said Yahweh, "In the place where the dogs licked up Naboth's blood, the dogs will lick up your blood, even yours."'" (1 Kings 21:17-19)

Elijah further speaks to Ahab in Yahweh's name: "I am bringing calamity to you, and will make a clean sweep of your descendants, and will cut off

---

[6]Translations hint at a variety of possible nuances for this Hebrew verb *(nhmty)* that underscore its slippery representation in English: "I regret" (njps), "I am sorry" (Moffat), "I am grieved" (niv), "I repent" (rsv).

[7]Nathan similarly reverses an earlier pronouncement. After Nathan tells David that he may build the temple, "for Yahweh is with you" (2 Sam 7:3), God sends Nathan back with the opposite message: "Thus said Yahweh, 'Are you the one to build me a house?'" (2 Sam 7:5). Unlike Isaiah, the first advice is not couched precisely as a divine oracle since it is not prefaced by "Thus said the Lord," and commentators often take Nathan's advice as simply his own uninformed opinion prior to hearing from God. But then why did not Nathan simply keep silent until he heard from God, instead of saying that Yahweh was behind David's efforts?

every male that belongs to Ahab" (1 Kings 21:21). The dynastic and personal doom is so overwhelming that—*mirabile dictu* for this most despicable king (1 Kings 21:25-26)—Ahab repents! This turn-about includes fasting, torn garments, sackcloth, and a total metamorphosis in demeanor and behavior (1 Kings 21:27). As a result, God rescinds at least part of the oracle when he informs Elijah:

> Have you observed how Ahab has humbled himself before me? Because he has humbled himself before me, I will not bring the evil in his days. In the days of his son I will bring the evil upon his house. (1 Kings 21:29)

As with Hezekiah's plaintive cry, so with Ahab's repentance comes a modification of the prophetic word because God himself is open to human choice, even when it comes to divine decrees.[8]

In the light of these examples, one must entertain the possibility that oracles in the writing prophets couched as apparent certainties may in fact be negotiable.[9] The word "perhaps" that occurs in the early writing prophets may simply be the occasional expression of what is everywhere implied. This notion is supported by Jeremiah's excursus:

> At one moment I might speak *('ădabbēr)* about a nation or a kingdom to pluck up and to break down and to destroy. Should that nation about which I have spoken *(dibbartî)* turn from its evil, I will relent *(wĕniḥamtî)* about the evil that I intended to do to it. At one moment I might speak *('ădabbēr)* about a nation or a kingdom to build and to plant. Should it do what is evil in my sight, without listening to my voice, I will relent *(wĕniḥamtî)*[10] about the good that I had said I would do to it. (Jer 18:7-10)

---

[8]This perspective is the fundamental presupposition of the story in 1 Kings 13, where God's orders to a nameless prophet include directions about eating and drinking. The prophet exhibits no surprise to hear later from a second prophet that the orders about dining were changed. Although the first prophet in this difficult passage is in the final analysis doomed for disobedience, both prophets before the oracle of doom speak with the assumption that God can change the orders he provides to his prophets.

[9]Richard Pratt ("Historical Contingencies and Biblical Predictions," in *The Way of Wisdom: Essays in Honor of Bruce K. Waltke*, ed. J. I. Packer and Sven K. Soderlund [Grand Rapids: Zondervan, 2000], pp. 180-203), provides a convenient elaboration of this notion with respect to the preexilic prophets.

[10]As in 1 Sam 15:11 above, translations here also show differing perspectives on this word in this context which vary even from the nuances evident in 1 Sam 15:11: "change my mind" (NJPS), "repent" (RSV), "relent . . . reconsider" ([T]NIV), "relent . . . think better" (NASB), "think again" (REB).

The Hebrew term translated here "I will repent" *(wĕnihamtî)* is the same verb that we saw in the preceding chapter that described God's change of plans when deliberating with Amos about the future (Amos 7:3, 6).[11] In this case God takes an additional step and here goes on record that even his most decisive affirmations about the future are subject to amendment. Even God's voice is not the final word, according to God himself, for human response can temper decrees that he has already promulgated. Should God affirm a rosy future which lulls humans into lethargy, that future can turn sour, or in God's words, "I will relent." Likewise, when God decrees doom, the specter of disaster may galvanize humans into a reformation that will move God to rescind the disaster. Because God is free to change his mind, even oracles that come from God himself can be overturned, as the repeated emphasis upon spoken decrees in Jeremiah 18 affirms. Therefore it poses no problem for Ezekiel to predict in the eleventh year that Nebuchadnezzar will plunder Tyre (Ezek 26:1, 7), while sixteen years later he reverses this oracle and insists that it is not from Tyre but Egypt instead that Nebuchadnezzar's booty will come (Ezek 29:17-20). Similarly, Isaiah can provide a positive oracle (Is 22:20-23) about the great future that lies ahead for Eliakim ("I will fasten him as a peg in firm place," Is 22:23), but at a later date appears a new oracle speaking of Eliakim's demise (Is 22:25).[12] An echo of this reversal of Eliakim's oracle appears in the Dtr History when God emphatically affirms that he overturns a statement that he made about Eli's house: "I did indeed say, 'Your house and your father's house will walk before me forever,' but now . . . days are coming when I will cut off your offspring and the offspring of your father's house" (1 Sam 2:30-31).

This broad consensus that the future is negotiable runs through a number of prophets, all of whom (among those whose dates are secure) appear before the postexilic period. But this consensus does not carry over into

---

[11]The readiness of God to change with respect to calamity in particular is enshrined in a formulaic statement that, in addition to its repetition elsewhere, recurs twice in the prophets: "relenting about calamity" (Joel 2:13; Jon 4:2; see variations in Jer 26:19).

[12]In the light of the conditional nature of prophecy, where statements about the future can be modified, some have noted that this compromises the usefulness of the criterion of fulfilled prophecy and non-fulfilled prophecy in separating out false prophets from true prophets (e.g., J. Crenshaw, *Prophetic Conflict: Its Effect upon Israelite Religion*, BZAW 124 [Berlin: de Gruyter, 1977], p. 51). See discussion below in chap. 15.

the postexilic period. A concomitant of the disappearance of the prophet's position in the divine council, which we observed in the preceding chapter, is the disappearance of the sense of open deliberation about the future. In the prophets after the exile who encourage repentance, the consequences are not hazy. The following statement appears only in two prophets—both postexilic—and in identical words: "Return to me and I will return to you" (Zech 1:3; Mal 3:7). This confident appraisal of the consequences of repentance is fleshed out with specific ways that God will bless his people when they behave as they are supposed to:

> With a curse you are cursed. I am the one you, the entire nation, are robbing! Bring the entire tithe to the storehouse, so that there is food in my house, and test me now in this. . . . I will surely open for you the windows of heaven! I will pour out for you a blessing until there is no more need. I will rebuke the devourer for you, so that it will not destroy. (Mal 3:9-11)

According to this late prophet, there is no hesitation about what will follow a reformation: looming destruction will be reversed, and the curse will be transformed into blessing. The same outlook informs the postexilic Haggai's appeals for repentance:

> Go up to the mountain and bring wood and build the temple, so that I may be pleased with it. . . . You expect much but it turns to little. You brought it home and I blew on it. Why? . . . Because of my house which is desolate, while all of you run, each to his own house. . . . I struck you, . . . every work of your hands. . . . From this day onward, . . . from this day I will bless you. (Hag 1:8-9; 2:17-19)[13]

Haggai's entire message is predicated upon the principle of cause and effect: if the people will repair the Temple, God will bless the people with

---

[13]The book of Haggai contains a prophecy identifying a descendant of King Jehoiachin in messianic terms (Hag 2:23) that marks a change of mind on God's part with respect to an earlier prophecy preserved in Jer 22:24-30 that doomed all of Jehoiachin's future descendants. What is noteworthy is not that Haggai brands the first prophecy as a false prophecy, but that he intentionally updates it as a perfectly legitimate enterprise consonant with a God who can change his mind (John Kessler, "Haggai, Zerubbabel, and the Political Status of Yehud: The Signet Ring in Haggai 2:23," in *Prophets, Prophecy, and Prophetic Texts in Second Temple Judaism*, ed. Michael H. Floyd and Robert D. Haak, LBH/OTS 427 [New York: T & T Clark, 2006], pp. 102-19). This is comparable to Micah's prediction of Zion's destruction (Mic 3:12) that Jews a century later saw as legitimate prophecy even though it was unfulfilled because, as they said, the king repented and Yahweh "changed his mind" (*wayyinnāḥem;* Jer 26:18-19).

abundant crops. There is no question of "perhaps" or "who knows?" for there is a new atmosphere concisely captured by Haggai's contemporary, Zechariah:

> As I intended to do you harm when your fathers provoked me to anger, . . . and I did not relent, so I have again intended in these days to do good to Jerusalem and to the house of Judah. Do not fear! These are the things you should do: speak truth, each person to his companion; judge with truth and full justice. (Zech 8:14-16)

Zechariah here explicitly distinguishes the way God treats the people after the exile from the way he dealt with his people before. The contrast conforms to the evidence noted above that God in the later period is disposed to a favorable treatment of his people, while in the earlier period such favorable treatment is not always a certainty, and in fact unpredictable. Among early writing prophets, one did not always know the consequences of repentance, but the later prophets know that God will bless.

I am not implying that among the preexilic prophets there were no pleas for repentance grounded upon a cause-and-effect scenario of future blessing for those who repent. On the contrary, such pleas did exist (e.g., Is 1:19-20; Jer 4:1-2). Rather, it is the complete confidence of the postexilic prophets that blessing is coming, untempered by any question of possible punishment, that distinguishes them from their predecessors.

If one continues this investigation into the apocalyptic literature of the Old Testament, it becomes clear that a developing trend has developed there to an extreme. Where future consequences could be presented as not entirely clear in the early prophets, and where it becomes less vague and more predictable in the later prophets, in apocalyptic the future becomes exceedingly predictable. In fact, the future in apocalyptic is already determined in its entirety. This notion dovetails closely with the decline of the divine council: there is no longer any need for debate about the management of the world. And if the future has been worked out in advance with such precision, one may be able to discover specific details, such as how many kings will reign and how they will behave (Dan 7:23-25; 8:21; 11:2-45), as well as how the righteous will fare (Dan 7:21, 25; 8:24; 11:32-35). The visions that Daniel sees or interprets are unlike anything seen in the early prophets, for his visions emanate from a worldview affirming that the future has already been decreed in its entirety. There is no more "perhaps" or "who knows?" about the future, for, behave as you will, what has been determined will come to pass.[14] God may have been able, according to the preexilic and exilic prophets, to change his mind in his dealings with his people, and according to the postexilic prophets he may have become more predisposed to bless his people. But with apocalyptic, history becomes a pre-programmed drama where the actors have their parts already written for them, and they neither miss their cues nor stray from their lines.

---

[14]In Dan 8:3 [2], Daniel is portrayed standing at the 'Ulay Gate (often rendered also as "canal" or "river") in Susa, a gate that derives its name from a nearby watercourse (Eulaeus River?), even though in Hebrew it sounds like this gate is the "Perhaps" Gate (cf. the Hebrew term *'ûlāy* discussed above in the earlier literary prophets). It is a minor irony that the apocalyptic vision that follows is subject to no amendment.

# 4

# WHAT DO YOU SEE?

WHEN WE DISCUSSED ABOVE the prophet's unique status as a member of God's council, we observed that a characteristic feature of God's relationship to his creatures was his habit of asking them questions. Not only would God ask questions of, or solicit advice from, the members of the council, but elsewhere in the Bible God frequently is depicted as one who approaches humans in general by asking questions. This communication technique was a significant feature of the preexilic prophets in a further very specific context that needs to be addressed at this point.

In the book of Amos, God asks Amos a question that will remain with the prophets in one form or another throughout the history of the literary prophets:

> He [i.e., Yahweh] showed the following to me. My Lord stood on a wall aligned with a plumb line, and in his hand was a plumb line.
> And Yahweh said to me, "What do you see *(rō'eh)*, Amos?"
> And I said, "A plumb line."
> My Lord said, "See, I am setting a plumb line among my people Israel. I will no more pass over him." (Amos 7:7-8)

Why does God ask the obvious? Why is such a simple—indeed mundane—answer acceptable? Amos was gifted with the special ability to see the significance of otherwise ordinary objects. If God had asked someone else not so gifted, the reply might have been, "I see a wall," or "I see a man with something in his hand," or "I see a man on a wall," and so on. But Amos distinguishes himself as a gifted prophet who immediately sees the relevant object undistracted by other features of the vision. And God uses Amos's insightful perception as a visionary—literally, one who sees the point of a vision—as the kernel of an oracle, the springboard for the message to follow. Amos focused precisely upon the plumb line (Heb *'ănāk*) and its resonance with Hebrew roots for groaning associated with pain and sorrow *(ne'nah, 'ānaq)* that God would no longer restrain from coming upon all Israel.[1]

On another occasion God approaches Amos in a similar fashion:

My Lord Yahweh showed the following to me: a basket of summer fruit.
He said, "What do you see *(rō'eh)*, Amos?"
I said, "A basket of summer fruit *(qāyis)*."
Yahweh said to me, "The end *(qes)* has come for my people Israel." (Amos 8:1-2)

This vision also requires some sophistication, for the answer to the question is again not obvious. Indeed, the point of the vision is not apparent from an English translation, which obscures the pun present in the Hebrew text. Answers such as "a basket of fruit," or "figs and pomegranates," or "fruit from trees" would totally miss the point and be useless answers for the oracle that God will communicate. What makes Amos special as a gifted prophet is that he immediately seizes upon the feature of significance: "summer fruit" *(qāyis)*, a word that sounds similar to the word for "end" *(qēs)*, the word that prompts the divine message that follows.

This ability to perceive such subtleties has roots in the depictions of prophets who lived before the literary prophets. When Saul tears *(wayyiqqāra')* the hem of the prophet Samuel's robe (1 Sam 15:27), Samuel sees the significance of the blunder as a pointer to the future: "Today Yahweh has torn *(qāra')* the kingdom of Israel away from you" (1 Sam

---

[1]Donald E. Gowan, *Theology of the Prophetic Books: The Death and Resurrection of Israel* (Louisville, Ky.: Westminster John Knox, 1998), p. 27.

15:28). Elisha is angry that the king strikes the ground with some arrows only three times: "To strike five or six times you would then have devastatingly struck Aram, but now you will strike Aram only three times" (2 Kings 13:19). After the prophetess Deborah informs the Israelite general Barak that he is to take the initiative in militarily confronting a Canaanite force, she discerns from his response the culminating event of the battle.

> Deborah: "Has not Yahweh, the God of Israel, commanded, 'Go and march to Mount Tabor, taking with you ten thousand men from the sons of Naphtali and from the sons of Zebulon. I will draw Jabin's military commander, Sisera, out to you at the Wadi Kishon, along with his chariots and his multitude. I will give him into your hand.'"
>
> Barak: "If you will go with me, I will go. If you will not go with me, I will not go."
>
> Deborah: "I will certainly go with you, although it will not be your renown on the road you take, for Yahweh will sell Sisera into the hands of a woman." (Judg 4:6-9)

Deborah sees that Barak's request has displaced his masculine leadership, which God had specified, for a feminine one. Deborah does not identify the woman who will deliver the *coup de grâce*, for the important clue that she sees in Barak's response is that Barak has substituted a female for a male leader. It would be no surprise for Deborah to discover that this story ends with the death of Sisera at the hands of the nomad woman, Jael (Judg 4:17-22; 5:24-27).[2]

The literary prophets thus continue a phenomenon that was seen to have had an already long pedigree: the prophet was one who could see the specific relevance of an event, an object, a comment in terms of what Yahweh was trying to accomplish. Jeremiah is another who follows in Amos's

---

[2]*Divination* is the term used to describe the observation of some variable aspect of reality in order to deduce the outcome of future events. Formal divination by experts is circumspectly controlled and regulated in the Hebrew Bible (e.g., Num 27:21; Ezra 2:63), even though informal divination is depicted throughout the Hebrew Bible as a commonplace without censure (cf. Gideon in Judg 6:36-40, Jonathan in 1 Sam 14:8-13, and Isaiah in 2 Kings 20:14-18). The verb "to observe, inspect" in Akkadian *(barû)* was the basis for the designation of the occupation of the "diviner" *(barû)* who inspected the entrails of animals in order to discern the future. See Frederick H. Cryer, *Divination in Ancient Israel and Its Near Eastern Environment: A Socio-Historical Investigation*, JSOTSS 142 (Sheffield, U.K.: Sheffield Academic, 1994).

shoes, for he also is required to demonstrate superior sight before the exile when the doom of Judah's destruction yet lies in the future:

> The word of Yahweh came to me, saying, "What do you see *(rō'eh)*, Jeremiah?
>
>    I said, "I see *(rō'eh)* an almond *(šāqēd)* branch."
>
>    Yahweh said to me, "You have seen well, for I am watching *(šōqēd)* over my word to perform it." (Jer 1:11-12)

Once again, a prophet is approached with a question whose answer is deceptively simple, but only the one gifted with a special insight can spot the details of relevance for the unfolding revelation. As in Amos, a pun between two Hebrew words lays the foundation for God's message. The point would have been missed had the object been described as simply a "branch" or a "staff" or a "piece of wood." It is not that Jeremiah has merely seen something, but as God says, he has "seen well."

A slightly different insight is required for Jeremiah's correct response to another question from God:

> The word of Yahweh came to me a second time, saying, "What do you see *(rō'eh)*?"
>
>    I said, "I see *(rō'eh)* a pot boiling with its top facing from the north."
>
>    Yahweh said to me, "From the north the evil will boil out upon on all the inhabitants of the land." (Jer 1:13-14)

The phonetic peculiarities of Hebrew are not necessary to understand the relevant point of this picture. Jeremiah does not describe the contents of the pot, nor the material of which the pot is made, nor that it is simply tipping over on one side. Instead he specifies the peculiarly appropriate direction from which it is tipping, for this is the key element that sets the following oracle in motion. But there is yet an additional bonus embedded in Jeremiah's responses, for the entire phrase translated "I see" (in both Jer 1:11 and Jer 1:13) appears in Hebrew as *'ănî rō'eh*, a phrase susceptible to another understanding that is particularly appropriate in this context: "I am a seer." Jeremiah's special gift and ability to see what God wants him to see allows him simultaneously to claim not only "I see" but also "I am a seer."[3]

---

[3]Cf. Samuel's retort to Saul: "I am the seer" (*ānōkî hārō'eh;* 1 Sam 9:19).

This insightful gaze, confidently discerning realities beyond the reach
of normal humans, accounts for a unique occasion where Jeremiah is
stunned into silence. He had been wearing a yoke to dramatize the subju-
gation of nations before the king of Babylon (Jer 27:2, 8) when suddenly
another prophet contradicted Jeremiah. The prophet Hananiah produced
a contrary oracle that he also claimed was from Yahweh: "Thus said Yahweh, . . . 'I have broken the yoke of the king of Babylon'" (Jer 28:2). To
underscore his message, Hananiah approached Jeremiah and broke the
yoke that was on Jeremiah's neck (Jer 28:11). Now what does Jeremiah
see? Does this stunning new development of a broken yoke signify an aspect of the future that Jeremiah must now integrate into his message? Has
the yoke of Babylon, that is, Babylon's oppressive power over the Near
East, been broken indeed? The text records that Jeremiah has nothing to
say. Instead of responding verbally, Jeremiah simply walks away, speech-
less. Why? Jeremiah has seen with his own eyes the broken yoke, and he
must determine what significance lies behind this surprising development.
Is the other prophet right? Is the yoke broken from off the nations? It apparently takes Jeremiah some time to assimilate this new development, for
his response is only forthcoming at a later date when he eventually replies
to the other prophet with the appropriate insight that is eventually vindicated: "You may have broken wooden bars, but you have made iron bars in
their place!" (Jer 28:13).

On another occasion preceding the destruction of Jerusalem and the
Temple, Jeremiah sees a vision similar to one seen by Amos. In this case,
it will not do for Jeremiah to repeat the response given by Amos. Times
have changed and a new response is needed. This time the prophet must
discern that some of the fruit have a different quality than some of the
other fruit.

> Yahweh said to me, "What do you see *(rō'eh),* Jeremiah?"
>
> I said, "Figs. The good figs very good, and the bad ones very bad, so bad
> that they cannot be eaten."
>
> The word of Yahweh came to me, saying: "Thus said Yahweh, the God
> of Israel: 'Like these good figs, so I will regard as good the Judaean exiles.
> . . . Like the bad figs, so bad that they cannot be eaten, . . . so I will treat
> Zedekiah, King of Judah.'" (Jer 24:3-5, 8)

It is clear from such a vision of fruit, common to more than one prophet, that a prophet cannot hitch a ride on the interpretations of prophetic visions that have gone before. Subtle changes prompt completely different messages. When Amos saw fruit, the key issue was neither the kind nor the quality but the season in which the fruit ripened: "summer fruit" was the essential element that gave the clue to coming judgment on all. For Jeremiah, however, it is precisely the quality of the fruit that he sees, and it is a quality that varies from fruit to fruit suggesting only a selective judgment that, unlike Amos, will not come upon all.

It is not an accident that prophets are asked to describe what they see, for some of the terms used to describe certain individuals with prophetic gifts can be translated quite appropriately by the English word "seer" (literally "see-er" or "one who sees"). *Hōzeh* and *rō'eh* are both Hebrew words that mean "one who sees." In all of the questions above when God asks, "What do you see?" we have noted that the Hebrew word God uses is precisely this word *rō'eh*. This designation "seer" is typically applied to individuals who are capable of seeing things that normal people cannot. In the case of Jeremiah and Amos, they clearly see in everyday objects a special significance which eludes the one who does not have the gift of special sight. In fact, this special gift of sight does not even require normal vision, as the experience of the blind prophet Ahijah makes clear when an individual tries unsuccessfully to disguise her identity from him (1 Kings 14:1-6).[4] First Samuel 9:9 suggests an identity between the "prophet" and the "seer" when it notes how "the 'prophet' today was formerly called the 'seer' *(rō'eh)*." Amos is in fact called a "seer" (*hōzeh*, Amos 7:12) by his enemies, a designation that he does not deny.[5]

This special vision is so fundamental that for many of the literary prophets, the introductory rubric or opening sentence for the entire book

---

[4]Cf. also blind Greek seers, e.g., Tiresias of Thebes and Phineus of Salmydessus, both of whom suffered blindness as a punishment. Versions of their stories in which the gift of prophecy, in essence a second sight, is a consequence of their blindness make it arguable that their special sight beyond the physical realm would probably be compromised if they had normal vision.

[5]The priority of Moses in the prophetic typology is preserved even with this motif, for Moses is portrayed as having greater sight than all other prophets (Num 12:6-8). Moses' first encounter with God is visual at the burning bush, seeing what no other human sees: "Let me turn aside now and see *(wĕ'er'eh)* this great sight, why the bush is not consumed" (Ex 3:3). Only after he turns to look does God call to him.

employs words associated with the act of seeing:

"The **vision** *(ḥăzôn)* of Isaiah son of Amoz which **he saw** *(ḥāzāh)*." (Is 1:1)

"which **he saw** *(ḥāzāh)*." (Amos 1:1)

"which **he saw** *(ḥāzāh)*." (Mic 1:1)

"The book of the **vision** *(ḥăzôn)* of Nahum." (Nah 1:1)

"which Habakkuk the prophet **saw** *(ḥāzāh)*." (Hab 1:1)

"The **vision** of Obadiah *(ḥăzôn)*." (Obad 1)

"I **saw visions** *(wā'er'eh mar'ôt)* of God." (Ezek 1:1)

An editorial summary in each case identifies succinctly the essence of the material in the following document. In the case of these seven prophets,[6] this editorial summary affirms that a focus upon the prophet's special sight is one of the single most helpful pieces of information for orienting readers to the material in the text that follows. For these orienting summaries, the one who communicates God's message is primarily one who has seen well.[7]

A surprising change occurs in the midst of the literary prophets. Visionary texts that are composed after the exile do not depict prophets with this same gift. Zechariah is approached by an angel and asked precisely the same question that God had earlier asked the former prophets:

He said to me, "What do you see *(rō'eh)?*"

I said, "I see that there is a lampstand entirely of gold, a bowl on top of it, seven lamps on it, seven spouts for the lamps that are on top of it, and

---

[6]The five books in the canonical sequence Amos, Obadiah, Micah, Nahum and Habakkuk (excluding Jonah) all contain a reference in their opening verse to this phenomenon with the Hebrew root *ḥzh*, a fact that may reflect an earlier compilation before becoming part of the twelve minor prophets.

[7]In spite of Jeremiah's frequent interpretations of the significance of what he sees (cf. Jer 18:1-12), it is remarkable that the Hebrew root *ḥzh* is not applied anywhere to his own insights and only occurs twice in the book of Jeremiah to denigrate the deceptive sight of misleading prophets (Jer 14:14; 23:16). This curiosity correlates with the identification of Jeremiah with the northern (Ephraimite) prophetic tradition (Robert R. Wilson *Prophecy and Society in Ancient Israel* [Philadelphia: Fortress, 1980], pp. 231-351, but see Herbert Huffmon, "Jeremiah of Anathoth: A Prophet for All Israel," pp. 261-72 in *Ki Baruch Hu: Ancient Near Eastern, Biblical, and Judaic Studies in Honor of Baruch A. Levine*, ed. Robert Chazan, William W. Hallo and Lawrence H. Schiffman [Winona Lake, Ind.: Eisenbrauns, 1999]).

two olive trees by it, one on the right of the bowl and one on its left."

I responded and said to the angel who was speaking with me, saying, "What are these, my lord?"

The angel who was speaking with me responded and said to me, "Do you not know what these are?"

I said, "No, my lord."

He responded and said to me, saying, "This is the word of Yahweh." (Zech 4:2-6)[8]

The succinct answers of the preexilic prophets Jeremiah and Amos, who quickly hone in on the particular elements of significance in a vision, are discarded by the postexilic prophet Zechariah. Instead, this later prophet gives a lengthy, verbose and meandering response, describing everything he sees in the vision, without a sense of proportion. Such a reply suggests that he really does not grasp the importance of the individual details or the way in which the details relate to the whole. This lack of understanding is confirmed when he asks the angel to tell him what they mean. When this passage is read against the background of the earlier vision narratives noted above, the angel's surprised reaction takes on a more profound significance. The angel expects Zechariah to comprehend. After all, a special insight was the qualifying factor for one to be a seer (a "see-er") and a prophet. But Zechariah does not have the insight that his predecessors once had. Rather humiliatingly he must confess to the angel that he does not see the point of the vision. The angel must explain what the earlier prophets grasped immediately and without tutoring.

One of the new and distinguishing features of Zechariah is his willingness to ask questions, even if the questions express his ignorance of what he, as a visionary, should know:

I said, "What are these, my lord?" (Zech 1:9)

I said to the angel who was speaking with me, "What are these?" (Zech 1:19 [2:2])

I said, "What are these coming to do?" (Zech 1:21 [2:4])

---

[8]Attempts to smooth the text, such as relocating Zech 4:1-3 elsewhere (e.g., before 4:11 as REB, NEB, NJB), soften but do not eliminate Zechariah's ineptitude in this segment.

I said, "Where are you going?" (Zech 2:2 [2:6])

I said, "What is it?" (Zech 5:6)

I said to the angel who was speaking with me, "Where are they taking the container?" (Zech 5:10)

I responded and said to the angel who was speaking with me, "What are these, my lord?" (Zech 6:4)

No prophet asks more questions than the postexilic Zechariah, and regrettably many of these questions were questions that God could earlier have asked his prophets and expected from them an informed reply. Now it is the ignorant prophet who is doing the asking, not God and not even the angel who after a few probes simply stops asking the apparently obtuse prophet.

On another occasion, an angel underscores that Zechariah is not living up to the expectations that one could have had of other prophets:

I responded and said to him, "What are these two olive trees on the right of the lampstand and on its left?"

I responded a second time and said to him, "What are these two growths of olive trees . . . ?"

He said to me, saying, "Do you not know what these are?"

I said, "No, my lord."

He said, "These are the two men consecrated with oil who attend the Lord of the whole earth." (Zech 4:11-14)

Once again, an angel expresses mild surprise at Zechariah's lack of insight. A prophet should be expected to have a higher aptitude of perception, but sadly Zechariah is no more insightful than most humans. Only once does Zechariah respond with an answer that seems to have some accuracy and reflects some insight on his part (Zech 5:2). Nevertheless, immediately afterward the angel hopefully presents another object for careful scrutiny to the prophet only to have it once again rebuffed with ignorance:

The angel who was speaking with me went out and said to me, "Lift up your eyes and observe what this is that is going out."

I said, "What is it?"

He said, "This is the container that is going out." (Zech 5:5-6)

The presentation of this prophet deliberately contrasts his behavior with the earlier prophets whose abilities were far more impressive. Not only the vocabulary, dialogue structure and scene presentation build upon the earlier more insightful prophets, but the text itself underscores the contrast with the earlier prophets as the book begins:

> Do not be like your fathers to whom the former prophets called out, saying, "Thus said Yahweh of hosts, 'Please return from your evil ways. . . .'" As for your fathers, where are they? And will the prophets live forever? Yet did not my words and my statutes that I commanded my servants, the prophets, overtake your fathers? (Zech 1:4-6)

There are several ominous suggestions in these words beyond the explicit warning to the people not to duplicate the spiritual rebellions of former generations. It is disconcerting, for example, that for the first time in a prophetic book there is a reference to "former prophets," suggesting a distinction that is certainly chronological but might also demarcate prophets of a different caliber. This phrase resurfaces elsewhere in the book as a minor motif: "Are not these the words which Yahweh proclaimed by the former prophets?" (Zech 7:7; cf. Zech 7:12, "the words which Yahweh of hosts had sent by his spirit through the former prophets"). This book is written with a backward glance that does not completely correlate the prophets of the past with the prophet Zechariah. There may be continuity, but there are features that point to them as a distinct group that is to be distinguished from Zechariah.

Even more suggestive is the query whose answer must be that the prophets do not live forever. Might there be an end to the prophetic gift? The former prophets are no more, and there is an ambiguity inherent in the question that could be construed as broader than a reference only to the past: "The prophets, do they live forever?" These verses that set off the former prophets in a distinct category are coupled disconcertingly with the subsequent consistent portrait of Zechariah as an inept observer of what any good seer or prophet should grasp immediately. This presentation undergirds the book of Zechariah, not unwittingly pointing out that this prophet is no longer representative of what prophets used to be. The book is explicitly aware of the prophets of the past even as it depicts Zechariah falling far short of their example in his perceptive abilities.

Zechariah's contemporary, Haggai, reflects the same decline in prophetic insight, albeit in a slightly modified format. Haggai is depicted as going twice to the priests with questions about ritual cleanliness, and both times the priests respond succinctly and unequivocally:

> "If a man should carry consecrated meat in a fold of his garment, and with the fold he touches bread, stew, wine, oil, or anything edible, will it become holy?"
>
> The priests responded and said, "No."
>
> Haggai said, "If someone who is unclean by contact with a corpse touches any of these, does it become unclean?"
>
> The priests responded and said, "It becomes unclean." (Hag 2:12-13)

The priestly responses become the basis for the prophetic oracle that follows, phrased as God's application of the insight to the moral issues facing the community. But it is remarkable that it is not the prophet who can supply the answers. Even more remarkably, he approaches classes of individuals—priests—whom other earlier prophets had condemned for their immorality and impoverished level of spiritual insight.[9] Although the sequence of Question-Answer-Application remains the same, God no longer expects his prophet to know the answer and must send him to someone else for the desired answer.

The decline in a prophet's ability to respond to divine questions is anticipated to a lesser degree in the earlier book of Ezekiel, composed during the exile. Ezekiel speaks very little in his book, but once God asks him a question about the valley of dry bones, a question to which Ezekiel pleads ignorance:

> He [i.e., God] said to me, "Son of man, can these bones come to life?"
>
> I said, "My Lord Yahweh, you know."[10]
>
> He said to me, "Prophesy to these bones and say to them . . ." (Ezek 37:3-4)

---

[9]E.g., Amos 7:10-17; Hos 5:1; 6:9; Mic 3:11; Is 28:7; Zeph 1:4; 3:4; Jer 2:8; 6:13; 32:32; Ezek 7:26; 22:26.

[10]This identical confession of ignorance surfaces later in response to another angel's question in Rev 7:14.

There once was a time when God could turn to his prophet for counsel or advice and expect an intelligent response (see chapter two). But when the prophet shrugs his shoulders with incomprehension ("God knows!"), the prophet is abdicating his responsibility to God and Israel. In Ezekiel one may also observe the beginnings of the trend where prophets can not adequately reply to angelic queries, for Ezekiel fails to answer when an angel asks, "Have you seen, son of man?" (Ezek 47:6). The old word that triggered awareness of prophetic insight, "see" *(rō'eh)*, resurfaces here but without receiving the time-honored response. Ezekiel in exile thus sets in motion what becomes a characteristic pattern for Zechariah after the exile. It is appropriate that Ezekiel, the first of the prophets to be removed to the periphery of the divine council, is precisely one who does not exhibit the characteristic insight that God requires for the deliberative process that is the very essence of God's council.

Even though the book of Ezekiel presents itself as the most consistently written autobiographical text in the Hebrew Bible, employing the first person singular to identify the writer and the one with whom God speaks, Ezekiel's voice is rarely heard in his own book. As the putative narrator he is, of course, everywhere present, but it is exceptional when he presents his own voice as an independent element in its own right on a part with God's voice. When on the six occasions he actually speaks unprompted by God, it is only briefly to underscore his revulsion at what he sees or to acknowledge his lack of comprehension and inability to grasp God's activity. In addition to his lame response to God's question above, he protests in the introductory chapters, "Oh, my Lord Yahweh, my person was never rendered unclean" (Ezek 4:14), "Oh, my Lord Yahweh, are you destroying all?" (Ezek 9:8), "Oh, my Lord Yahweh, are you completely devastating?" (Ezek 11:13).[11]

The momentum of this transformation from the insightful gaze of pre-exilic prophets[12] to the increasingly flustered incompetence of exilic and

---

[11]The remaining two occasions when the reader hears Ezekiel's voice as a distinct element are Ezek 20:49 [21:5]; 24:2.

[12]This is not to say that earlier prophets could not lose their insight. Samuel, so perceptive in his first encounter with Saul (1 Sam 9), is misled by outward appearances when he comes to anoint David, prompting Rashi to paraphrase God's mild rebuke in 1 Sam 16:7: "Even though you called yourself a seer when you said to Saul, 'I am the seer' (1 Sam 9:19), now I inform you that you are

postexilic prophets can be traced within the Hebrew Bible to its final manifestation in the apocalyptic material of the book of Daniel. No longer does God or an angelic messenger even bother to ask Daniel questions, for Daniel understands nothing of what he sees. Angelic figures assume that Daniel does not understand (they express no surprise as they did with Zechariah), for now it is a completely perplexed Daniel who is asking all of the questions. As he admits, "I was shocked by the vision, and there was no one who understood it" (Dan 8:27):

> "Gabriel, explain the vision to this fellow." He came near to where I was standing, and as he came, I began to tremble and fell upon my face. He said to me, "Understand, son of man . . ." (Dan 8:16-17)

> As for me, Daniel, my spirit was agitated within me, and the visions of my head frightened me. I approached one of those who were present and inquired of him the truth about all this. He said to me that he would inform me of the interpretation of the matter: "These great beasts . . ." (Dan 7:15-17)

> Then I wanted to know the truth concerning the fourth beast. . . . He said as follows: "As for the fourth beast . . ." (Dan 7:19-23)

It is particularly disappointing when Daniel asks for clarification and stunningly is denied a response:

> I heard but I did not understand. I said, "My lord, what will be the outcome of these things?" He said, "Go, Daniel, for the words are to be secret and sealed until the time of the end." (Dan 12:8-9)

Revelation from God has come a long way from the time of Amos where God "will do nothing unless he has revealed his secret to his servants the prophets" (Amos 3:7) to the book of Daniel where God and his angels refuse to divulge further information about the future, even when asked. Although Daniel attempts to understand the words of earlier prophets such as Jeremiah, Daniel is unable to exegete the text and requires a special angel to explain (Dan 9:1-4, 20-23). Apocalyptic literature in general will continue to present the visionary as one with underdevel-

---

not a seer." Elijah also, brusquely removed from his prophetic office and replaced by Elisha when he no longer can respond with insight to God's questions, is unable to discern the point of what God asks him to observe, and fails to see the greater reality of what is taking place in Israel: he is not alone as he self-indulgently claims (1 Kings 19:9-18).

oped insight.[13] The poor perceptive ability of the later prophets and individuals who receive divine revelations corresponds well with a theme discussed earlier, specifically the prophet's gradual loss of a position on the divine council. It is no surprise that the later prophets are not depicted as active on the divine council, for their insight does not count for much in comparison to their predecessors. Indeed, later Jewish mystical texts are explicit that any visionary who displays his ignorance by daring to ask for an explanation of what God reveals deserves to be stoned by the angels among whom he stands.[14]

A final curiosity will serve to conclude this investigation. As one looks back over the citations above where God asks questions of Jeremiah and Amos, God calls these prophets by name: "Jeremiah!" or "Amos!" This recalls depictions of God's summons to prophets early in Israel's history when he calls out in the Dtr history, "Samuel!" (1 Sam 3:6, 10) or "Elijah!" (1 Kings 19:9, 13). When addressing the exilic prophet Ezekiel, however, God no longer uses the prophet's name but instead calls him by the considerably less intimate and more austere appellative, "Son of man!" one of the distinguishing characteristics of this book.[15] Moving further in time, God address no prophet after the exile by name or by any other designation.[16] It may be that the appellations used to address the prophet reflect in their own way the increasing distance between God and the prophet that is demonstrable in the declining ability of the prophet to see the significance of what God is doing in human history.

---

[13]E.g., Rev 7:13-14; I Enoch 22:6-9; 23:3-4; 25:1-3; 27:1-2; 4 Esdras 2:44-47. Note the angel's words to Ezra: "Your understanding has utterly failed regarding this world, and do you think you can comprehend the way of the Most High?" (4 Esdras 4:1).

[14]Gershom G. Scholem, *Major Trends in Jewish Mysticism* (New York: Schocken, 1946), pp. 52-53.

[15]Over ninety times (e.g., Ezek 2:1, 3, 6, 8; 3:1, 3-4, 10, 17, 25).

[16]Daniel is addressed as "Daniel" and "son of man" (Dan 8:17, as Ezekiel) in the apocalyptic material of the book of Daniel, but it is angels and not God that address him in this fashion. His proper name appears in two visions ("Daniel!" Dan 9:22; 10:11-12; 12:4, 9), in addition to other unparalleled appellations such as "greatly beloved" (Dan 10:19).

# 5

# THE MANNER OF REVELATION

IN THE PRECEDING CHAPTERS WE HAVE SEEN how God is intent upon
interacting with humans in the administration of the cosmos. God's instrument for such interaction is the divine council, a forum where he interacts with his creatures, asking questions and listening to the responses
his creatures provide. We saw that when he asks the gathered council,
"Whom shall I send, and who will go for us?" (Is 6:8), he is speaking for
himself as well as the council members ("us") who have gathered, a style
of speech that probably goes back even to the opening chapters of Genesis:
"Let us make man in our image" (Gen 1:26).[1] Because of this interaction,
God seeks for humans who have insight and discernment and can take
their position on the divine council, interacting with God. The prophet is
just such a unique individual, one whom God queries and who responds
in synchrony with God's perspective.

---

[1]Cf. Gen 3:22; 11:7. This understanding of the verse is quite ancient (cf. *Genesis Rabbah* 8.4; Philo,
*De Opficio Mundi* 24 [75] and *De Mutatione Nominum* 33-35 [168-79]). Humans, angelic beings
and God are all mutually intelligible as partners in dialogue. From the perspective of the Hebrew
Bible, angels are made in the image of God no less than humans, and probably more so: one way of
referring to supernatural beings in the Hebrew Bible is simply to call them *ʾĕlōhîm*, the same word
that is typically used to identify God (Ps 82:1; 1 Sam 28:13; cf. Ps 8:5 [6] as quoted in Heb 2:7).
"Sons of God" is another way of referring to angelic-type beings that unambiguously affirms the
image of the father in the son (Job 1:6; 2:1; 38:7; Ps 29:1).

In the Deuteronomistic history (Joshua, Judges, 1–2 Samuel, 1–2 Kings), most prophets speak with God and God speaks with his prophets in congenial dialogue reflecting a relationship that might obtain between intimate friends. This presentation is consistent with the prophet's privileged position as a member of the divine council, for in this capacity the prophet is expected to interact vigorously, and at times even disagree, with God. But rarely in such portrayals does the prophet ever evince awe or fright at the potentially precarious position in which he finds himself. The creature talks intimately with the creator of the universe, yet feels as comfortable as if he were addressing his next-door neighbor. It is as if the prophet has managed to retrieve the intimacy that characterized the relationship of Adam and Eve with God in the Garden before their disobedience ruptured the friendship.

Any number of examples will confirm this general picture. God does not overwhelm the boy Samuel when he first calls to him at night as Samuel sleeps. The voice that Samuel hears is as faint and unobtrusive as old Eli's calling from a distant room, which Samuel mistakes for God's voice (1 Sam 3:1-15). Ever after, Samuel and God constantly dialogue with one another almost as equal partners.[2] Similarly, when God informs the prophet Ahijah of the queen's arrival, the reader is simply told that "Yahweh said to Ahijah" (1 Kings 14:5). Elsewhere, Elijah and God banter back and forth when they disagree over the appropriateness of Elijah's flight from queen Jezebel (1 Kings 19:9-18).

Sometimes the Deuteronomistic history provides further details to enhance the context, such as the time that, just as in God's initial revelation to Samuel, God reveals himself to Nathan at night (2 Sam 7:4). But in Nathan's case (unlike Samuel's) it still is unclear if this encounter takes place in a dream or vision, or if it is just like any other conversation that these prophets have with God while they are awake in broad daylight. This lack of interest in defining the manner of revelation is also apparent in the frequent phrase, "and the word of Yahweh came to [prophet's name]."[3] How the word of Yahweh came is not even hinted at, and the

---

[2]1 Sam 8:6-9; 9:15-17; 16:1-3, 12. A nocturnal verbal revelation from God comes to Samuel again in 1 Sam 15:10-12, 16.

[3]To Samuel (1 Sam 15:10), to Nathan (2 Sam 7:4), to Gad (2 Sam 24:11), to Shemaiah (1 Kings

response of the recipient is unknown. Indeed, the word translated "came" in this phrase is literally the completely nondescript word "was" *(hāyāh)*.

Although revelation is typically pictured as conversational in format, this is not to say that there are not revelations of a more exalted or spectacular nature. We noted in an earlier chapter that the divine council that Micaiah describes was an awesome spectacle. But how Micaiah saw this assembly is not made clear. Was it a dream? A vision? A trance? Was he physically transported? He records no personal sense of awe or fright (1 Kings 22:19-23). God's revelation to Elijah on Mt. Horeb in 1 Kings 19 (to be discussed below) has some peculiar elements, and in this case an unusual description unfolds of the prophet's response to an unparalleled theophany: "He wrapped his face in his mantle and went out and stood at the entrance of the cave" (1 Kings 19:13). Elisha has an unusual request for a musician to play before he receives a revelation (2 Kings 3:15). Although there are a few such peculiar aspects to some revelations from God, their very infrequency in the Dtr history underscores the otherwise typical presentation of congenial dialogue between God and prophet.

This low-profile portrayal of the supernatural element in revelation in the Dtr history is reinforced on another level. Prophets are frequently depicted as if they possessed natural talents and innate abilities to see more than most humans. Stories where this is apparent are in those places where the prophet is portrayed as acting without consulting God and exercising a formidable control in his own right over nature and history. Elisha is depicted as acting on his own in providing miraculous quantities of oil for a poor widow (2 Kings 4:1-7). When Elisha wants to reward a wealthy woman for her kindness, and after asking his own servant what she needs, he promises her—with no mention of a consultation with God—that she will bear a son within a year (2 Kings 4:11-17). How did Elisha know that his servant was lying behind his back and to his face? He affirms his un-

---

12:22), to the old deceptive prophet (1 Kings 13:20), to Isaiah (2 Kings 20:4) and to Elijah (1 Kings 17:2, 8; 18:1; 19:9; 21:17, 28). On one occasion, a direct revelation to the patriarch Jacob is recalled in this fashion (1 Kings 18:31) in contrast to the book of Genesis which recorded this revelation as divine speech in a dialogue between God and Jacob ("he said" Gen 32:28; 35:10). Since the phrase is also used to describe prophetic revelation that comes to a king such as Solomon (1 Kings 6:11), the ambiguity of the process in this case further underscores how unhelpful the phrase is for exploring the revelatory process.

usual knowledge by noting, "Did I not go with you in spirit?" (2 Kings 5:26). Prophets can also interpret the significance of certain omens without explicitly turning to God for the interpretation. When Saul tears Samuel's garment, Samuel immediately interprets this action as signifying that God has torn the kingdom from Saul (1 Sam 15:27-28), just as Elisha immediately interprets king Joash's striking the ground as a sign of only a partial conquest of his enemies (2 Kings 13:14-19). As we saw in chapter four, the prophet has a special gift in seeing the significance of apparently mundane objects and events. Special powers associated with the prophet himself continue even after death, for Elisha's bones can revive the dead simply by making contact with the corpse (2 Kings 13:21).[4]

It is evident, therefore, that prophets are depicted as spiritually potent in their own right. Of course, prophets can also be described in other contexts as powerless and lacking insight without God's continual assistance. Elisha confesses his inability to perceive the cause of a woman's grief because "Yahweh has hidden it from me and has not told me" (2 Kings 4:27). God "uncovered Samuel's ear" in advance of Saul's arrival, revealing to his prophet that "about this time tomorrow I will send to you a man." When he arrived a day later, God informed Samuel, "Here is the man I told you about!" (1 Sam 9:15-17). Sometimes prophets must pray to God before their actions become efficacious: Samuel prays before a battle (1 Sam 7:9-10) and in summoning thunder and rain (1 Sam 12:18), while Elisha prays before reviving a dead boy (2 Kings 4:33-37) and in order to have his servant's eyes see the protective angelic forces that surround the prophet (2 Kings 6:17-20). Prophets can also speak of how God "shows" them the future (2 Kings 8:10, 13). Some cases are difficult to evaluate, such as the popular theology placed on the lips of non-Israelites who affirm that "Elisha . . . tells Israel's king the words you [i.e., the king of Syria] speak in your bedroom" (2 Kings 6:12). In this case it is not clear if the prophet is understood to be intrinsically gifted with formidable knowledge or has access to divine promptings.[5]

---

[4]See also Elisha's purging a stew of its lethal contents (2 Kings 4:41), his advice to Naaman on how to cleanse his leprosy (2 Kings 5:8-14), and his retrieval of a sunken ax head (2 Kings 6:6-7), all of which are accomplished without mentioning any consultation with God.

[5]Some see two different perceptions of prophets conveyed by distinct genres (e.g., Rofé, *Prophetical Stories*, pp. 13-30). The distinction may be real but unreliable: the fact that the naturally gifted

The fact that narrators so frequently describe prophets as spontaneously gifted with insight or power underscores the privileged plane on which the prophet was seen to function. The interplay between a prophet's innate ability and gifts and the special revelation that comes from God is best captured in 2 Samuel 7 when David expresses his desire to build a temple for God's ark. Without consulting God, Nathan encourages David to proceed with divine approval: "Go, do everything that is in your heart, for Yahweh is with you" (2 Sam 7:3). As one reads, one discovers that this statement is rather presumptuous, but Nathan is not rebuked when that same night a revelation comes to Nathan informing him that the opposite is the case: "Go and say to my servant, David, 'Thus said Yahweh, "Will you be the one to build for me a house to live in?"'" (2 Sam 7:5). This example elucidates the balance between a natural prophetic gift on the one hand and its limitation on the other hand by God. The prophet really does act independently of God, a feature one should expect in the light of the prophet's behavior on the divine council as a free-thinking agent. At the same time, the prophet is not given carte blanche, for God always has the last word, again a reflection of the divine council where it is God who is seated on a throne while all others stand.

The depiction of God's typically friendly and even casual encounter with his very gifted prophets in the Dtr history never becomes overwhelming to the point where the prophet cringes in fright. Where one can discern prophets receiving God's revelation in the literary prophets before the exile, this pattern seems to continue. We have already discussed those occasions where the divine council is presupposed and the prophet comfortably acts out his part (chapter two), or those times that God asks his prophets questions to which they reply (chapter four). To these one may add Jeremiah's call to service where the young Jeremiah's apparent first encounter with the divine is portrayed as a dialogue in which Jeremiah feels comfortable in declining God's offer:

> I said, "Ah, my Lord Yahweh! I do not know how to speak, for I am just a lad."

---

prophet appears in both Rofé's simple legenda as well as in his ethical legenda (e.g., 2 Kings 5) compromises the usefulness of the distinction, a matter to be discussed further below (e.g., Nathan in 2 Sam 7, Habakkuk and Jeremiah).

> Yahweh said to me, "Do not say, 'I am just a lad,' for you will go to all to whom I send you."
>
> Yahweh stretched out his hand and touched my mouth, and Yahweh said to me, "I hereby put my words in your mouth." (Jer 1:6-7, 9)

Even the remarkable contact between God's hand and man's mouth does not prompt any physical recoil by Jeremiah. In such intimate encounters, it is important to note that never does God approach a prophet in the Dtr history or the preexilic literary prophets with the initial advice, "Fear not!" There is nothing to fear.

The pattern set by Jeremiah's initial encounter with God appears elsewhere in his book and other preexilic literary prophets.[6] For example, another prophet with whom God is depicted as having an affable relationship is Hosea. The reader of Hosea's marital biography simply hears how "Yahweh said to Hosea" what Hosea was to do and how Hosea carried it out (Hos 1:2-9; 3:1-2). Jeremiah seems to have had a dreamlike revelation that was actually refreshing, for he notes: "I awoke and saw *(wā'er'eh),* and my sleep was pleasant to me" (Jer 31:26). It is actually quite rare that a preexilic literary prophet describes any aspects of the form that a revelation takes. When features such as the above are noted on exceptional occasions, they are unimpressive and mundane. Because the preexilic literary prophets rarely describe the means by which God reveals himself, it is not surprising that there are hardly any descriptions of the physical consequences that such revelation had upon the prophet in question: they do not faint or tremble in fright.

Although an innate ability or divine gift distinguishes the prophet as one who has an extraordinary insight (discussed above in chap. 4), the literary prophets also reflect at times the prophet's need to be informed by God. The prophet, although gifted, is a creature with limitations, and his

---

[6]E.g., Jer 13:1-9; 14:11-14; Is 7:3; 8:1, 5, 11. Habakkuk 3:16 is not to be taken as Habakkuk's response to a prophetic revelation that he received from God; it is the characteristic response of any worshiper to a typical recital of God's deeds as is narrated in the preceding verses (see Theodore Hiebert, *The God of My Victory: The Ancient Hymn in Habakkuk 3,* Harvard Semitic Monographs 38 [Atlanta: Scholars, 1986], pp. 109-13). Isaiah's cry of woe in Isaiah 6 results from an awareness of his own sinfulness but no physical response such as fright or physical collapse is noted. Jonah's belligerent disagreement in his dialogue with God can only take place in a context where prophet and God are assumed to have a relationship that tolerates such daring ease of access.

thoughts are not to be identified with God's thoughts. This fact is precisely what makes the divine council such a lively affair. Habakkuk's verbal give-and-take with God undergirds the first part of the book that bears his name:

> (Habakkuk): "How long, O Yahweh?
> (God): "Look (plural) among the nations! Observe (plural)! Be astonished (plural)! Wonder (plural)! Because I am doing something in your (plural) days . . .
> (Habakkuk): "Are you not from everlasting, O Yahweh, my god. . . . Why do you look upon the treacherous? Why are you silent?" (Hab 1:2, 5, 12-13)

This interchange assumes that the prophet does not fathom God's intent. And this failure of two minds to connect becomes explicit when this dialogue closes with the words: "I will stand at my post and station myself on the watch-tower, I will keep a lookout to see what He will speak to me, and what I should reply when I am reproved" (Hab 2:1). Eventually God replies ("Yahweh answered me and said, 'Write the vision . . .'" Hab 2:2), but it is crucial to note that the prophet knows he must be prepared to wait for a response. Here there is no instantaneous comprehension as the prophet is put on hold. This suspension of communication echoes what we saw above in the Dtr history when Elijah noted how "Yahweh has hidden it from me and has not told me" (2 Kings 4:27), or when Nathan gave permission to David to build the temple only to be told later that night that—to the contrary—God did not want David to build the temple (2 Sam 7:3-5).

Jeremiah also behaves in a similar fashion when homeless Judahites ponder what to do after the destruction of Jerusalem, asking Jeremiah to disclose God's will to them. He must wait ten days before "the word of Yahweh came to Jeremiah" (Jer 42:7), only then being able to relay to the people a response from God. On another occasion, Jeremiah is strangely but justifiably silent when he observes another prophet break the symbolic yoke under which Jeremiah had been staggering. Jeremiah simply does not know how to respond to this new development (Jer 28:10-11). From Jeremiah's perspective, the broken yoke could conceivably point to the termination of the "yoke" of Babylonian rule, much as other prophets witnessed similar surprising and unexpected actions with historical repercussions (e.g., Samuel in 1 Sam 15:27-28 observing Saul tearing his garment and noting, "Today Yahweh has torn the kingdom of Israel away from you"). Jeremiah makes no immediate response to the newly smashed yoke, waiting until some undisclosed period of time later when "the word of Yahweh came to Jeremiah after Hananiah the prophet had broken the yoke" (Jer 28:12).

There is therefore a general homogeneity of presentation in the Dtr history and the preexilic classical literary prophets. God and his prophet have a comfortable dialogic relationship. At times the prophet exercises a certain independence of action or confidence that he understands something of what God desires, even though this confidence is not always justified. At other times, the prophet is aware of his need to be informed, that there are arenas of divine activity beyond his ken. But always the prophet knows that he is able to communicate reciprocally with God as with a close companion.

All of this begins to change in the exilic book of Ezekiel. Now God comes with the storm clouds from the north (Ezek 1:4) in an overwhelming display of power that forces Ezekiel to collapse and fall to his face (Ezek 1:28). In the rest of the book, Ezekiel can dialogue with God just as the earlier prophets had done,[7] but further grand theophanies do appear in which Ezekiel once again falls to his knees for a total of four times. The phrase, "I fell on my face," repeats (Ezek 1:28; 3:23; 43:3; 44:4) in dramatic, stark contrast to earlier prophets who never react in this manner to God's presence, even in the face of accompanying convulsions of nature. When Elijah, for example, saw Yahweh "passing by" (1 Kings 19:11), accompanied by storm and earthquake, he remained emphatically standing (1 Kings 19:11, 13).

Ezekiel, therefore, marks the beginning of a gradual change in the presentation of the manner in which God reveals himself to his prophets. Although the book of Haggai still retains the vague phrase "and the word of Yahweh came to Haggai saying" (e.g., Hag 2:10, 20), after the exile a

---

[7]E.g., Ezekiel speaks to God (Ezek 4:14; 9:8; 11:13; 20:49 [21:5]; 37:3) and God speaks to Ezekiel (Ezek 3:1; 4:13; 8:5, etc.). The vague phrase, "and the word of Yahweh came to me saying" appears regularly in the book (e.g., Ezek 3:16; 6:1; 7:1; 11:14).

trend continues away from the congenial dialogue between God and prophet. In Zechariah, the encounters between Zechariah and the angels are emphatically in the context of night visions: "In the night I saw . . ." (Zech 1:8). Unlike rare comments in early prophets that God revealed himself at night,[8] the nocturnal setting is absolutely crucial for Zechariah's revelation, for the images that he sees are the building blocks of dreams and not everyday objects that the earlier prophets saw in their visions. When Zechariah notes that "the angel who was talking with me returned and roused me like a man is roused from his sleep" (Zech 4:1), one is mildly surprised that a prophet can fall asleep while receiving a revelation from God. This is a novel development, for one can hardly picture Amos or Jeremiah slumbering in the presence of God. When Jeremiah speaks of wakening refreshed (Jer 31:26), he seems to be coming out of a revelatory condition. Zechariah's sleep, on the other hand, incapacitates his ability to receive revelation. The manner of revelation has moved into a new mode where a prophet can be overcome with drowsiness while angels speak.

The most extreme form of these new developments in biblical texts occurs in Daniel's revelations. As in Zechariah, some are emphatically at night:[9]

> Then the mystery was revealed to Daniel in a vision of the night. (Dan 2:19)

> Daniel saw a dream on his bed, with visions of his head. Then he wrote down the dream . . . : "I was seeing in my vision by night. . . . I was seeing in the visions of the night." (Dan 7:1-2, 13)

Even revelations to non-Jews occur in dreams at night, such as Nebuchadnezzar (Dan 2:1; 4:5, 10, 18 [2, 7, 15]), detracting from any special gift that Daniel might be presumed to have in this regard. The effect of the

---

[8]In addition to 1 Sam 3:2-15 and 2 Sam 7:4 in the Dtr history discussed above, note also 1 Sam 15:10-12, 16.

[9]The perception of the reliability of dreams as a mode of divine communication in the Bible is a larger topic that requires significant nuancing. Jean-Marie Husser, *Dreams and Dream Narratives in the Biblical World*, Biblical Seminar 63 (Sheffield, U.K.: Sheffield Academic, 1999), provides a convenient access and discussion, notably observing with relevance to the matter at hand that during the exile and postexile a change is evident in biblical literature where dreams are rehabilitated as an acceptable mode of revelation.

revelation upon the recipient represents the most dramatic departure from the early prophets, for now Daniel goes even further than Ezekiel in describing the physical trauma he undergoes:

> My spirit was agitated within me, and the visions of my head frightened me. . . . My thoughts greatly frightened me, and my face turned pale. (Dan 7:15, 28)

> I began to tremble and fell upon my face. . . . I, Daniel, . . . was sick for days. (Dan 8:17, 27)

> No strength remained in me, and my appearance was marred, and I retained no strength. I heard the sound of his words, and as I heard the sound of his words, I fell into a trance with my face to the ground. . . . As he spoke this word to me, I stood up trembling. . . . I turned my face to the ground and was speechless. . . . "No strength remains in me, neither is there any breath left in me." (Dan 10:8-9, 11, 15, 17)

It is no wonder that the words "Do not fear!" now appear for the first time to encourage the prophet to receive the vision to come. Neither God nor any angel ever addressed the early prophets with these words by the very nature of the friendly conversation that characterized the relationship between God and prophet.[10] Indeed, the fright that characteristically begins to accompany angelic revelation corresponds to the distancing of the prophets from the divine council where prophets once regularly rubbed shoulders with all varieties of supernatural creatures without any recorded discomfort. Now the appearance of a solitary figure, even in human form, is disconcerting, for prophets without access to the divine council are no longer acclimated to the rarified air of the divine realm.

The manner of revelation is, therefore, another prophetic theme whose manifestation vacillates through time. The manner by which God revealed himself to the prophets reflects a variability that correlates with the way that a prophet related to the divine council, with a prophet's ability to see, and with the degree to which the future remained negotiable. As with the other themes, the exile resurfaces as the crucial period in which a transition is apparent between earlier and later prophets. The variable

---

[10]God does say it earlier, but it is advice not to fear the ones to whom the prophet is sent, not the present vision and its accoutrements (Is 8:12; Jer 1:8; Ezek 2:6; 3:9).

manner of revelation cannot be a coincidental feature of prophetic literature, for it indexes the fundamental relationship of the prophet with God.
What is surprising is the candor of the later prophets in portraying the
loss of intimacy and ease which had characterized the earlier prophets
who preceded them. The forms that precede the exile are consistently presented, just as are the forms that emerge from and follow the exile, but
there is no question that the earlier reflect a more desirable relationship
between God and man.

# 6

# ANGELS

WE BEGAN THIS INQUIRY WITH A LOOK at the divine council where the prophet stood with other privileged creatures, supernatural beings that also dialogued with God in administering the cosmos. One of the more stunning transformations in the perception of the prophet's role is his relationship with these supernatural, mediating beings that pass between God and man, those other members of the divine council to which the prophet is privy. One might think that, in the light of the prophet's unique status as a human being on the divine council discussed above, angels would be a dispensable element in a prophet's career. After all, of what need is an angelic intermediary when one has direct access to the throne of God himself?

And this is precisely the picture that emerges in the earliest depictions of prophetic activity. There is not a single literary prophet before the exile who receives a message from an angel. If this were even a minor part of the divine revelation, one would still expect some mention of what would have been a supernatural vindication that the message was not merely human. But angels are completely lacking in the revelatory process for literary prophets before the exile. Indeed, accounts about angels in any capacity are sparse in the extreme in these texts. There are those places where supernatural beings are depicted in the divine council as discussed earlier (cf. the seraphim in Is 6). And there is one account of an "angel of Yahweh" who massacres 185,000 Assyrian soldiers besieging Jerusalem (Is 37:36). But this verse, along with the entire story in which it is found, is copied largely verbatim from its original context in 2 Kings 19:35.[1] Otherwise, there are no angels depicted as active contemporary with the lives or messages of the literary prophets before the exile.[2] For these literary prophets, angels are a largely ignored phenomenon.

When one turns to narratives in the Dtr history, it may come as a surprise that there are very few accounts of angelic activity here also.[3] In the 102 chapters that comprise the books of 1–2 Samuel and 1–2 Kings, books that also contain extensive and rich material on prophetic activity, only once is an angel depicted delivering a message to a prophet. In this exceptional passage, an "angel of Yahweh" comes to Elijah with a message from God that Elijah is supposed to deliver in turn to the king of Israel (2 Kings 1:3, 15). This passage is so unusual[4] in these books that there is good reason to see here influence from some other source, perhaps a scribal modification of the text.

In the first place, Elijah (along with other prophets in these books) is repeatedly given divine messages, and in all cases apart from this passage the message comes straight from Yahweh. In addition to the prophet Micaiah who reports words that he heard Yahweh speak (1 Kings 22:17, 20,

---

[1]It is also arguable that the two books had access to a common source (cf. J. Alec Motyer, *The Prophecy of Isaiah: An Introduction and Commentary* [Downers Grove, Ill.: InterVarsity Press, 1993], pp. 285-86).

[2]Literary prophets do discuss the activity of angels in the past (Hos 12:4; cf. Is 63:9).

[3]There are only two accounts of angels who are clearly supernatural beings who quickly destroy large populations in a manner reminiscent of the tenth plague preceding the Exodus: (1) the angel who decimates the Assyrian army besieging Hezekiah in Jerusalem (2 Kings 19:35 // Is 37:36 // 2 Chron 32:21), and (2) the angel who brings a plague upon Israel as a consequence of David's misguided census (2 Sam 24:16-17 // 1 Chron 21:12,15-16, 20, 27, 30). In 1 Kings 19:5, 7 an angel (or is it a human "messenger" from Yahweh?) provides Elijah with food on his journey. A fourth narrative may appear in 1 Kings 13:18 where a prophet whose credibility is questionable claims that an angel spoke to him, but this whole chapter is a hotly debated account that stands out as an exceptional narrative on every count. Whether any of the "spirits" that one finds active as an "evil spirit" or a "lying spirit" (1 Sam 16:14-16, 23; 18:10; 19:9; 1 Kings 22:21-23) are to be associated with angelic or demonic beings is moot, but the term "angel" *(malʾāk)* is never applied to them in these passages.

[4]For a careful discussion of the late features and the uniqueness of this account on many levels see Rofé, *Prophetical Stories*, pp. 34-39.

22), "Yahweh said" his words directly to the prophets Ahijah (1 Kings 14:5), Elijah (1 Kings 19:15) and Samuel (1 Sam 3:11; 8:7, 22; 9:17; 16:1, 2, 7, 12). In the case of Samuel in particular, the speech is described as audible and hardly distinguishable from other human voices (1 Sam 3:4, 6, 8, 10). This continues a pervasive tradition that begins in the Garden of Eden with Adam and Eve and continues through the primeval history and into the stories of the patriarchs and beyond: "Yahweh said" directly to humans what he wanted to say. There was typically no angelic mediation.[5]

A less precise phrase can also be used to describe divine revelation to prophets: "The word of Yahweh/God 'came' to [person's name]." As we noted earlier, the verb in this phrase is actually not the verb "come," which is simply an English compromise to make more intelligible the Hebrew word that means "to be, become" *(hāyāh)*. Literally the phrase communicates that "the word of Yahweh was to" the prophet in question, a very vague indication that in some fashion the prophet and God's word crossed paths. This could refer to participation in the divine council, perceiving a vision, hearing an aural communication, or any other form of revelation. The ambiguity may be deliberate, preserving as a mystery the mechanism by which the prophet was apprised of God's perspective on human affairs. This phrase is used when God communicates with the prophets Samuel (1 Sam 15:10), Nathan (2 Sam 7:4), Gad (2 Sam 24:11), Shemaiah (1 Kings 12:22), Elijah (1 Kings 17:2, 8; 18:1; 19:9; 21:17, 28), Isaiah (2 Kings 20:4), the old nameless prophet who misleads the young prophet (1 Kings 13:20), and perhaps that young prophet as well (1 Kings 13:1, 5, 9, 17). What is important for our present discussion, however, is that in none of these passages is there any hint that angelic mediation is present.[6]

In the second place, there is a possible mechanism for a scribal modification that is attested elsewhere in the Bible, specifically with regard to the phrase "angel of Yahweh." Only a single four-consonant Hebrew word *mal'āk* makes the difference in meaning between "Yahweh said" and "the/

---

[5]Adam and Eve (e.g., Gen 3:13), Cain (e.g., Gen 4:6), Noah (e.g., Gen 7:1), Abraham (e.g., Gen 13:14), Hagar (e.g., Gen 16:9), Jacob (e.g., Gen 31:3), Moses (e.g., Ex 7:1), Balaam (Num 22:9), Joshua (e.g., Josh 3:7), Gideon (Judg 7:2).

[6]In 1 Kings 13:18, it is not the narrator but the deceptive old prophet who notes how "an angel spoke unto me by the word of Yahweh," a unique case underscoring the glaring omission of angels in all other divine communications.

an angel of *(mal'ak)* Yahweh said." This word *mal'āk* is a word that later
scribes could insert into a biblical passage when they wished to make God
more transcendent or to dissociate God from activities that might seem
too profane for later readers (or for other theological reasons).[7] If this word
is removed from these two verses, this account reads like all others in the
books of Samuel and Kings: "The [omit 'angel of the'] LORD said to Elijah
. . ." (2 Kings 1:3, 15).

However one accounts for the idiosyncratic story of Elijah and an angel
of Yahweh in 2 Kings 1, the overwhelming evidence of the early prophets
remains that angels are a peripheral phenomenon.[8] In the exilic period,
however, a dramatic change first begins to make its appearance. No angels
are mentioned in the book of Jeremiah, a text that is completed in exile but
for the most part describes the last days of Judah before the destruction of
the temple in 586 B.C. Jeremiah's contemporary, Ezekiel, however, records
a new development.

An entire chapter in Ezekiel (Ezek 9) is devoted to a description of
supernatural beings (one of whom speaks to God in Ezek 9:11) who pass
through Jerusalem at God's bidding in order either to destroy or to spare
certain of its inhabitants. Furthermore, although Ezekiel's book is overwhelmingly cast in the form of God's speech addressed to Ezekiel, angelic
guides are introduced in Ezekiel 40 who speak to Ezekiel as a revelation
unfolds about the future temple complex.[9] Throughout Ezekiel 40–42,
God is not mentioned as the source of the revelation as these supernatural

---

[7]As an example, in Ex 4:24 the Hebrew text reads "Yahweh" but the Septuagint reads "angel of
Yahweh." It is the inconsistent insertion of this word in some places that causes confusion so that it
is not clear if it is Yahweh or an angel of Yahweh who is speaking, even though both are mentioned
and there is only one speaker (e.g., Ex 3:2-7; Judg 6:12-14). For further discussion see Sam Meier,
"Angel of Yahweh," in *Dictionary of Deities and Demons in the Bible*, ed. Karel van der Toorn, Bob
Becking and Pieter W. van der Horst, 2nd ed. (Leiden: Brill, 1999), pp. 53-59.

[8]Indeed, Alexander Rofé, *Israelite Belief in Angels in the Pre-Exilic Period as Evidenced by Biblical
Traditions*, Ph.D. Dissertation, Hebrew University of Jerusalem (1969), pp. 112-19, 313-42, even
treats the attitude toward angels in the prophets as a polemic. However, in order to do so he prob-
lematically treats references to cherubim and seraphim as a typologically different phenomenon,
notes that Ezekiel mentions angels without calling them "angels" (see the next note), and treats
Jeremiah's references to the "council" in Jer 15:19; 23:18-22 not as God's council but as a reference to intimates among the prophets, even as he admits that an entourage of angels does appear
prominently in Zechariah.

[9]Ezekiel 40–48 is commonly distinguished from the rest of the book of Ezekiel for this and other
reasons.

beings unveil the various aspects of the future temple, and it is only their voices that are heard in chapters 40–42.[10] God's voice again begins to be heard addressing Ezekiel in Ezekiel 43:7, but because there is now more than one revelatory voice, it can become ambiguous as to who is speaking to Ezekiel if it is not clearly specified, and it may require at times several readings for clarification (e.g., Ezek 43:18). These angelic voices surface here and there later in Ezekiel (Ezek 46:20, 24; 47:6, 8).

What begins in Ezekiel in sporadic fashion becomes the predominant means of revelation after the exile in the book of Zechariah. Although the short postexilic books of Haggai and Malachi show no angels giving revelation, God's voice is hardly heard in the first eight chapters of Zechariah[11] as angels become the primary relays for communicating (and explicating) what the prophet needs to know. It now becomes clear why there is no reference to Zechariah attending the divine council: he receives his information from the supernatural messengers *(mal'ākîm)* whom God dispatches to relay God's plans that have already been decided upon. The status of the prophet has undergone a major reevaluation, indeed what may be described as nothing less than a demotion. He no longer interacts directly with God in the decision-making process, instead receiving information secondhand from God's angelic messengers.

It is appropriate to carry the investigation on to the book of Daniel, for the book of Daniel represents a culmination of the developing trend which began in the exile and gained momentum after the exile. Daniel is never addressed by God. Only angels bear messages and revelations to him. Each prophet before Daniel is either personally addressed by God or at least proclaims God's message with appropriate indicators that God's

---

[10]Ezek 40:3-4, 45; 41:4, 22; 42:13. These personages are never identified as "angels" *(mal'ākîm),* but their extraordinary appearance is determinative in identifying them as belonging to the category of supernatural emissaries (cf. "appearance of bronze" in Ezek 40:3). Ezekiel does not employ the term "angel" to refer to such supernatural figures in the book bearing his name, using instead simply the term "man," a common convention elsewhere as well (e.g., "the man Gabriel" Dan 9:21; "one like the appearance of a man" Dan 10:18; cf. Dan 10:5; 12:6, 7; Judg 13:3-23, especially Judg 13:6, 8, 10, 11).

[11]Zech 1:3-6. Often when God's words are present in the opening chapters of Zechariah, it is because an angel has relayed them (Zech 1:14-17; 2:4-5; 4:6-7). When the phrase "the word of Yahweh came to me" appears in Zechariah (Zech 1:1; 4:8; 7:4, 8; 8:1, 18), the ambiguity already present in earlier texts is compounded: does this refer to a direct communication from God or is the word, as often in Zechariah, mediated through an angelic figure?

words are being quoted: "Thus said Yahweh," "declares Yahweh" or "the word of Yahweh came to me." These elements, so characteristic of prophets, are conspicuously absent in the book of Daniel. Although Daniel may see a vision of God at work in the future (Dan 7:9-14), he never hears God speak. Consequently angels must play an unusually significant role in this book. For the first time in the Bible, one discovers in the book of Daniel that angels have individually distinct names such as Michael and Gabriel,[12] and, reciprocally, only here does an angel address God's prophet by his proper name (Dan 9:22; 10:11-12; 12:4, 9). In none of the literary prophets does God send an angel to deliver his prophet from calamity, but Daniel does receive this distinct privilege.[13] The increasing significance of angels is further underscored by the appearance in Daniel of a particular type known as the "watchers," otherwise unmentioned in the Hebrew Bible although amply attested in pseudepigraphical works.[14]

In conclusion, then, a total reversal has taken place in comparison to the preexilic period where the literary prophets never mention angels as a part of the revelatory process, and where the Dtr history finds angelic commissions to be unusual in the extreme. In the book of Daniel angels become the only means by which a verbal message comes to a human. The gradual transformation of the revelatory process can first be detected in the exilic period (Ezekiel). This transition and development corresponds to developments that we have witnessed in preceding chapters. We have already noted that the intimate relationship between prophet and God sustained in the earlier prophets was replaced by a distancing in the later prophets, a distance which was bridged by angels. A concomitant of this distancing seems to be the prophet's numbed sensitivity to the revelation he is granted. It is so numbed that Zechariah is even guilty of falling asleep while receiving a vision: "Then the angel who talked with me came again, and wakened me, as one is wakened from sleep" (Zech 4:1). Most notably, the prophet's declining relationship to the divine council correlates precisely with the increase of angelic activity in the revelatory pro-

---

[12]Michael in Dan 10:13, 21; 12:1; Gabriel in Dan 8:16; 9:21.

[13]Dan 6:22; cf. Dan 3:28. Isaiah 37:36 is different in that there it is an angel of Yahweh who is not said to be sent by God nor is it specifically the prophet who is rescued; see also note above.

[14]Dan 4:13, 17, 23 [4:10, 14, 20]; Jubilees 4:15, 22; 1 Enoch 12:4; 14:3; 15:2; 2 Enoch 18; Damascus Document 2.18; *Genesis Apocryphon* 2.1, 16.

cess. With the prophet no longer having access to the divine council, and with the prophet's declining ability to see clearly what God wishes him to see, the role of angels as explicating mediators between God and man becomes correspondingly of utmost importance. Where God had earlier asked the prophet, "What do you see *(rō'eh)?*" now it is an angel who asks the prophet this same question. Such developments, however, prompt the query: If the very means of revelation is in a process of transformation, is this reflected also in the means by which God's voice is described?

# 7

# THUS SAID YAHWEH

THERE IS A MISINFORMED IMPRESSION that all prophets employ the phrase "Thus said Yahweh" and related expressions. One even finds entire books on the prophets titled *Thus Says the Lord*, as if the phrase in some fashion encapsulates the essence of all the prophets.[1] However, such phrases by which God's words are identified in the prophets are not characteristic of all the prophets, or even most of them. On the contrary, there appears to be a development comparable to the transformations already discussed in the preceding chapters: the literary prophets who are associated with the period before the exile only rarely and sporadically employ such phrases. It is with those prophetic works associated with the exile and moving into the postexilic period where a dramatic increase is observable in the usage of such phrases, so much so that they become a major feature of prophetic speech only among the later prophets.

In table 7.1 are listed seven literary prophets for whom such phrases have little significance. This is apparent in the thirty-five chapters (552 verses) represented by these books where such phrases appear only twenty-

---

[1]James M. Ward, *Thus Says the Lord: The Message of the Prophets* (Nashville: Abingdon, 1991). "The important point for our purposes is that, with very few exceptions, prophetic poetry is formally presented, usually with an introductory formula like 'thus saith the Lord,' as a divine discourse" (Robert Alter, *The Art of Biblical Poetry* [New York: Basic Books, 1985], p. 141).

one times, or on an average less than once per chapter or once for every 26 verses.

**Table 7.1.**

| | Declares Yahweh (n'm-yhwh) | Said Yahweh (non-initial) ('mr yhwh) | Thus said Yahweh (kh 'mr yhwh) | And the word of Yahweh came to [name], saying (hyh dbr yhwh l'mr) |
|---|---|---|---|---|
| Habakkuk | 0 | 0 | 0 | 0 |
| Micah | 2[a] | 0 | 2[b] | 0 |
| Obadiah | 2[c] | 0 | 1[d] | 0 |
| Joel | 1[e] | 0 | 0 | 0 |
| Hosea | 4[f] | 0 | 0 | 0 |
| Nahum | 1[g] | 0 | 1[h] | 0 |
| Zephaniah | 5[i] | 1[j] | 0 | 0 |
| **TOTAL** | 15 | 1 | 4 | 0 |

[a]Mic 4:6 and Mic 5:9.
[b]Mic 2:3; 3:5.
[c]Obad 4, 8.
[d]Obad 1.
[e]Joel 2:13.
[f]Hos 2:15, 18, 23; 11:11.
[g]Nah 2:14; 3:5.
[h]Nah 1:12.
[i]Zeph 1:2, 3, 10; 2:9; 3:8.
[j]Zeph 3:20.

Most of these prophets that can be dated with some confidence represent works that are associated with preexilic prophets. Only Joel and Obadiah are difficult to date, and it should be noted that Obadiah's twenty-one verses do contain a higher percentage of the use of these phrases to identify God's voice. But what is important in all of these books is not simply the sparse use of these phrases to point to God's words. What is crucial to observe is that there is little concern to distinguish the words of God from the words of the prophet. In these books it is frequently difficult to determine when God speaks and when the prophet speaks, for the voices blend and merge with a freedom that is disorienting for one who wishes greater precision in knowing the source of each articulation. For example, consider the first eight verses of the book of Micah:

**A** The word of Yahweh that came to Micah, . . . which he saw concerning
Samaria and Jerusalem.

**B** Listen, all peoples!
Take heed, earth, and all that is in it!

**C** May my Lord Yahweh be a witness against you,
the Lord from his holy temple.
For behold, Yahweh is coming from his place.
He will descend and tread upon the high places of the earth.
The mountains will melt under him
and the valleys will be split
like wax before fire,
like waters poured down a steep place.

**D** All this is for Jacob's transgression
and for the sins of the house of Israel.
What is Jacob's transgression?
Is it not Samaria?
What is Judah's high place?
Is it not Jerusalem?

**E** I will turn Samaria into a ruin in the open country,
a place for planting vineyards.
Her stones I will pour down into the valley . . .
and all her idols I will turn into a desolation. . . .

**F** For this reason will I lament and wail.
I will go barefoot and naked.
I will raise a lamentation like the jackals. (Mic 1:1-8)

Section A speaks of both Micah and God in the third person, introduc-
ing the book as a whole. The speaker of section B is not initially clear, since
it could be either Micah or God. Because God is described in the third
person after a few lines (section C), one presumes that it is Micah's voice
after all. This continues for several lines until section D in which there are
no pronominal referents to God, or anyone for that matter. One could presume that Micah is still speaking in section D were it not for the fact that in
section E it is Yahweh who is clearly speaking. But the transition between
Micah's voice to God's voice was never made clear, making one less confi-

dent about the identity of the voice in section D. Finally, although the person speaking in section F continues to identify himself as "I," it is clear from the content that it is no longer God but a human (presumably Micah) speaking. Once again, the transition between speakers is not clearly marked.

It is this lack of concern for sorting out competing voices that makes the omission of phrases such as "Thus said Yahweh" quite dramatic in the early prophets. In most of the seven prophets noted in table 7.1 above, there is a general lack of concern to distinguish God's words from the prophet's. This ambiguity of attribution is actually a function of poetry, for the same phenomenon happens in the book of Psalms, where God's voice is often formally undistinguished from the psalmist's.[2] If speech attribution is related to the poetic genre, it is not surprising and, indeed, reinforces another theme that we will discuss in the next chapter.

But the identification of the speech of God goes beyond a mere writing convention, for what is at stake is the very definition of what constitutes God's word. Is the prophet's voice to be separated from God's? In the preexilic prophets there is little effort expended by writers to disentangle the two and one must presume that it was not an issue. However, compare the following introduction (again eight verses, like the Micah passage above) to the postexilic book associated with the prophet Haggai where one immediately becomes aware of new priorities in clearly specifying precisely what constitutes God's word:

> In the second year . . . **the word of Yahweh came by the prophet** Haggai to Zerubbabel. . . . **Thus said Yahweh of hosts**, saying, "This people says, 'The time has not come for Yahweh's house to be rebuilt.'" **The word of Yahweh came by the prophet** Haggai, saying, "Is it time for you yourselves to live in your paneled houses while this house is in ruins?" Now, **thus said Yahweh** of hosts, "Consider your ways. . . ." **Thus said Yahweh** of hosts, "Consider your ways. Ascend to the mountains, bring wood and build the house, so that I may be pleased with it and be honored," **said Yahweh**. (Hag 1:1-8)

---

[2]For example, God is not speaking in Ps 91:11 but he is speaking in Ps 91:14, with no clear mention that the speaking voice has changed. The same occurs in Ps 95 where the psalmist is speaking in the opening verses (Ps 95:1-7) but the psalm closes (Ps 95:8-11) with God's words. Only the content makes the transition clear. For further discussion see Meier, *Speaking of Speaking*, pp. 32-41.

The contrast between Micah and Haggai is dramatic: where no indication of speaker appeared in the former, the latter is emphatic, and repeatedly so, in clarifying what words belong to God. The ambiguity present in Micah is no longer tolerated in Haggai, and on the contrary there is an aggressive desire to highlight that these words are divine in origin. In table 7.2 the postexilic books of Haggai, Malachi and the first eight chapters of Zechariah are presented with the evidence for the use of the same phrases that were noted in table 7.1:

**Table 7.2.**

| | Declares Yahweh (n'm-yhwh) | Said Yahweh (non-initial) ('mr yhwh) | Thus said Yahweh (kh 'mr yhwh) | And the word of Yahweh came to [name], saying (hyh dbr yhwh l'mr) |
|---|---|---|---|---|
| Haggai | 12[a] | 3[b] | 5[c] | 5[d] |
| Zechariah 1–8 | 13[e] | 4[f] | 19[g] | 7[h] |
| Malachi | 1[i] | 24[j] | 1[k] | 0 |
| TOTAL | 26 | 31 | 25 | 12 |

[a]Hag 1:9; 2:4a, 4b, 4c, 8, 14, 17, 23a, 23b; and at the conclusion of an oracle in Hag 1:13; 2:9, 23c.
[b]Hag 1:8; 2:7, 9.
[c]Hag 1:2; 2:11; and in mid oracle in Hag 1:5, 7; 2:6.
[d]Hag 1:1, 3; 2:1, 10, 20. Contrast the introduction to the books of Zephaniah, Micah, Joel, and Hosea.
[e]Zech 1:3, 4, 16; 2:9, 10, 10, 14; 3:9, 10; 5:4; 8:6, 11, 17.
[f]Zech 1:3; 4:6; 7:13; 8:14.
[g]Most appear in chapters 1 and 8 (Zech 1:3, 4, 14, 16, 17; 8:2, 3, 4, 6, 7, 9, 14, 19, 20, 23). Note also Zech 2:12; 3:7; 6:12; 7:9.
[h]Zech 1:1, 7; 4:8; 7:4, 8; 8:1, 18.
[i]Mal 1:2.
[j]Appearing in mid-oracle (Mal 1:2, 6, 10, 11, 13, 13, 14; 2:2, 4, 8, 16, 16; 3:5, 7, 10, 11, 12, 13, 17, 19, 21), although it is unclear if Mal 1:8, 9; 3:1 appear in mid-oracle.
[k]Mal 1:4.

In these 14 chapters (214 verses), the 94 occurrences of phrases that mark God's speech appear on the average of six or seven times in each chapter, or once in every two verses. This is an extremely high density, underscoring that the lack of markers for divine speech in the earlier prophets is now being over-compensated by a proliferation of such phrases in the later prophets.[3]

---

[3]Zechariah 9–14 behaves much like the seven minor prophets discussed above that show little concern for identifying the divine voice (Zech 10:12; 11:4, 6; 12:1, 4; 13:2, 7-8), a fact that corresponds

The earliest extensive evidence for an overt concern to identify God's speech by the use of such phrases occurs in the prophetic books that emerge from the exile, specifically Jeremiah and Ezekiel. Some parts of Jeremiah, predictably poetic, are reluctant to clarify speaking voices, much like the book of Micah.[4] But other parts, especially prose sections but also in much poetry, exuberantly use these phrases, as these eight verses illustrate:

> "Behold, the days are coming," **says Yahweh**, "when I will make a new covenant with the house of Israel and with the house of Judah, not like the covenant . . . that they broke, though I was their husband," **says Yahweh**. "But this is the covenant that I will make with the house of Israel after those days," **says Yahweh**. "I will put my law within them . . . for all of them will know me, from the least of them to the greatest of them," **says Yahweh**, "for I will forgive their iniquity, and their sin I will remember no more."
>
> **Thus said Yahweh**, . . .
>
> "If these fixed orders ever depart from my presence, **says Yahweh**,
> so also the seed of Israel will cease from being a nation before me for forever."
>
> **Thus said Yahweh**,
>
> "If the heavens above can be measured, . . .
> so also even I will reject all the seed of Israel
> because of all that they have done," **says Yahweh**.
>
> "Behold, the days are coming," **says Yahweh**, "when the city shall be rebuilt. (Jer 31:31-38)[5]

The mixture in Jeremiah of voices that are marked by clear phrases and other voices that are unmarked is very complex.[6] In any case, Jeremiah

---

with a scholarly consensus with respect to the literary unity of the book on other grounds (see note 7 in chap. 1).

[4]E.g., Jer 4:28–5:8; 46:6-12; 47:3-7; 48:2-11.

[5]The increasing use of these formulae over time is especially observable in the book of Jeremiah where the Septuagint preserves a text that is more restrained in this regard than the Masoretic text (cf. Emanuel Tov, *Textual Criticism of the Hebrew Bible*, 2nd ed. [Minneapolis: Fortress, 2001], pp. 319-23).

[6]See discussion in Meier, *Speaking of Speaking*, pp. 258-72, supplemented with H. Van Dyke Parunak, "Some Discourse Functions of Prophetic Quotation Formulas in Jeremiah," in *Biblical Hebrew and Discourse Linguistics*, ed. Robert D. Bergen (Winona Lake, Ind.: Eisenbrauns, 1994), pp. 489-519.

bears the impression of a transitional work in this regard, preserving much of the earlier ambiguity side by side with other passages that aggressively mark God's speech as the postexilic prophets will do.

Jeremiah delivered his oracles orally before the exile, their written form and editing beginning toward the end of his career and continuing after the destruction of Jerusalem in 586 B.C.[7] In contrast to Jeremiah, Ezekiel's work began in exile in Babylon, a few years before the destruction of the temple. Also unlike Jeremiah's book, Ezekiel's is far more regular—at least in Ezekiel 11–39—in its application of phrases such as "Thus said Yahweh" and "The word of Yahweh came to me, saying." These two phrases regularly mark the beginning of God's speech,[8] which is often interspersed with explicit reminders that God is speaking (e.g., "Said the Lord Yahweh"[9]). Whatever the reason for the distinctively different forms in the first ten chapters and the final nine chapters of Ezekiel, the book as a whole still exhibits a transitional stage in the application of such phrases.[10] In both Ezekiel and Jeremiah, the interest in identifying the voice of God has become more explicit and more regular with hundreds of appearances of these phrases.[11]

It may seem ironic that the emphatic specification of God's words comes when the prophet is on the brink of being distanced from the divine council. It is precisely at the transitional time of the exile, as we have seen earlier, when the prophet's relationship to the divine council becomes tenuous and less clear that one finds a developing interest in explicitly identifying the voice of God. Would not one intuit, contrarily, that the prophet who sits on the divine council should be the one with

---

[7]The account in Jer 36 underscores two issues in this regard, both of which are remarkable as perspectives emanating from a written text: (1) the emphatically oral nature of Jeremiah's communications, and (2) the secondary nature of the written format, something to which one resorts only when the oral medium is stifled.

[8]E.g., Ezek 11:14-16; 12:8-10, 17-19, 21-25, 26-28; 13:1-3; 14:1-4.

[9]E.g., Ezek 11:21; 12:25, 28; 13:16; 14:11, 23.

[10]For detailed discussion, see Meier, *Speaking of Speaking*, pp. 230-42.

[11]We have not mentioned the books of Amos and Isaiah, both of which are quite complex in this regard. Amos represents a curious mixture of a number of conventions in different parts of the book that show a high priority for marking explicitly God's voice, but other parts of the book show a contrary reticence (see Meier, *Speaking of Speaking*, pp. 226-29). The first half of Isaiah (Is 1–35) shows little concern to identify speakers in contrast to the last half of the book (Is 40–66) where the voice of God overwhelmingly predominates and is often, although not consistently, marked (see Meier, *Speaking of Speaking*, pp. 242-58).

the most confidence and authority, and the most likely to affirm, "Thus said Yahweh"? It is likely that another related issue requires attention before we can address this question, specifically the very form in which prophetic oracles are composed. For that, we will need to inquire into the nature of Hebrew poetry.

# 8

# POETRY, PROSE AND THE PROPHETS

HEBREW POETRY IS NOT AN EASY TOPIC TO DISCUSS, for scholars are not in agreement about all of its essentials.[1] Hebrew poetry certainly does not rhyme sounds as does traditional English poetry, even though it does rhyme ideas. All agree that these conceptual rhymes, where one statement is reformulated in different words and expanded, are one of the common, although not necessary, features of poetry.[2] Psalm 114:1-4 can provide a useful illustration:

| When **Israel** went out | **from Egypt,** |
| The **house of Jacob** | **from a people of foreign tongue,** |
| **Judah** became | **his sanctuary,** |
| **Israel** | **his dominion.** |

---

[1]For a survey of its essentials see Wilfred G. E. Watson, *Classical Hebrew Poetry: A Guide to Its Techniques* (Sheffield, U.K.: JSOT, 1984). Part of the problem in pinning down the contours of Hebrew poetry is that Hebrew poetry, like the Hebrew language, changes over time and the Bible preserves multiple stages in its evolution. On this still problematic area, see Frank Moore Cross Jr., "Toward a History of Hebrew Prosody," in *Fortunate the Eyes That See: Essays in Honor of David Noel Freedman in Celebration of His Seventieth Birthday*, ed. Astrid B. Beck, Andrew H. Bartlet, Paul R. Raabe and Chris A. Franke (Grand Rapids: Eerdmans, 1995), pp. 298-309.

[2]For a magisterial discussion of this phenomenon see James Kugel, *The Idea of Biblical Poetry: Parallelism and Its History* (New Haven, Conn.: Yale University Press, 1981).

| | |
|---|---|
| **The sea** | looked and **fled**; |
| **The Jordan** | **turned back**. |
| **The mountains** danced | **like rams**, |
| **The hills** | **like lambs**. |

In each pair of lines, the second line is a reformulation and/or expansion of the first line. The precision of the reformulation is evident in the words in each pair that are boldface, these words or phrases representing synonyms or words with overlapping, congruent meaning. With this stereophonic, double representation of a single concept, Hebrew poetry achieves a high literary style that can be quite distinct from prose and narrative elsewhere in the Bible. Sometimes the rhyming of a single idea or concept can contrast two opposite notions, as in Psalm 18:27 [28]:

For **you save** an afflicted people
But **you abase** haughty eyes.

Such devices are among many that are representative features of Hebrew poetry. The problem in defining poetry comes when one begins to wrestle with recovering features that do not seem to be preserved in literary traditions, such as meter, elision of vowels, or any accompanying music. There is also the problem of the changes that Hebrew poetry underwent through time, and even detecting the boundaries between poetry and prose when some texts sit comfortably between the two categories. Unfortunately, biblical poetry is not traditionally written in stanza form with parallel lines clearly indicated, as is true in the formatting of English poetry. When Hebrew poetry appears in biblical manuscripts, it is formatted to look formally no different from Hebrew prose.[3]

With this in mind, the reader is encouraged to pick up a Bible and scan through the book of the prophet Micah, observing how the printers of the

---

[3]The Biblia Hebraica Stuttgartensia (and related texts) do format the Hebrew text as poetry, but this is a modern convention and an interpretive device. A few passages in the Bible regularly display a peculiar formatting device dubbed in rabbinic terminology, "log over brick, brick over log" and "log over log, brick over brick" (Ex 15:1-18; Deut 32; Judg 5; 2 Sam 22). Exceptions include some scrolls from Qumran that format the book of Psalms by separating cola (e.g., some parts of the Psalms scroll from Cave 11). That ancient Semitic poetry could be formatted for the eyes of the reader to see the parallels is evident in some cases in Akkadian and Ugaritic texts, but the device seems not to have been treated as necessary.

English Bible have formatted these seven chapters. Most modern English Bibles that make a distinction between prose and poetry will format Micah's entire book as poetry (usually with the exception of the very first verse). One may contrast this consistent poetic formatting with the book of Haggai, where most English Bibles present the entire book as prose. If one looks at yet a third example, the book of Jeremiah, one discovers that the first half of the book tends to be formatted as poetry (with a few prose sections) while the last half of the book tends to be primarily prose (with a few poetic sections). It is clear from these three examples that not all of the prophets employ prose and poetry with the same consistency.

Despite the awkwardness in some places of distinguishing poetry and prose, English Bibles, regardless of the translation, tend to agree on which passages are to be formatted as prose and which are to appear as poetry. If one continues the exercise just begun with the three prophets Micah, Haggai and Jeremiah, one can begin to discern that some prophets tend to behave in similar fashions with regard to their use of poetry or prose. One can place the literary prophets on a chart (see table 8.1) representing a continuum spanning those which evince mostly prose to those which are composed of mostly poetry (according to English Bible conventions).

**Table 8.1.**

| Poetry   - - - - | Mixed Poetry/Prose | - - - -Prose |
|---|---|---|
| Hosea | Isaiah 1–35 | Haggai |
| Joel | Jeremiah | Malachi[a] |
| Amos | Ezekiel | |
| Obadiah | | Zechariah 1–8 |
| Micah | Zechariah 9–14 | |
| Nahum | | |
| Habakkuk | | |
| Zephaniah | | |
| Isaiah 40–66 | | |

[a]Most Bibles format Malachi as prose. Although there are a few translations that present it as poetry (e.g., NKJV and NAB), a comparison of these will indicate how problematic this is. See the appendix.

In interpreting table 8.1, one can see that Jeremiah shows a generally equal amount devoted to both poetry and prose,[4] Ezekiel shows a more

---

[4]As noted above, most of the poetry in Jeremiah appears in the first half of the book, while most of the prose appears in the second half, but a notable exception is the corpus of poetic oracles against

significant use of prose, and Zechariah is mostly prose with some poetic sections in one part of the book.

There is a curious correlation between table 8.1 above and table 8.2 below that identifies the prophets according to the general time in which they were active:[5]

**Table 8.2.**

| 8th century | 7th century | 6th century | 5th century |
| --- | --- | --- | --- |
| Amos | Nahum | | Haggai |
| Hosea | Habakkuk | Ezekiel | Zechariah 1–8 |
| Isaiah 1–35 | Zephaniah | | Malachi |
| Micah | Jeremiah | Isaiah 40–66 | |

Those prophets identified as clearly eighth–seventh century prophets have their oracles preserved in texts that are associated with a poetic format. Those prophets active after the exile in the 6th century are exclusively or primarily prosaic. Those prophets overlapping the exilic period (Jeremiah and Ezekiel) represent a curious mixture of prose and poetry together, suggesting a possibly transitional nature.[6]

In other words, the genre or literary medium in which a prophet's words are recorded seems to roughly correlate with the time in which the prophet was active. Specifically, poetry is the primary medium for the preexilic prophets, prose for the prophets after the exile, while the prophets associated with the exile show a mixture of both. It must be stressed that this is not a rigorous analysis but an observation of an obvious general trend. One can not make the claim that prophets only spoke in poetry in the preexilic period nor that they stopped composing poetry in the postexilic period. The poetry of Isaiah 40–66, for example, is a reminder of just such

---

the nations in Jer 46–51. An alternate arrangement of the text of Jeremiah appears in the Septuagint, which places these oracles after Jer 25 and so more closely juxtaposes the poetic sections of Jeremiah. For a survey of attempts to relate the prose and the poetry in the book of Jeremiah, and continuing perplexities in this regard, see Robert R. Wilson, "Poetry and Prose in the Book of Jeremiah," in *Ki Baruch Hu: Ancient Near Eastern, Biblical, and Judaic Studies in Honor of Baruch A. Levine*, ed. Robert Chazan, William W. Hallo and Lawrence H. Schiffman (Winona Lake, Ind.: Eisenbrauns, 1999), pp. 413-28.

[5]Joel, Obadiah, and Zechariah 9–14 are not easily dated and so are not included in table 8.2.

[6]The so-called prose sermons of Jeremiah represent a distinctly new phenomenon in the literary prophets (e.g., Jer 7:1–8:3; 11:1-14; 16:1-18; 18:1-12; 19:1-13; 31:27-34; 33:1–34:5; 34:12-22; 35:12-17), just as does the prosaic and entirely autobiographical format for Ezekiel's book.

an overlap in the transitional period of the exile. Nevertheless, this curious general correlation between a prophet's date and the medium in which
the book is written must be explained. Such a correlation being associated
with so many figures and so many texts is not likely to be accidental.[7]

The clear preference for poetry as a characteristic medium of communication for prophets associated with early Israel receives further support
from circumstantial evidence from elsewhere. It is very rare for the Bible
to relate the preliminary ritual by which a prophet prepared for or solicited
a revelation from Yahweh. But when Elisha wishes to learn the divine
response to a king's question about the future, he makes the following
request which results in the events described:

> "And now bring me a musician." It happened that as the musician played,
> the hand of Yahweh came upon him [i.e., Elisha], and he said, "Thus said
> Yahweh, 'Make lots of trenches in this dry river bed.'" (2 Kings 3:15-16)[8]

Before Elisha can receive Yahweh's revelation in this account, he requires a musician to play. If music could be a significant dimension of
prophecy, the poetic genre in which oracles were cast is therefore quite
appropriate. The rhythmic cadence and measured structure of music finds
an appropriate partner in the metrical or regulated complexes of poetry.
The book of Psalms, for example, as a collection of poetry, contains works
that were designed to be sung.[9] It is not an accident, therefore, when other

---

[7]Robert Lowth, who laid the foundation for all subsequent work in Hebrew poetry, in his lectures in
the mid-eighteenth century already noted the correlation between poetry and prophecy, and more
particularly the decline of poetry in prophetic texts after the Babylonian exile (e.g., his lecture #21
[*Lectures on the Sacred Poetry of the Hebrews*, vol. 2, trans. G. Gregory, (London: J. Johnson, 1787) p.
100]). The development of the insight that literary prophets were poets was a special contribution
of B. Duhm beginning a century later in his commentary on Isaiah (*Das Buch Jesaia*, HKAT 3/1
[Gottingen: Vandenhoeck & Ruprecht, 1892]).

[8]Although Bibles format Elisha's oracle as prose, it is demonstrably poetry: "Make this dry riverbed
full of trenches. / For thus said Yahweh, / You will not see wind, / and you will not see rain, / but
that dry riverbed will be filled with water, / and you will drink, you / and your cattle and your
animals. / And this is but a light matter in Yahweh's eyes, / and he will give Moab into your hand,
/ and you will strike every fortified city, / and every choice city, / and you will fell every good tree,
/ and stop up all water sources, / and ruin every good piece of land with stones" (2 Kings 3:16-19).
The highly picturesque language and poetic parallelism in many prophetic speeches in the Dtr
history has been noted (Gerhard von Rad, "The Deuteronomic Theology of History in 1 and 2
Kings," pp. 154-66, in *From Genesis to Chronicles: Explorations in Old Testament Theology*, ed. K. C.
Hanson [Fortress: Minneapolis, 2005], p. 159).

[9]The term *mizmôr* that appears at the beginning of over one-third of the psalms in the book of
Psalms (e.g., Pss 3–6; 8–9; 12–13; 15; 19–24) may signify music accompanied by an instrument,

prophets are depicted as prophesying in the context of music:

> You will meet a band of prophets coming down from the high place. Before them will be a harp, a tambourine, a flute, and a lyre, and they will be prophesying. The spirit of Yahweh will alight upon you, you will prophesy with them, and you will be transformed into another man. (1 Sam 10:5-6)

> David set apart . . . for the service the sons of Asaph, Heman and Jeduthun, who prophesy with lyres, harps, and cymbals . . . under the authority of their father Jeduthun with the lyre, who prophesied by thanksgiving and praised Yahweh. (1 Chron 25:1-3)

The three individuals singled out in the last citation from the late biblical book of Chronicles are elsewhere called "the king's seers,"[10] who give directions to the singers in the temple service (2 Chron 35:15). The Chronicler indicates that the positioning of Levites "with cymbals, with harps, and with lyres" was "a command from Yahweh through his prophets," among whom are mentioned "Gad the king's seer and Nathan the prophet" (2 Chron 29:25). The only time that Moses' sister, Miriam, is called a prophetess is after crossing the Red Sea when "she took a tambourine in her hand" and sang (Ex 15:20-21). It may be significant that the prophetess Deborah (Judg 4:4) had a song of hers preserved in Judges 5, lyrics that begin with the phrase, "And Deborah sang" (Judg 5:1), correlating with words of Isaiah that similarly commence, "I will sing a song" (Is 5:1). Ezekiel's reputation is not surprising from this perspective when his hearers perceive him as "just a singer of bawdy songs, who has a sweet voice and plays skillfully" (Ezek 33:32 NJPS). In the poetic "last words of David" (2 Sam 23:1), David is described as the "sweet psalmist of Israel" (2 Sam 23:1 KJV[11]) who as a poet and musician says, "The spirit of Yahweh

---

even though it is often translated as simply "psalm." Nevertheless one must be wary of etymology, for lyric poetry is not accompanied by a lyre. Not only are some psalms specifically called "songs" *šîr* in their introductions (Ps 18; 30; 45; 46; 48; 66–68; 76), numerous cryptic directions that are apparently musical are scattered throughout the psalter (cf. the introductions to Ps 4; 5; 6; 7; 12; 54–55; 61; 67; 76), in addition to specific references to their being sung (see the introduction to Ps 7; cf. Ex 15:1; Judg 5:1).

[10]The MT reads "Asaph, Heman, and Jeduthun, the king's seer (Hebrew *ḥōzēh*)," as if only Jeduthun is the seer. There are Hebrew manuscripts, however, which read the plural *ḥōzê* "seers," along with the LXX (cf. 1 Esdras 1:15), and in any case Heman is called the "king's seer" elsewhere (*ḥōzēh*, 1 Chron 25:5).

[11]Cf. "The singer of Israel's songs" (REB). The translation is not secure, for the Hebrew root *zmr*,

spoke through me, and his word was on my tongue" (2 Sam 23:2).

Asaph appears first in the above list of three individuals who are said to be appointed by David "to prophesy with lyres, harps, and cymbals." This Asaph is the figurehead to whom the group known as the "sons of Asaph" looked as their founder and model, an individual whose name appears at the beginning of twelve psalms in the book of Psalms (Pss 50; 73–83). His emphatic connection with music is a leitmotif of the books of Chronicles, Ezra and Nehemiah, the single most significant feature that distinguishes him.[12] There is a comfortable congruence, therefore, between this feature and the fact that the Chronicler calls him a "seer" (Hebrew *hōzeh*) whose words should be used in the context of temple worship when the Levites sing praises to God (2 Chron 29:30).[13] It has been argued that a preexilic (and later) ancient Israelite "audience would have understood a prophet speaking in the first performance of these psalms . . . and they would have understood a singing performance of prophetic speech on subsequent occasions, or perhaps a prophetic liturgist breathed into the speech a new freshness on the occasion of each performance."[14] In this light, it is even more remarkable that the literary prophets exhibit a notable decline in poetic format in contrast to the emphatic postexilic liturgical connection with prophecy reflected in the books of Chronicles.

A connection between music and prophecy in Israel is reinforced by other cultural phenomena. Assyrian sources support "the compatibility of

---

"sing with accompaniment," may mean "strength, protection" (cf. "the favorite of the Strong One [i.e., God] of Israel," NRSV).

[12]1 Chron 15:16-19; 16:5, 7, 37; 25:1, 2, 6; 2 Chron 25:12; 35:15; Ezra 2:41 (// Neh 7:44); 3:10; Neh 11:17, 22; 12:35.

[13]One of the distinctive features of the books of Chronicles is the peculiar emphasis upon the connection between prophets and the temple liturgy. See for example Harry V. Van Rooy, "Prophet and Society in the Persian Period According to Chronicles," in *Second Temple Studies. 2. Temple and Community in the Persian Period*, ed. Tamara C. Eskenazi and Kent H. Richards, JSOTSS 175 (Sheffield, U.K.: JSOT, 1994), pp. 163-79, who argues for the decline of the prophetic institution in the Persian period with aspects of its roles assumed by the temple Levites. The passages in Chronicles that describe the Davidic period in this regard pose problems in their descriptions of prophecy: (1) to what degree does the Chronicler's understanding of prophecy correspond with the preexilic understanding of prophecy, and (2) when the Chronicler, a postexilic writer, insists that there is a correlation between music and prophecy, to what degree is he reflecting a first or second temple perspective? See Sara Japhet, *I & II Chronicles* (Louisville, Ky.: Westminster John Knox, 1993), pp. 439-41.

[14]John W. Hilber, *Cultic Prophecy in the Psalms*, BZAW 352 (Berlin: de Gruyter, 2005), p. 184.

genuine prophecy with psalmody."[15] Classical Arabic poetry was precisely the medium of expression before the seventh century A.D. among pre-Islamic seers or soothsayers.[16] In the modern Middle East, the Rwala bedouin continued to believe that Allah sent celestial spirits with a message for men only during a dream which could be either natural or artificial, and in order to receive God's message through an artificial dream, one induced such a dream by music or dancing.[17] In Greece, music itself was a divine gift[18] that Socrates explicitly compares to the gift of prophecy: "God takes away the minds of poets, and uses them as his ministers, as he also uses diviners and holy prophets" (*Ion* 534). Plutarch observed by the beginning of the second century A.D. that the older oracles in Greek shrines were cast in poetic form, prompting a variety of responses to the question why the prose format was predominant in his day. As a priest of Delphi, his dialogue, "Why are Delphic Oracles no Longer Given in Verse?" can be taken as an informed analysis of what was perceived to be a significant contrast with the past.[19]

Such a substantial attestation connecting prophecy and music may have relevance for the Hebrew Bible. Why is it that poetry should be so extensively associated with a divine message, and correspondingly with books in the Bible attributed to prophets? And if poetry (and perhaps its partner, music) was a significant dimension for Hebrew prophecy before the exile, why did the format become dispensable after the exile?

One may initially observe that poetry is generally recognized cross-

---

[15]Ibid., p. 226.

[16]Michael Zwettler, *The Oral Tradition of Classical Arabic Poetry: Its Character and Implications* (Columbus: Ohio State University Press, 1978), pp. 101, 133, 139, 166, 201. Muhammed's utterances in the Qur'an were identified by his opponents as poetry, although he justly claimed otherwise (ibid., pp. 156-61).

[17]Alois Mursil, *The Manners and Customs of the Rwala Bedouins*, Oriental Explorations and Studies 6 (New York: American Geographical Society, 1928), p. 411.

[18]In the Odyssey, Alcinous describes Demodocus as a "divine minstrel" to whom god has given the gift of minstrelsy (8.43-45), for after all it is a divine Muse who teaches all minstrels (8.480-81). Plato has Socrates observe that poets "are simply inspired to utter that to which the Muse impels them, and that only; and when inspired, one of them will make dithyrambs, another hymns of praise, another choral strains, another epic or iambic verses . . . for not by art does the poet sing, but by power divine" (*Ion* 534).

[19]Of related interest is his dialogue, "The Oracles in Decline." On the other hand, Plutarch's contemporary Tacitus records that the oracle at Colophon continued to provide metrical prophecies (*Annals* 2.54).

culturally as a more formal register of human speech—indeed, a human universal[20]—a more sophisticated mode of verbalization that requires special skills in its production. As such, it becomes a more appropriate medium for mediating divine communications that by definition transcend ordinary human patterns. The medium is very much the message, and can even become one criterion by which one can discern a supernatural origin.[21] The medium in which Hebrew prophetic texts are written is central to the message they convey. Poetry in many ways is not even optional for prophetic texts, for in poetic texts, the sounds of words take on a heightened significance. Phonetic images contribute to all aspects of the prophetic message. For example, the following dismal portraits are intricately bonded by phonetic links that tie one word to another. Along with the translation, a transliteration of the corresponding Hebrew phrase permits these phonetic congruencies to be seen:

Terror, pit, and trap
*paḥad wāpaḥat wāpāḥ* (Is 24:17 // Jer 48:43)

For justice . . . bloodshed, for righteousness . . . an outcry
*lĕmišpāṭ . . . mišpāḥ liṣdāqāh . . . ṣĕʿāqâ* (Is 5:7)

A day of destruction and desolation
*yôm šōʾâ ûmĕšôʾâ* (Zeph 1:15)

Plundered, pillaged, and stripped
*bûqâ ûmĕbûqâ ûmĕbullāqâ* (Nah 2:10 [2:11])

As destruction from the Almighty
*kĕšōd miššadday* (Is 13:6 // Joel 1:15)

Bitter and impulsive
*hammar wĕhannimhār* (Hab 1:6)

---

[20]Donald E. Brown, *Human Universals* (Philadelphia: Temple University Press, 1991), p. 132.

[21]Plato has Socrates opine that poets speak in poetic form "in order that we who hear them may know them to be speaking not of themselves who utter these priceless words in a state of unconsciousness, but that God himself is the speaker, and that through them he is conversing with us" (*Ion* 534). For further discussion of the tensions inherent in the relationship between prophecy and poetry, see Stephen A. Geller, "Were the Prophets Poets?" *Prooftexts* 3 (1983).

In the case of Is 24:17 (// Jer 48:43) the similar sounds become the basis of an expanded explanation:

> The one who flees from the terror *(paḥad)* will fall into the pit *(paḥat),* and the one who ascends from the pit *(paḥat)* will be caught in the trap *(paḥ).* (Jer 48:44; cf. Is 24:18)

It is the way that these words appear in Hebrew that constitutes the basis of this prophecy. This prophecy would not be generated in another language, for it arises from the phonetic shape of these words in Hebrew. We saw earlier that the keen prophetic sight ("What do you see?") often depended upon a prophet's ability to connect an object with a divine message, such as Amos's vision of the "summer fruit" *(qāyiṣ)* that grounded an oracle focused on the "end" *(qêṣ),* or Jeremiah's identification of the "almond branch" *(šāqēd)* that launched God's assertion of his determination to "watch over" *(šōqēd)* his word (see above p. 41). Because poetry places a higher premium on the texture of words themselves, and prophetic poetry exploits these sounds to generate visions of both present and future, it is clear that a shift from poetry to prose as noted above in the formulation of prophetic texts represents a fundamental shift in how prophecy was perceived.[22]

Thus, in the same way that a prophet could see the cosmic significance of ordinary objects, early prophets were also able simply to hear the name of a person or place and identify the fate that lay in store for the object so named. Names gave clues to destiny ("As is his name, so is he," 1 Sam 25:25), evident from the intense concern in the Bible for naming children and even renaming adults. It is therefore no accident in the prophetic perspective that Ahab son of Qolayah is roasted by Nebuchadnezzar (Jer 29:21-22). Why? This is the only place in the entire Bible where the finite verb "roast" *(qālâ)* appears. Why was this unusual verb used? It depicts a fate appropriate for a man whose father's name (Qolayah) sounded similar to this verb.

In similar fashion, the names of the following cities, locations, or peoples are seen by the prophets as pointing to their fates:

---

[22]An easily accessible and illuminating experiment in transforming poetic oracles into prose, and the consequent loss and gain, appears in Alter, *Art of Biblical Poetry,* pp. 160-62.

| | |
|---|---|
| Beth-Le'aphrah | "Roll yourself in the dust *('āpār)*" (Mic 1:10) |
| Sa'anan | "Does not go out *(yāṣĕʾâ)*" (Mic 1:11) |
| Lakish | "Harness chariot to horse-team *(lārekeš)*" (Mic 1:13) |
| 'Akzib | "Deception *('akzāb)* to the kings of Israel" (Mic 1:14) |
| Mareshah | "I bring on you the dispossessor *(hayyōrēš)*" (Mic 1:15) |
| Gilgal | "He will surely go into exile *(gālōh yigleh)*" (Amos 5:5) |
| 'Azah (= Gaza) | "Will be abandoned *('azûbāh)*" (Zeph 2:4) |
| 'Eqron | "Will be uprooted *(tēʿāqēr)*" (Zeph 2:4) |
| Keretim (= Cherethites) | "Will be caves *(kĕrōt)*[23] for shepherds (Zeph 2:5-6) |
| Ma'barah[24] | He has passed by *('ābar)*" (Is 10:29) |
| 'Anathoth | "Answer her *('ăniyyâ)*" (Is 10:30) |
| Madmenah | "Is in flight *(nādĕdâ)*" (Is 10:31) |
| Nob | "He shakes *(yĕnōpēp)*" (Is 10:32) |
| Tekoa | "Blow *(tiqʿû)* the horn!" (Jer 6:1) |
| Valley of Jehoshapat | "I will enter into judgment *(nišpaṭtî; lišpōt)*" (Joel 3:2, 12 [Heb 4:2, 12]) |

It may happen that what a prophet sees is at dissonance with the name by which the person or object is identified. Since the future fate is markedly different from the present status of the person or object in view, it is not a great stretch to see a new name as a sign of the change of circumstances that will take place. Because Jeremiah foresees a dismal fate for a certain priest, he tells him, "Pashhur is not the name Yahweh has called you, but rather Magor-missabib ('Terror all around')" (Jer 20:3).

For a similar reason, prophets name their children with care. Prophetic children become walking sermons, so to speak:

| | |
|---|---|
| Shear-yashub | "A remnant will return" (Is 7:3; 10:21-22) |
| Immanuel | "God with us" (Is 7:14; 8:8, 10) |
| Maher-shalal-hash-baz | "Swift is the booty, speedy is the prey" (Is 8:1, 3) |
| Lo-ruhamah | "Not pitied" (Hos 1:6) |
| Lo-ammi | "Not my people" (Hos 1:9) |

---

[23]This word appears only here in the entire Bible, underscoring that it is the mention of the Cherethites that has prompted its use here.

[24]So NEB, REB; most translations do not take this as a place name.

Since individuals can be renamed in accord with an unfolding destiny, one finds prophets even renaming their own children when a message changes. Hosea anticipates a different and more hopeful future, which prompts him to provide his daughter Lo-ruhamah ("Not pitied") with a new name, Ruhamah, "Pitied." His son Lo-ammi ("Not my people") similarly becomes Ammi "My people" (Hos 2:1 [3]).

At other times, a prophet's child need not be renamed for the simple reason that the name is inherently ambiguous, requiring interpretation in accord with the circumstances. The names that Isaiah gave to his children can be interpreted both optimistically and pessimistically. Immanuel ("God with us") may signify either that God is with Israel in judgment (as in Is 8:8) or that he is with Israel as their protection (as in Is 8:10). In the case of Isaiah's son Maher-shalal-hash-baz ("Swift is the booty, speedy is the prey"), is it the enemy's booty or Israel's booty that is swift? Does Isaiah's son Shear-yashub ("A remnant will return") give comfort that at least a remnant will return, or are there tragic overtones that not everyone but only a remnant will return? Hosea's son Jezreel has such a name that simply requires reinterpretation: in judgment it means that God brings punishment for the massacre of the valley of Jezreel (Hos 1:4-5), in hope it means that *yizrě'e'l* "he [God] will sow" Israel once again in her own land (Hos 2:22-23 [2:24-25]).

In such cases, which meaning was the relevant one? Discerning in such ambiguous cases which option is the appropriate message for his audience is precisely what makes a prophet. In the same way that the prophet saw the immediately appropriate significance of ordinary objects, so the prophet heard in a name the sign of judgment or of hope that God had decreed. By a pun or a play on words, the prophet indissolubly linked a person or place with a specific future. Because the early prophetic texts are poetic, placing a high premium upon the sound of words themselves, it is likely that the prophetic penchant for focusing on the sounds of names is related to the poetic format. This may explain why this device is largely abandoned in the later prophetic books of the Old Testament. In the same way that the later literary prophets do not depict themselves as particularly insightful (visually), neither do they continue the earlier tradition of having ears finely tuned to detecting the nuances of fate embedded in names.

An exceptional case from later biblical books does appear in the apocalyptic book of Daniel, but it is likely related to a new phenomenon that is a feature of apocalyptic, namely the coding of revelations in terminology and symbols that deliberately cloud and obscure understanding for non-initiates.[25] When a disembodied hand writes on the wall of the palace in Babylon, there are two insurmountable hurdles for the observers that prevent comprehension of the communication: no one can read it and no one can interpret it.[26] Daniel, however, is able to do both. The reading of the text, itself a problem for the bystanders, presents a list of four monetary terms in a sequence that is not even a sentence and which contains no verb: "A mina, a mina, a shekel, and half-minas" (*mĕnē' mĕnē' tĕqēl ûparsîn*; Dan 5:25). Unlike the Babylonian diviners who would be able to see no significance in these three different weights, Daniel understands them as puns of judgment, for he both hears the appropriate phonetic puns and sees their relevance for the present situation. Although they are all nouns, they sound like verbs: God twice numbered (*mĕnâ* "he numbered" Dan 5:26) the days of the kingdom, the king was morally weighed (*tĕqal* "he weighed")[27] and found deficient, and the kingdom was divided (*pĕras*, "he split")[28] and given to the Medes and Persians (Dan 5:25-28).

We ended the preceding chapter with the observation that God's voice was explicitly and regularly marked ("Thus said Yahweh") only in the writing prophets associated with the exile and later. Because the earlier writing prophets were reluctant to tag God's words with specific markers, we raised

---

[25]D. S. Russell, *The Method and Message of Jewish Apocalyptic* (Philadelphia: Westminster Press, 1976), pp. 122-27.

[26]"Read this inscription and tell me its interpretation" (Dan 5:7); "read this writing and make known its interpretation" (Dan 5:8); "read this writing and make known its interpretation" (Dan 5:15); "read the writing and make its interpretation known" (Dan 5:16); "read the writing to the king and make known the interpretation" (Dan 5:17). The only suggestion that the script might be legible, and that only the interpretation is in doubt, appears in Dan 5:15 when the king notes that his best men "could not declare the interpretation of the message." But this comment must be read in light of the repeated double focus on both reading and interpreting. The fact that the writing itself is not given to the reader until Dan 5:25 also suggests that the words themselves were not accessible until Daniel read them out. Since the words are in Aramaic, the lingua franca of the Babylonian and Persian empire, the implication is that they were not written in Aramaic script but in some kind of cipher (archaic Hebrew characters?).

[27]Daniel actually interprets this as a second person singular passive verb referring to the king, "You have been weighed" *(tĕqîltâ)*.

[28]Daniel interprets this as a third feminine singular passive verb referring to the kingdom, "it has been divided" *(pĕrîsat)*.

the possibility that the contrast may have been a function of their use of poetry. Poetry elsewhere in the Bible exhibits a similar reluctance to bracket God's words in any special way. For example, God's voice is interjected into a speech spoken by a human in Psalm 46:9-11 [10-12]:

> (A) He [God] makes wars cease to the end of the earth.
> He breaks the bow and shatters the spear; chariots he burns in the fire.
> (B) Surrender and know that I am God.
> I will be exalted among the nations, I will be exalted in the earth.
> (C) Yahweh of hosts is with us, the God of Jacob is a bastion for us.

The excerpt begins (A) and ends (C) with a human speaking, but in the middle (B) God unambiguously begins to converse in the first person. Because this feature is a characteristic of biblical poetry,[29] it hardly comes as a surprise that there is little concern to distinguish God's voice in the early literary prophets, who write predominantly in poetry.

It is inevitable that confusion will surface in such environments. Not only may it be a matter of speculation as to who is speaking at times, but equally disorienting may be the problem as to when God begins to speak. A passage dedicated to the divine council provides an appropriate example in Psalm 82:

> v. 1 God has taken his stand in the divine council;
> He judges in the midst of the gods.
> v. 2 How long will you judge perversely,
> And show partiality to the wicked?
> v. 3 Give justice to the weak and the orphan,
> Vindicate the poor and the destitute,
> v. 4 Deliver the weak and the impoverished,
> Rescue them from the hand of the wicked.
> v. 5 They do not know nor do they understand,
> They walk around in darkness;
> All the foundations of the earth are shaken.
> v. 6 I say, "You are gods, sons of the Most High, all of you;
> v. 7 Nevertheless, you will die like men, and you will fall like any prince."
> v. 8 Arise, God judge the earth;
> For all the nations are your possession.

---

[29]The voice of God begins to speak without an explicit introduction, for example, in Ps 75:2 [75:3]; 81:6 [81:7]; 95:9; 132:14.

The piece begins and ends with the poet's voice, first describing God's activity (Ps 82:1) only to conclude with a petition to God for justice (Ps 82:8). But in between, a shifting platform obscures the identity of the speaking voice. Is it God's voice addressing the council that we hear in Psalm 82:2? The shift from second person ("you") to third person ("they") in Psalm 82:5 suggests that if God speaks in verses 2-4, God is no longer speaking in verse 5 and once again a human is heard as in verse 1. The authoritative first person in verse 6 sound likes God speaking once again, but if so, the cryptic pronoun "I" does not elucidate (cf. Zeph 3:7). There is no narrative context by which the statement that contains "I" can be evaluated.

It is not only contexts where human voices may alternate with the divine where such unmarked speech surfaces in poetry. The book of Lamentations provides examples of voices other than God's that break into a poetic recitative. Personified Zion is readily identifiable in a number of cases by shifts of person and the distinctive content of her words, even though none of the words are explicitly introduced as belonging to her (e.g., Lam 1:9b, 11b, 18). Here, too, identifying the speaker and the boundaries of the speech is not always an easy task. Lamentations 2:20-22 is such a problematic speech apparently by Zion, but the fact that she speaks is not transparent until verse 21.

In the preceding chapter it became clear that the rise of the explicit marking of God's speech as distinct from the prophet's words was observable as a phenomenon whose watershed was the exile in the sixth century B.C. This development correlates with the decline of poetry and an increasing use of prose in the literary prophets, a phenomenon whose watershed was likewise the exile. These changes in prophetic speech and presentation are mutually reinforcing, underscoring that prophecy was not a static phenomenon and that the exile is a significant chronological boundary in its numerous transformations.[30]

---

[30]Alter, *Art of Biblical Poetry*, pp. 137-62, devotes an entire chapter to "Prophecy and Poetry," arguing that "one cannot plausibly attribute this uneven drift toward prose to changing literary preferences in the decades around and following the destruction of the First Commonwealth, since, after all, one of the most brilliant of prophetic poets was . . . Deutero-Isaiah" (p. 137). English poetry provides an illuminating example to counter Alter's claim, for a formal rigor in structuring words (e.g., combinations of meter, rhyme, line-length) was once mandatory in English poetry.

Among these transformations, one should recall that the ambiguity of the divine voice in poetry and early prophecy corresponds to the ambiguity of the early prophetic view of the future ("perhaps!"). We saw in an earlier chapter how it was precisely the early prophets who held the most ambiguous view of the future. It was the later prophets, precisely those who most profusely demarcated God's words with confidence, who have the most confident view of the future. An increasing degree of confidence in identifying God's words is contemporary with the decline of poetry and the rise of prose where speech identification is less optional, and possibly also with a constricting of the options open for the future.

This analysis of the ways in which God's words are identified has resulted in a confirmation of some transitions that occur with other themes already discussed above. As the transitions in these themes under discussion continue to accumulate, a consistent pattern emerges: the exile repeatedly marks the temporal watershed that distinguishes one set of prophetic texts from the other. Some prophetic themes from the preexilic period contrast with postexilic prophetic themes so dramatically that it becomes obvious that the writers are addressing different issues, different realities, different social conditions, and ultimately a different world.

---

Beginning in the 19th century, this readily identifiable, distinguishing feature of poetry was compromised by innovative free verse with its abandoning of predictable structuring, a feature that became one of the hallmarks of twentieth-century English poetry. We are fortunate in being able to trace closely the general transformation of poetry over the past century and a half, as well as the particular developments of individual poets, so that the cultural contexts and rationales are explorable (most noteworthy as avant-garde expressions). Are there poets who today still write under the older constraints? Yes, and they are some of the best who in varying degrees can express varying degrees of disdain, nostalgia, or regret for the clear shift in contemporary culture's production of poetic forms (e.g., Amy Clampitt, "Robert Frost and the Better Half of Poetry," in *Written in Water, Written in Stone: Twenty Years of Poets on Poetry*, ed. Martin Lammon [Ann Arbor: University of Michigan Press, 1996], pp. 11-16; Charles Wright, "Improvisations on Form and Measure," pp. 27-29 in Lammon [1996]; David Lehman, "Notes on Poetic Form," pp. 46-49 in Lammon [1996]). We are unable to explore, as we can in English poetry, the cultural contexts that prompted a shift in the production of poetry among Hebrew prophets. The fact of such a change is present in the texts that remain, comparable to the observable change that one can see in any anthology covering the past two centuries of English poetry. As noted earlier, I am hardly arguing that prophets stopped producing poetry any more than poets who write in English stopped writing metrically predictable verse. Thus, one can not use the poetry of Is 40–66 to argue any chronological priority to the prose of Ezekiel. We simply do not know the literary context of each prophet, let alone the larger context of prophecy apart from the texts now in our hands. Yet the fact remains that one can not obscure—in spite of not unexpected exceptions—an overwhelming general tendency in the production of poetry as the early medium of choice for written prophetic communiqués, a preference that changed in the sixth century.

# 9

# Writing the Prophets

Up to this point, we have investigated a number of themes and issues that distinguish earlier prophecy from later prophecy. The investigation in the last chapter focused upon changes in the very format in which prophetic words were recorded. This feature prompts an inquiry into the ways in which the prophets' words were actually written down. Unfortunately, we know nothing about the process of composition for most books in the Hebrew Bible. Who wrote these books, how they were written, precisely when they were written and why they were written remain matters for informed speculation. This fact applies especially to those books that now bear the names of specific men who have been identified as prophets. It is true that writing was a fully developed phenomenon throughout the Near East by the third millennium B.C., and the invention of the consonantal alphabet in the second millennium B.C. further facilitated the widespread use of writing. Nevertheless, in spite of the well-established role that writing played in the ancient Near East by the first millennium B.C., there are very few specific indicators that writing played a major role in early Israelite prophetic circles.[1]

---

[1]It has been claimed that the earliest prophetic material comes from the eighth century B.C. because writing in ancient Israel and Judah only became widespread in that century (Alexander Rofé,

It is instructive to contrast the situation in the New Testament where the actual process of writing has moved to the fore as an essential component of the message itself. The books of Luke and Acts, for example, begin with a self-conscious reference to the author and his purpose in composing a narrative account for the sake of someone less acquainted with the events under consideration:

> Since many have attempted to set in order an account of those matters that have been fulfilled in out midst, . . . it seemed appropriate for me also, having investigated everything carefully from the beginning, to write it out for you in order, most excellent Theophilus. (Lk 1:1-3; cf. Acts 1:1)

The book of John, in addition to referring to the author and speaking of other events in Jesus' life that were not included in this specific document (Jn 21:24-25), includes self-conscious statements of purpose for the material that was written:

> In the presence of the disciples, Jesus performed many other signs that are not written in this book, but these have been written in order that you may believe that Jesus is the Christ. (Jn 20:31)

Most of the documents in the New Testament are letters with clearly identified authors and addressees. Even (especially!) the Apocalypse contains repeated and emphatic pointers to the importance of writing and documents:

> Blessed is the one who reads and those who hear the words of the prophecy and heed those things that are written in it. (Rev 1:3)

> Write in a book what you see and send it to the seven churches. . . . Write, therefore, those things that you have seen. (Rev 1:11, 19)

> Write . . . Write . . . Write . . . Write . . . Write . . . Write . . . Write. (Rev 2:1, 8, 12, 18; 3:1, 7, 14)

> I was about to write, and I heard a voice from heaven saying, "Seal up the things that the seven thunders have spoken, and do not write them." (Rev 10:4)

---

*Introduction to Prophetic Literature*, trans. Judith H. Seeligmann, The Biblical Seminar 21 [Sheffield: Sheffield Academic, 1997], pp. 11-12). But the eighth century as a watershed for the broad use of writing is debatable, and we will see below that there was little interest in writing prophetic material even in the eighth–seventh centuries.

"Go, take the book. . . ." And I went to the angel, saying to him that he should give me the little book. And he said to me, "Take and eat it. . . ." And I took the little book from the angel's hand and ate it." (Rev 10:8-10)

Write, "Blessed are the dead who die in the Lord from now on." (Rev 14:13)

Write, "Blessed are the ones who have been invited to the Lamb's marriage supper." (Rev 19:9)

And I saw the dead, great and small, standing before the throne, and books were opened. And another book was opened, which is the one of life, and the dead were judged from the things which were written in the books. (Rev 20:12)

Write, for these words are faithful and true. (Rev 21:5)

Do not seal up the words of the prophecy of this book. (Rev 22:10)

I bear witness to everyone who hears the words of the prophecy of this book: if anyone adds to them, God will add to him the plagues that have been written in this book, and if anyone removes any of the words of the book of this prophecy, God will remove his portion from the tree of life and from the holy city, which are written in this book. (Rev 22:18-19)

This focus upon writing throughout most of the New Testament[2] disappears when one goes back in time to the prophetic texts of the first millennium B.C. in the Hebrew Bible. There, prophetic narratives find writing to be of no importance at all. The extensive accounts of prophets like Samuel, Elijah and Elisha in the books of Samuel and Kings tell us nothing about how the information about them has been preserved,[3] nor does the phenomenon of writing itself even appear in those stories. Allusions to writing in other contexts in these books make it clear that it was an available technology (e.g., 2 Sam 1:18; 1 Kings 11:41; 14:19, 29; 2 Kings

---

[2]Not every work in the New Testament places an equal stress upon writing. Neither Matthew nor Mark, for example, focuses upon the composition of the document itself, in contrast to Luke and John and other New Testament texts. Such exceptions do not detract, however, from the larger picture where a general emphasis pervades the culture in which these texts were composed, an emphasis that finds it important to identify the process of writing in contrast to preexilic prophetic texts to be discussed below.

[3]Unlike the kings whose narratives are typically concluded with reference to written sources in which information about the king is available (e.g., 1 Kings 11:41; 14:19, 29; 15:7, 23, 31).

23:2-3, 21, 24), but its absence in stories about prophets underscores the lack of focus upon it. The only possible exception occurs at the point when kingship is inaugurated, for the reader is informed that "Samuel spoke of the law of the kingdom to the people and wrote in the book and deposited it before Yahweh" (1 Sam 10:25). But this narrative of a public and formal event has little to say about writing as a function of prophecy, especially since this is the only time that writing is ever mentioned in conjunction with a prophet in the books of Samuel and Kings.

One may speculate that sayings by, and stories about, charismatic figures such as Samuel, Elijah and Elisha were written down by their followers. As models for such hypothetical written sayings and exemplary lives one may offer the much later Gospel writers recording the words and deeds of Jesus in the New Testament, the dialogues of Socrates written by his student Plato, or the stories of rabbis in the Talmud originally passed down by word of mouth. If these examples are relevant, they attest to a master's, teacher's or prophet's lack of concern to put into writing during his lifetime any definitive corpus.

It is this stress upon the oral transmission of a prophet's words and deeds, not the written format, that is reflected in a story about Elisha's servant, Gehazi, who is asked by the king of Israel, "Tell *(sappĕrâ)* me, please, all the great things that Elisha has done" (2 Kings 8:4). Unlike the later insomniac king of Persia, Xerxes, who has his courtiers read to him from written chronicles (Esther 6:1), this king of Israel receives an oral recollection from a prophet's follower. In this case, an added bonus materializes when one of the oral accounts dovetails with the experience of a woman who comes across the king's path:

> It so happened that as he (i.e., Gehazi) was telling *(mĕsappēr)* the king how he (i.e., Elisha) had restored the dead to life, behold, the woman whose son he had revived was crying out to the king for her house and field. Gehazi said, "My lord the king, this is the woman, and this is her son whom Elisha restored to life." (2 Kings 8:5)

This story presumes as a matter of course that access to a prophet's deeds and words can be found in the oral renditions that his followers pass on. Significantly, and in accord with the rest of the books of Samuel and Kings, there is no document here to provide an answer to the king's query about the prophet. A document cannot further elaborate, clarify or respond to interrogation. It is rather the oral dimension that in this case gives the king the opportunity to cross-check the reliability of Gehazi's account: the king can hear the woman's account as well: "The king asked the woman, and she told *(wattĕsapper)* him" (2 Kings 8:6). The repetition here of the verb "tell," Hebrew *spr*, sustains the episode's focus upon the oral interplay that brings all of the characters together in dialogue, even the absent Elisha who is present through the words that the characters speak.

In such an environment, one will not expect an archive or library to be the source that one consults to explore what prophets have said.[4] The fund of prophetic deeds and oracles will more readily be found with those who, like Gehazi, have an immediate recall of what they heard or saw of the prophet himself, or what they had heard from someone who had. When Jeremiah is on trial for his life as a traitor to his country, words of a former prophet are invoked when the trial convenes. The accusation against Jeremiah is unequivocal: "A death sentence for this man because he prophesied against this city" (Jer 26:11). The defense is also equally clear:

> Men from among the elders of the land arose and said to the entire gathering of the people, saying, "Micah from Moresheth prophesied in the days of Hezekiah, King of Judah, and said to all the people of Judah, saying, 'Thus said Yahweh of hosts, "Zion will be plowed as a field, and Jerusalem will become ruins, and the temple mount high places of the forest."' Did Hezekiah, King of Judah, and all Judah in fact put him to death? Did he not fear Yahweh?" (Jer 26:17-19)

A precedent for the court is retrieved from the memories of some of the older men[5] who recall a prophetic message spoken over a century

---

[4]Although it is certain that prophetic utterances were archived in seventh-century Assyrian royal contexts, something that is "plausible for eighth-century Judah" (Matthijs de Jong, *Isaiah Among the Ancient Near Eastern Prophets: A Comparative Study of the Earliest Stages of the Isaiah Tradition and the Neo-Assyrian Prophecies*, VTS 117 [Leiden: Brill, 2007], p. 460; cf. pp. 171-90), such biblical accounts about this period stress the retrieval as an exercise in recall in contrast to later biblical accounts such as that noted above in Esther 6:1 that focus on archives.

[5]The contrasting behavior and interplay of social groups in this passage—priests (Jer 26:7, 8, 11, 16), prophets (Jer 26:7, 8, 11, 16), all the people (Jer 26:7, 8, 9, 11, 12, 16, 17), princes (Jer 26:10, 11, 12, 16) and elders (Jer 26:17)—highlights the peculiar focus upon the elders who appear only once in this account for the precise purpose of resurrecting an historical memory overlooked by the other groups.

earlier. The rhetorical questions posed by these elders assume that the audience is also expected to remember the event: "Did Hezekiah . . . in fact put him to death? Did he not fear Yahweh?" (Jer 26:19). It may or may not be that Micah's words were written down by this time, but accessing these words and the royal response in Jeremiah 26 is depicted not as a search among documents (contrast Ezra 4:15, 19; 6:1-2) but as a recollection of a shared memory. Micah's communication is itself portrayed as oral and not written: "He said to all the people of Judah" (Jer 26:18). Prophetic words, particularly those with a vindicated reputation, did not have to be written down when their common currency could be assumed as a matter of course. These narratives presuppose a reader's familiarity with this social phenomenon as something that is neither extraordinary nor of dubious reliability.

Therefore, like the narratives about prophets in the books of Samuel and Kings, one finds an echo in the literary prophets themselves of an oral dimension for the preservation of prophetic oracles. In most of the books of the literary prophets there is no concern for writing in connection with prophetic activity. There is not a word about writing in the sixty chapters of Hosea, Joel, Amos, Obadiah, Jonah, Micah, Nahum, Zephaniah, Haggai and Zechariah. It is true that there is a great deal about God's word and his communication with Israel and Judah in these chapters, but the emphasis in each of the these prophetic books is upon its oral dimension (highlighted below), not the written form:

> The word of Yahweh which came to Hosea. . . . When Yahweh first **spoke** through Hosea, Yahweh **said** to Hosea, "Go . . ." (Hos 1:1-2)

> The word of Yahweh that came to Joel, . . . "**Hear** this, O elders . . ." (Joel 1:1-2)

> The words of Amos . . . which he saw in visions. . . . And **he said**, "Yahweh roars. . . ." Thus **said** Yahweh, "For three transgressions of Damascus . . ." (Amos 1:1-3)

> **Hear** this word which Yahweh has **spoken** against you, sons of Israel . . . (Amos 3:1)

> Thus **said** Yahweh God concerning Edom . . . (Obad 1)

The word of Yahweh came to Jonah . . . **saying**, "Arise, go to Nineveh . . ." (Jon 1:1-2)

The word of Yahweh which came to Micah . . . which he saw concerning Samaria and Jerusalem. "**Hear**, O Peoples . . ." (Mic 1:1-2)

Thus **said** Yahweh concerning the prophets who lead my people astray . . . (Mic 3:5)

Yahweh has **issued a command** concerning you . . . (Nahum 1:14)

"Therefore, wait for me," **declares** Yahweh . . . (Zeph 3:8)

Then the word of Yahweh came by Haggai the prophet **saying** . . . (Hag 1:3)

The angel **speaking** with me **said** . . . (Zech 1:9, 14)

The word of Yahweh of hosts came to me **saying**, "**Say** to all the people of the land . . ." (Zech 7:4-5)

In the books of Isaiah, Habakkuk and Malachi a similar profile emerges, although four isolated comments in these three books hint at a role for writing that is not otherwise elaborated.[6] In three of these four exceptional contexts the focus seems to be upon writing down a prophetic vision so that at some future date the vindication of its foresight can be confirmed:

Yahweh said to me, "Take for yourself a large text *(gillāyôn)* and write *(kĕtōb)* on it with a man's stylus, 'For Maher-shalal-hash-baz.' And I summoned for myself Uriah the priest and Zechariah the son of Jeberechiah as reliable witnesses." (Is 8:1-2)

Write *(kotbāh)* it on a tablet *(lûaḥ)* with them and inscribe it on a scroll *(sēper)* that it may serve as a witness for a later day forever. (Is 30:8)

Yahweh answered me and said, "Write *(kĕtōb)* the vision and inscribe it on the tablets *(hallūḥôt).* . . . For the vision is yet for the appointed time; . . . if it delays, wait for it, for it will certainly come. It will not be late. (Hab 2:2-3)

Then those who feared Yahweh spoke together, each with his neighbor,

---

[6]As in the Dtr history, isolated references to the technology associated with written documents appear in the book of Isaiah, but these references have nothing to do with the prophet and his message (Is 10:1, 19; 29:11-12, 18; 34:4, 16; cf. Is 50:1).

and Yahweh gave heed and listened. A book *(sēper)* of remembrance was written *(wayyikkātēb)* before him for those who feared Yahweh and esteemed his name. (Mal 3:16)

In the first case, the prophet is told to write only four cryptic Hebrew words whose import will gradually unfold. The second and third cases employ similar language to describe a single revelation whose long-term validity requires a written document as a testamentary confirmation. That is, in these three cases a specific oracle has a long-term significance whose vindication will be uniquely sustained by a written and duly witnessed text. The significance of the "book of remembrance" in the fourth case above is not associated with the prophetic word at all; it is a heavenly book written in response to the community's obedience.[7]

In sum, therefore, the voice of God is found throughout thirteen prophetic books with only a few exceptional references to peculiar oracles that required specific commands for their written format. The very need for the command to write in a few exceptional cases highlights the complete absence of writing elsewhere in the prophets. The sustained emphasis upon oral communication clarifies that it is not writing that is the medium of choice, for it appears only peripherally. How, then, and why did the oral prophetic word become the written prophetic word?

There are two prophetic books where a sudden focus upon writing God's revelation becomes central to the message of the prophet. It is no accident that this occurs in both the books of Jeremiah and Ezekiel, for they are largely contemporaneous and both books depict events that take place during the crisis years of Jerusalem's fall. In the book of Jeremiah, for example, one finds the prophet ordered to write down not just some but all of his communications from God: "Thus said Yahweh, the God of Israel, 'Write for yourself all the words that I spoke to you in a book, for behold, days are coming,' declares Yahweh, 'when I will restore the fortunes of my people'" (Jer 30:2-3). The motivation sounds very much like the three isolated references to writing in most of the prophets noted above, i.e., there will be a future vindication for which the written words

---

[7]Cf. Ex 32:32-33; Ps 69:28 [69:29]; 139:16; Jer 17:13; Ezek 13:9; Dan 12:1 (cf. Andrew E. Hill, *Malachi* [New York: Doubleday, 1998], pp. 339-40).

will stand as a confirmation of the prophet's foresight. But three other contexts in Jeremiah attest to a new development.

A distinctly different situation emerges in Jeremiah 29. The bulk of this chapter is devoted to a letter composed by Jeremiah for Jews forcibly exiled to a conquering land. A large number of details fill out the extended narrative, including the occasion for writing the letter (to expose false hopes of a quick return), the place from which Jeremiah writes (Jerusalem), the missive's specific destination (Babylon), the approximate date (after the exile of King Jehoiachin, i.e., after 587 B.C.), and the individuals through whom the letter was delivered (two royal messengers, Elasah and Gemariah). The letter itself is provided either verbatim or in a condensed format. In this case, however, the prophet's words are written down for a very specific reason: the prophet is unable to deliver this message in person. The written message becomes a surrogate for the prophet, going where the prophet cannot.

A second event in Jeremiah provides a similar perspective but with some unique twists, adding to the accumulation of contexts where writing becomes a primary concern for the prophet. In the case of Jeremiah 51:59-64, however, we are told that "Jeremiah wrote on a single document all the evil which will come to Babylon, all these things that are written against Babylon" (Jer 51:60). He handed this scroll to a sympathetic royal bureaucrat, Seraiah, who was traveling to Babylon, with the instructions that Seraiah was to read it aloud in its entirety. Having read it, Seraiah was instructed then to recite a brief prayer to God with regard to the contents of the document, to find a stone to tie to the document, and then to throw the document into the Euphrates. As the stone carried the text to the river bottom, Seraiah was to recite a divine oracle: "Babylon will sink like this and will not rise because of the evil that I am bringing against it" (Jer 51:64). Again, the prophet does not make the trip but can record the appropriate words for someone else to read. The document again becomes a surrogate for the prophet himself. The unique twist that climaxes the account is the document itself perishes—intentionally—in the process.

Yet another occasion surfaces in Jeremiah, reflecting a similar response to a comparable problem. In chapter 36, Jeremiah's inability to deliver his message personally results from the fact that the king has placed him under house arrest in Jerusalem. The order from God is targeted precisely to the written format that the prophecy is to take:

> This word came to Jeremiah from Yahweh, saying, "**Take for yourself a scroll and write** on it all the words which I spoke to you about Israel, Judah, and all the nations from the time I spoke to you from the days of Josiah up to this day. . . ." Jeremiah called Baruch the son of Neriah, and **Baruch wrote** at Jeremiah's dictation all Yahweh's words which he spoke to him, **on a scroll**. Jeremiah ordered Baruch, saying, "I am restricted; I cannot go to the house of Yahweh. So you **go and read from the scroll which you have written** at my dictation." (Jer 36:1-6)

Like Jeremiah's letter to Babylon in chapter 29, and like the scroll entrusted to Seraiah in chapter 51, the written text here responds again to a physical reality: the prophet needs a substitute for his own vocal chords when he can not be present to deliver the message. When Jeremiah's opponents who want to stifle his message deliberately destroy this document (Jer 36:23), Jeremiah has a replacement scroll made—with appropriate supplements in light of new circumstances:

> Jeremiah took another scroll and gave it to Baruch the son of Neriah, the scribe, and he wrote on it at Jeremiah's dictation all the words of the document which Jehoiakim king of Judah had burned in the fire, and many similar words were further added to them. (Jer 36:32)

The single most illuminating aspect of God's words to Jeremiah in this last context, however, is that the writing is comprehensive, designed to include "all the words" about Israel and Judah ever delivered by Jeremiah. What is presented here is consequently nothing less than an explanation for the genesis of the book of Jeremiah. Twenty-three years are said to elapse (Jer 25:3) from the thirteenth year of Josiah's reign when Jeremiah began to speak (Jer 1:2) up to the time when this comprehensive scroll is written in King Jehoiakim's fourth year (Jer 36:1). Unfortunately there are no specific oracles in the book of Jeremiah associated with any precise date in Josiah's reign (640–609 b.c.) apart from two comments noting that Jeremiah began his activity in the thirteenth year of Josiah's reign (Jer 1:2; 25:3). Otherwise one simply finds a vague reference to how "Yahweh said to me in the days of Josiah the king . . ." (Jer

3:6). This lack of precision in dating is what one would expect for prophetic activity where no written records were kept and only afterwards was a decision made to compile the material (we will look at this in greater detail in the next chapter).

The book of Jeremiah is thus the first prophetic book where there is a focus upon the written text itself, where there are references even within the book to itself, (cf. "all that is written in this document that Jeremiah prophesied against all the nations," Jer 25:13).[8] The special character of the book as a written document emerges from the crisis that prompts a forcibly constrained prophet to communicate by the written word. The initial compilation of all Jeremiah's earlier oral oracles is supplemented with further (often dated) oracles along with narratives about Jeremiah. This continues until one reaches the point where a conclusion to the collection is noted: "Thus far are the words of Jeremiah" (Jer 51:64). There is even a special oracle composed as an encouragement for the scribe who wrote the document for Jeremiah:

> The word that Jeremiah the prophet spoke to Baruch, son of Neriah, when he wrote these words on a document at Jeremiah's dictation in the fourth year of Jehoiakim . . . : "Thus said Yahweh: '. . . I will give your life to you as booty in all the places to which you go.'" (Jer 45:1, 5)

The opening rubric of the book itself specifies that the oracles begin with King Josiah's thirteenth year and extend to the final—eleventh—year of King Zedekiah (Jer 1:2-3). One should also keep in mind the other circumstances in this book where writing plays an indispensable role, such as the occasion when Jeremiah composed another scroll of oracles against Babylon which he entrusted to Seraiah to carry to Babylon in King Zedekiah's fourth year (Jer 51:59), and when Baruch read Jeremiah's scroll publicly in the ninth month of Zedekiah's fifth year (Jer 36:9).

The proliferation of dates in the latter half of Jeremiah's book, in contrast to the paucity in the first half, is instructive in dramatically preserving the explicit transition made in the middle of the book from an oral to

---

[8]Cf. the unparalleled use of the procedure involved in the production, use and preservation of a legal document by Jeremiah (Jer 32:6-44).

a written format. The first half of the book preserves the culture of the earlier prophets where there is no focus upon writing, while the latter half of the book presents the culture of the prophets of the exile (and after) where writing can be of central importance. It is possible that the book of Jeremiah preserves the kind of catalyst that made the transition possible or even necessary, for it was a crisis that shifted Jeremiah's message from the spoken to the written word. If Jeremiah is paradigmatic, it may have been the crisis of the exile that crystallized the written format for many of the other literary prophets. Words that had long been transmitted orally by a prophet's followers, even transmitted orally from generation to generation, could easily be lost in times of national upheaval such as the Babylonian invasions of the early sixth century. Similar crises have encouraged oral literatures to be written down, as in the case of the Mishnah by the end of the second century A.D. and the Talmud by the sixth century A.D. The book of Jeremiah is evidence that a parallel phenomenon was at work also in ancient Judah: for the first part of his prophetic career, this prophet showed no concern to preserve any of his words in writing. It is only when he is incarcerated and his prophetic word in danger of being stifled that writing becomes the means of communicating God's word. Otherwise, writing is not the preferred medium.

A moment's pause will clarify the less than desirable role that writing plays for a prophet. There is no need to write down a prophet's words, as long as the prophet himself is accessible. For clarification or a reminder, an ancient Israelite or Judaean needed only to ask the prophet himself, or his successor or disciples. As long as specific prophets are identifiable in ancient Israel, it is of no great consequence to write their words down, and even less so if their prophetic messages are continually being delivered. Quite the contrary, writing down the prophet's words while the prophet is alive is counterproductive in that it tends to focus on what is past. It becomes a high priority to record a prophet's words in writing if prophets and their disciples become scarce or even vanish. Then the backward glance to what the prophet once said becomes the next best thing, a substitute for ready access to prophets themselves. It is precisely at the time that Jeremiah lived that such social upheavals occurred, for the population decimation accompanying the Babylonian invasions correlates well with the awareness that prophecy itself is changing, as we have seen. [9]

At the same time that Jeremiah is making his transition from oral prophet to literary prophet, another prophet also restricted in his freedom to speak[10] is making a similar transition. Ezekiel, a priest like Jeremiah (Jer 1:1; Ezek 1:3), but one who is forcibly exiled from Jerusalem to Babylon, is the first prophet whose book from start to finish is composed intentionally as a written communication.[11] Unlike all other prophetic books up to this time, Ezekiel's voice is heard entirely from his own perspective.[12] Ezekiel is not described by some faceless narrator who observes him. Rather, Ezekiel's "I" dominates the narrative:

> While I was by the River Chebar, . . . I saw visions of God. . . . And as I looked . . . I also heard. . . . I opened my mouth. . . . I came to the exiles. . . . I was sitting in my house. . . . I dug through the wall. . . . I went out in the dark. . . . Some elders of Israel came to me and sat down before me. . . . I spoke to the people in the morning, and in the evening my wife died. (Ezek 1:1, 4, 24; 3:2, 15; 8:1, 8; 12:7; 14:1; 24:18)

The final chapters of the book exist as a response to a supernatural command to write down a vision ("write for their eyes," Ezek 43:11), and Ezekiel elsewhere receives a divine order to write down a specific revelation ("write for yourself the name of the day, this very day," Ezek 24:2). Most dramatic of all is the inaugural vision that launches Ezekiel's revelations, for it is climaxed when Ezekiel eats an inscribed scroll from God's

---

[9]The very fact that it is a literary document that stresses the primacy of the oral component, an element that could undermine the derivative authority of the document itself as a secondary phenomenon, is awkward to account for unless it reflects a genuine reality. Explicit examples of divine oracles that continue in oral formats include Jeremiah in the temple court (Jer 26:1-16), Jeremiah's address to the Rechabites (Jer 35:1-19), Jeremiah speaking to survivors of Jerusalem's destruction (Jer 42:1–43:3) and to Jewish refugees in Egypt (Jer 44:15-26), and Zechariah addressing the high priest in public (Zech 6:9-14).

[10]Ezek 3:25-26; 4:8; 24:27; 33:22.

[11]Ellen F. Davis *Swallowing the Scroll: Textuality and the Dynamics of Discourse in Ezekiel's Prophecy*, JSOTSS 78 (Sheffield: Almond, 1989), provides an extended focused analysis of this issue, observing that Ezekiel's distinct speech forms arose as a function of writing, which was a response to a new environment and a new challenge to communicate God's message, essentially marking the end of one kind of prophecy and the beginning of another. See also Joachim Schaper, "The Death of the Prophet: The Transition from the Spoken to the Written Word of God in the Book of Ezekiel," in *Prophets, Prophecy, and Prophetic Texts in Second Temple Judaism*, ed. Michael H. Floyd and Robert D. Haak, LBH/OTS 427 (New York: T & T Clark, 2006), pp. 63-79, for further nuancing of this perspective.

[12]An exceptional editorial comment in this book refers to Ezekiel in the third person in Ezek 1:3.

hand so that God's words may become Ezekiel's (Ezek 2:7–3:4). As a result of this event, even Ezekiel's spoken words presume an origin in a written text.

This image of the ingested scroll is a convenient dramatization of the shift that has taken place between the earlier prophets and these later prophets. When Isaiah inaugurated his prophetic life, God presented no such document to him. Instead, a supernatural being—a seraph—grasped a burning coal with tongs from the sacred altar and "touched my mouth and said, 'Behold, this has touched your lips'" (Is 6:7). God's command followed: "Go and **say** to this people." (Is 6:9). This earlier prophet's mouth, lips and the spoken word were the focus of his commission. The later prophet Ezekiel, on the other hand, focused upon the written form of the communication that was handed to him and which he replicated in the form of his own autobiographical prophetic book: "Write *(kĕtōb)* for their eyes" (Ezek 43:11).[13]

It is therefore no accident that God impairs Ezekiel's speech so that he cannot speak for much of the time covered by the book: "I will cause your tongue to cling to the roof of your mouth so that you will be dumb" (Ezek 3:26). God not only warns Ezekiel that he will be unable to speak—although he is not told that it will end up lasting seven years[14]—but God

---

[13]Jeremiah's commissioning corresponds to Isaiah's in this regard when God touches Jeremiah's lips (Jer 1:9), with a focus on the oral dimension of the communication that is only later modified by changing circumstances.

[14]From the fifth year (Ezek 1:2) to the twelfth year (Ezek 33:21-22) of Jehoiachin's exile. The precise nature of Ezekiel's verbal restraint is not clear, for Ezekiel seems to be vocal with denunciations during the time he is supposed to be unable to speak (e.g., Ezek 11:25; 12:9-11, 22-23, 27-28; 13:1-2; 14:1-4; 17:2, 12; 20:1-3, 49; 24:18-21). Could he only condemn but not function as a mediator with God on the people's behalf, similar to Jeremiah's inability to pray for Judah in Jer 7:16 (e.g., Paul Joyce, *Divine Initiative and Human Response in Ezekiel,* JSOTSS 51 [Sheffield: JSOT, 1989], pp. 58-59)? Did Ezekiel speak, but only and repeatedly of Jerusalem's destruction as an idée fixe (Moshe Greenberg, "On Ezekiel's Dumbness," *JBL* 77 [1958]: 101-5), or only God's oracles and nothing of his own thoughts as a guarantee in a time of proliferating false oracles that whatever he said was from God (Millard C. Lind, *Ezekiel* [Scottdale, Penn.: Herald, 1996], pp. 44-46)? Does the problem result from textual disarray that only now makes it seem that his dumbness overlaps with his denunciations (a consensus in the mid-twentieth century; see Greenberg, "Ezekiel's Dumbness," for discussion), or is 3:25-27 a piece of late interpretation among Ezekiel's disciples speaking of hostile fellow exiles binding him, along with Yahweh's striking him dumb (Walther Zimmerli, *Ezekiel I,* trans. Ronald E. Clements [Philadelphia: Fortress, 1979], pp. 160-61)? Is this inability to speak a literary creation and not a literal sign at all (Davis 1989)? Or did the people's stubbornness prevent him from speaking as he wished (Calvin)? Being struck dumb is elsewhere attested as a sign of divine displeasure: another priest, Zechariah, the father of John the

also informs him what event will bring an end to his impaired condition, namely when the reports arrive in Babylon of Jerusalem's destruction: "In that day the refugee will come to you to bring news for your ears; in that day your mouth will be opened with the refugee, and you will speak, and you will no longer be dumb" (Ezek 24:26-27). Events unfold accordingly:

> It happened that in the twelfth year, tenth month, and fifth day of our exile, the refugee came to me from Jerusalem, saying, "The city has been devastated." The hand of Yahweh was upon me in the evening before the arrival of the refugee, and he opened my mouth by the time he reached me in the morning; my mouth was opened and I was no longer dumb. (Ezek 33:21-22)

The restriction of Ezekiel's speech corresponds to the new preferred medium by which God communicates. The written word now becomes the best medium of communication in the same way that Jeremiah's incarceration elevated the written word to a new status: it was the only way for the prophet's verbal message to reach the public. For both prophets, the written format correlates with some type of compromise with the oral dimension. With Jeremiah and Ezekiel the verbal dimension itself undergoes a transformation from an emphasis upon the spoken word to a preference for the written word. It is the text that will survive as the gift of prophetic speech changes.

The primacy of the written word that pervades the New Testament, and which we observe gradually unfolding in a prophetic context in the Hebrew Bible, continues in later books in the Hebrew Bible after Jeremiah and Ezekiel. In the book of Daniel, earlier prophets such as Jeremiah are now readily accessible through their writings: "I,[15] Daniel, discerned in the documents the number of the years which was the word of Yahweh to Jeremiah the prophet" (Dan 9:2). God's revelation now may come not as a voice but as a writing on a wall (Dan 5:5-8, 15-17, 24-28). When strange visions disturb Daniel's sleep, he immediately writes down what he sees so

---

Baptist, is stricken dumb throughout the period of his wife's pregnancy because he did not believe the angel when informed of the miracle (Lk 1:20, 22, 62-64).

[15]An extensive use of the authorial "I" with reference to a prophet appears first in the book of Jeremiah (especially in the first half of the book, e.g., Jer 1:4-14; 2:1; 3:6, 11; 4:10; 11:6, 9, 18; 13:1-3; 14:11-14; 15:1; 16:1; 17:19; 18:3-5) and then prominently in Ezekiel, a feature that will become characteristic of apocalyptic and pseudepigraphical texts.

that he remembers what he has seen in an attempt to understand it (Dan 7:1), even though some of what Daniel writes is to be hidden (Dan 12:4).

The very limited material at our disposal therefore suggests that a change to a new focus upon the written word as a medium of prophecy is attested at the time of Jeremiah and Ezekiel, that is, at the end of the seventh century and the beginning of the sixth century. This is not to say that some prophetic circles could not continue to stress the oral and minimize the written medium. Postexilic prophetic books such as Haggai, Zechariah and Malachi show varying degrees of emphasis upon written and oral media.[16] One should not suggest that one can predict from a text's emphasis upon writing that it was written either before or after the crisis events that focus upon the destruction of the first temple in 586 B.C. But biblical literature points to a consistent lack of concern for writing among prophets before this date, with a shift in emphasis that can be closely observed at this time.

This perspective may be useful in appreciating what seems to be a flourishing of prophetic books attested in 1–2 Chronicles, in contrast to the minimal explicit attestation of such books in the Deuteronomistic history (Joshua, Judges, 1–2 Samuel, 1–2 Kings). The composer of the Dtr history is not averse to pointing to sources that can be used—and perhaps that he used—to investigate events which he narrates: he refers to the Chronicles of the Kings of Israel (e.g., 1 Kings 14:19; 15:31), the Chronicles of the Kings of Judah (1 Kings 14:29; 15:7), and a document relating the Acts of Solomon (1 Kings 11:41). These sources may be related in some fashion to royal records that are well attested in the palace bureaucracies of other monarchies in the ancient world. But there is no explicit reference to any written prophetic narratives. Even though the Dtr historian records numerous prophetic stories, he never cites a prophetic source for these.[17]

---

[16]We will discuss in the next chapter Haggai's and Zechariah's novel sustained interest, unlike Malachi's, in recording specific dates connected with prophetic oracles, a phenomenon that correlates with the focus upon literary prophetic oracles. Although the inscribed flying scroll that Zechariah observes in a vision (Zech 5:1-3) may be a reflection of the new prophetic interest in this medium, the book of Zechariah itself preserves no self-referential comments about its own status as a written text.

[17]A written prophetic source (or sources) may lie behind these stories, as some have proposed, most notably A. F. Campbell, *Of Prophets and Kings: A Late Ninth-Century Document (1 Samuel 1—2*

It is otherwise with the later biblical book of Chronicles, for in addition to using the Dtr history as a source, as well as texts that bear names similar to those used by the Dtr historian,[18] he also includes a wide variety of texts that are associated with prophetic figures:

Chronicles of Gad the Seer (1 Chron 29:29)

Chronicles of Samuel the Seer (1 Chron 29:29)

Chronicles of Nathan the Prophet (1 Chron 29:29; 2 Chron 9:29)

The Prophecy of Ahijah the Shilonite (2 Chron 9:29)

Visions of Iddo the Seer (2 Chron 9:29)

Chronicles of Iddo the Seer (2 Chron 12:15)

Midrash of the Prophet Iddo (2 Chron 13:22)

Chronicles of Shemaiah the Prophet (2 Chron 12:15)

The postexilic context of the Chronicler's writing and his focus upon written prophetic sources corresponds well with what we have seen above. He is writing in a period, unlike the Dtr historian, when written prophetic sources have apparently become a major resource. None of these are accessible to us, but their availability to the postexilic Chronicler underscores that the phenomenon of a written text as a primary medium for prophetic words, first attested with Jeremiah and Ezekiel, had blossomed by the time of the Chronicler. It is this availability of the written word that makes it possible for a figure like Daniel to access a prophet long after he is dead, as the text notes, "I discerned in the documents the number of the years which was the word of Yahweh to Jeremiah the prophet" (Dan 9:2).

We are able to witness, then, the transformation of prophecy from a primarily vocal phenomenon to a primarily visual and literary phenomenon. From the classical preexilic prophets for whom the word "Hear!" was the central issue, a new development takes place with an increasing insistence upon the new commands, "Read!" (Jer 36:6, 15; 51:61; cf. Jer 36:10,

---

*Kings 10)*, CBQMS 17 (Washington, D.C.: Catholic Biblical Association of America, 1986). The Dtr historian simply never draws attention to it as an explicit source that one can consult for further information as he does the royal archives.

[18]E.g., "Book of the Kings of Israel" (2 Chron 20:34), "Book of the Kings of Judah and Israel" (2 Chron 25:26; 28:26; 32:32), "Book of the Kings of Israel and Judah" (2 Chron 27:7; 35:27; 36:8).

13-14, 21, 23) and "Write!" (Ezek 24:2; 43:11; Jer 30:2; 36:2). This transformation is observable in the works of Jeremiah and Ezekiel as they stand at the boundary between the last years of the Davidic monarchy on the one hand and the beginning of the Jewish diaspora on the other. Although we do not know when other prophetic books apart from Jeremiah and Ezekiel were actually written down, the crisis of the Judaean destruction and exile, coupled with the new emphasis upon written oracles favoring wide dissemination as evidenced in Jeremiah and Ezekiel, provides the type of environment in which it could easily take place. As we have come to expect on the basis of the preceding chapters, the exile resurfaces as a time that marks the transformation of prophecy in ancient Israel.

# 10

# DATING THE PROPHETS

THE PRECEDING CHAPTER ADDRESSED what we know of the process by which prophetic texts in the Bible were written down. A related concern that contributes to this discussion is the means by which one can attempt to date the literary prophets. One of the more taxing problems in the early prophets is the lack of dates associated with their oracles. It is this fact that prompts a bewildering variety of interpretations for passages that depend upon a specific year in which individual scholars prefer to place a given oracle. Such scholarly fine-tuning has its place, but the impression left by the early prophetic books themselves is that dating is largely an irrelevant context for the words recorded. The six chapters of the books of Habakkuk and Nahum provide no chronological orientation, their dates of composition depending solely on the reader's deductions from random comments. Not a single specific date appears in the books of Hosea, Amos, Micah and Zephaniah even though some chronologically sensitive person has provided an introductory verse to each book that gives a vague context for the prophet's life "in the days of king . . ." (e.g., Hos 1:1; cf. Is 1:1). But no single oracle is fixed in a particular moment in time in the thirty-three chapters of these four prophets. Even stories about the prophet's activities are not focused in time: when Amos interacts with a very specific priest of

Bethel (Amaziah) who corresponds with King Jeroboam II (Amos 7:10-17), no clue is provided as to when this occurs in the reign of this longest-reigning Israelite king (forty-one years according to 2 Kings 14:23).

One may counter that there are a few passages where there is a clear concern to provide a quite narrow time frame for the words recorded. Amos 1:1 identifies at least some words in the book—but which ones?—that relate to a vision that he saw "two years before the earthquake." This is a valuable chronological marker, but only for contemporaries who remember which earthquake is in view. It has little value for those who live long after the event and do not know to which of hundreds of earthquakes that have since occurred it relates (in what year of King Jeroboam did it happen?).[1] Recording this incident probably had little real significance for chronology, its appearance instead buttressing the prediction in the book that God will "shake" those who are doomed (Amos 9:1). The datum itself provides little chronological value beyond this possible setting for that oracle.

Isaiah 6:1 and Isaiah 14:28 are similar in specifying that a particular vision occurred "in the year that King Uzziah/Ahaz died." Again, there is no interest in chronology here *per se*, for it is not the date that is important but the event that is mentioned: the king's death. This is significant for Isaiah's message, for Isaiah is reminded in chapter 6 that the divine king (Yahweh) remains enthroned despite the passing of Judah's king. Similarly, in Is 14:28 Philistia is warned that the Judaean sovereign's death should not be seen as an opportunity to rebel from vassalage. It is the event—not its date—that is important for understanding each oracle.

Isaiah 20:1 confirms this perspective. This verse appears to reflect a chronological interest when it dates the oracle "in the year that the commander came to Ashdod, when Sargon king of Assyria sent him and he fought against Ashdod and captured it." Unfortunately, this is a largely worthless chronological marker unless one is a contemporary of the events that happened. In what year of Sargon's reign? In what year of the king of Judah's reign? Who was the king of Judah? Rather, it is the fact that an

---

[1]On the basis of archaeological evidence of an earthquake at excavated sites, estimates of a date in the first half of the eighth century have been proposed for this earthquake (David Noel Freedman and Andrew Welch, "Amos's Earthquake and Israelite Prophecy," in *Scripture and Other Artifacts: Essays on the Bible and Archaeology in Honor of Philip J. King*, ed. Michael D. Coogan, J. Cheryl Exum and Lawrence E. Stager [Louisville, Ky.: Westminster John Knox, 1994], pp. 188-98.

Assyrian king conquered a city—not the date it occurred—that provides the context for the oracle that insists a similar experience will happen to Egypt. For those of us living long after the events, the chronological data to satisfy our curiosity as to the time mentioned must be imported into the text, deduced from documents of the Assyrian empire and the remnants of destruction uncovered by archaeologists. The fact that we must go elsewhere to uncover this information simply underscores the point: the early prophetic books show no interest in dating their words.

Isaiah 7:1 likewise shows no real chronological interest, for it is simply establishing for the reader the relevant actors in the narrative to follow:

> And it happened in the days of Ahaz, son of Jotham, son of Uzziah, king of Judah, that Rezin king of Syria and Pekah, son of Remaliah, king of Israel, went up to Jerusalem to war against it, but he was unable to conquer it. (Is 7:1)

Again: in what year of which king? The text presents no interest in chronology itself. The entire sixty-six chapters of the book of Isaiah contain only one clear date whose purpose is without doubt to establish chronology:

> And it happened in the fourteenth year of King Hezekiah that Sennacherib king of Assyria came up against all the fortified cities of Judah and captured them. (Is 36:1)

This is the only verse in the books associated with early literary prophets whose explicit motivation is to identify a specific point in time for a prophetic activity. But the anomaly is easily explicable: this verse is a quotation from 2 Kings 18:13 (as most of Is 36–39 is excerpted from 2 Kings 18–20),[2] a book where chronology and synchronisms between kings are all-important. This anomalous bolt from another horizon only serves to underscore how little concern for chronology captures the attention of those who wrote down the oracles of the early prophets. There are 105 chapters (this figure includes all of Isaiah) where no oracles are provided with specific chronological markers for the benefit of readers who might be living long after the events were otherwise forgotten, the sole exception being one verse whose origin lies in a text outside the

---

[2]On this issue, see chapter six, n. 1.

prophets, a text dedicated to chronological concerns.

This lack of chronological focus in early prophetic books can be better visualized by turning to the postexilic prophets for whom precision in dating is a high priority. Haggai's two short chapters insist on dating every oracle that is recorded. In addition, the year of the revelation is not enough, nor is the month, for even the day on which the revelation came is worthy of attention:

1st day, 6th month, 2nd year of Darius the King (Hag 1:1)

21st day, 7th month (Hag 2:1)

24th day, 9th month, 2nd year of Darius (Hag 2:10)

24th day (Hag 2:20)

Zechariah also specifies the very day on which visions came to him:

8th month, 2nd year of Darius (Zech 1:1)

24th day, 11 month, 2nd year of Darius (Zech 1:7)

4th day, 9th month, 4th year of Darius (7:1)

What motivates a sudden concern for chronology in these prophets that is not duplicated in the prophets discussed above?

This concern is actually not sudden, for one can see the transformation gradually unfold in the transitional book of Jeremiah. This book begins in a fashion similar to the early prophets with a vague notice positioning Jeremiah "in the days of king . . ." (Jer 1:3). But unlike the early prophets there is also in the introduction a notice that the revelation occurred in a specific year of a specific king:

> The words of Jeremiah . . . to whom the word of Yahweh came in the days of Josiah, son of Amon, king of Judah, in the thirteenth year of his reign. (Jer 1:1-2)

This curious orientation both backwards (with little chronological concern like the early literary prophets) and forwards (a concern for chronology like the two postexilic prophets noted above) characterizes the book of Jeremiah as a whole. After the opening dates, numerous oracles and events from the life of Jeremiah are recorded with no chronological markers apart from what one might have expected from the early prophets, for example:

That which came as the word of Yahweh to Jeremiah in regard to the drought . . . (Jer 14:1)

The word which came to Jeremiah from Yahweh when King Zedekiah sent to him Pashhur son of Malchijah and Zephaniah the priest son of Maaseiah, saying . . . (Jer 21:1)

After Nebuchadnezzar king of Babylon had carried away captive Jeconiah son of Jehoiakim king of Judah, and the officials of Judah with the craftsmen and smiths from Jerusalem and had brought them to Babylon, Yahweh showed me . . . (Jer 24:1)

As with the early prophets, this information is chronologically inadequate even though it serves its purpose in providing the necessary historical background for the particular events and oracles that follow in each case. Such notices appear throughout the book.[3]

The first precise chronological marker for an oracle appears only in the second half of the book (Jer 25:1). From this point onward, a total of eight date formulas provide the year of a king's reign as the date for Jeremiah's words, for which one date formula even preserves a month:

4th year of Jehoiakim (=first of Nebuchadnezzar; Jer 25:1)

Beginning of Zedekiah's reign (Jer 26:1)[4]

5th month, 4th year of Zedekiah (Jer 28:1)

10th year of Zedekiah (=18th of Nebuchadnezzar; Jer 32:1)

4th year of Jehoiakim (Jer 36:1)

4th year of Jehoiakim (Jer 45:1)

4th year of Jehoiakim (Jer 46:2)

Beginning of Zedekiah's reign (Jer 49:34)

---

[3]Jer 29:1; 33:1; 34:1,6-8; 35:1; 40:1; 47:1; 49:28. Jer 39:1-2 and 41:2 introduce no oracles but are excerpted with the following verses from 2 Kings 25:1-7, 25 or a common source (Mordechai Cogan and Hayim Tadmor, *II Kings* [Garden City, N.Y.: Doubleday, 1988], pp. 320-21). All of Jer 52 with its extensive dating clearly is excerpted from 2 Kings 24:18–25:30, because the Dtr evaluation of Jehoiakim (Jer 52:2) and the presentation of the manner of punishment by exile (Jer 52:3, 27) are typical of 1–2 Kings but foreign to Jeremiah (ibid., p. 120).

[4]Some texts read "Jehoiakim." "Beginning" is a reference to the year in which the king comes to the throne and should not be interpreted as a vague generalization.

Other dates appear that are associated with specific events, such as the fourth year of Zedekiah when Jeremiah gives a scroll to Seraiah to carry to Babylon (Jer 51:59). The transitional character of Jeremiah is evident, for no specific dates appear in the first half of the book where most of the poetry is found. And although specific dates are found in the second half of the book where prose predominates, they are infrequent and most oracles are not introduced with a reference to a specific date.

Ezekiel is another prophet who, like Jeremiah, also began his prophetic career before the fall of Jerusalem and finished it after its destruction. Ezekiel, too, appears to be in this transitional phase where dating of prophetic oracles becomes important, for, although most of Ezekiel's oracles are not introduced with a specific date, he provides a few more dates than does Jeremiah. Most of these appear in only a very small portion of the book (Ezek 24–32), a section concerned for the most part with the oracles against the foreign nations. In the first 23 chapters, on the other hand, only two such dates are provided (Ezek 1:1; 8:1). This uneven attention to dating oracles points to only a selective concern that does not permeate the entire work. Like Jeremiah, some parts of the book look backward to the early prophetic disregard for dated oracles while other parts of the book anticipate the postexilic passion for precise dating of visions. In this latter regard, Ezekiel goes further than Jeremiah in precision, citing in almost every case the very day of the vision:

**Table 10.1.**

| Day | Month | Year | Reference |
|---|---|---|---|
| 5 | 4 | 30 | (Ezek 1:1) |
| 5 | 1 | 5 of Jehoiakin's exile | (Ezek 1:2) |
| 5 | 6 | 6 | (Ezek 8:1) |
| 10 | 5 | 7 | (Ezek 20:1) |
| 10 | 10 | 9 | (Ezek 24:1) |
| 1 | 1 | 11 | (Ezek 26:1) |
| 12 | 10 | 10 | (Ezek 29:1) |
| 1 | 1 | 27 | (Ezek 29:17) |
| 7 | 1 | 11 | (Ezek 30:20) |
| 1 | 3 | 11 | (Ezek 31:1) |
| 1 | 12 | 12 | (Ezek 32:1) |
| 10 | 1 | 25 of exile (=14th year after Jerusalem destroyed) | (Ezek 40:1) |

The new focus upon recording the specific time when an oracle was given appears with a divine command to Ezekiel that is unattested in earlier prophets: "Write for yourself the name of the day, this very day" (Ezek 24:2). It should be noted as well that the apocalyptic book of Daniel predictably partakes of the later penchant for dating in supplying dates—none more precise than the year—for the visions he sees (Dan 2:1; 7:1; 8:1 9:1; 10:1) but curiously not for the stories that appear in the book.[5]

There is, therefore, a clear pattern of disregard for the dating of oracles among the early literary prophets. This disregard is modified slightly in the transitional books of Jeremiah and Ezekiel (written or completed in exile), a trajectory that continues with an increasing interest after the exile in not only dating oracles but dating them to precise days in a month. This shift in focus is probably not a minor feature, for it does not appear randomly as if it were optional. It is evident that the dates of early oracles were not preserved; had they been, later generations who found precise dating important would have passed them on.

We describe this feature as a "pattern" since there is a demonstrable general correlation between the explicit dating of a book and its temporal setting. But it must be stressed that this is only a pattern—that is, a general correlation that may be subject to aberrations. The book of Malachi, for example, is universally recognized as a distinctly postexilic book, even later than Haggai and Zechariah, but it preserves not a single date. This book makes it clear that one can not argue the reverse proposition, namely that the presence or absence of a concern for dates is a certain indicator of a temporal context. Two other books, Obadiah and Joel, are notoriously difficult to date, partly as a result of the lack of any date notation, even in their opening verses. Good reasons can be posited for dating them early, and good reasons are available to date them later. Although one could argue that these two books align more closely with the earlier prophets than with the later prophets in light of the clear pattern discussed in this section, there are many more issues that must be scrutinized in dating the content of a literary prophet. The example of Malachi, therefore, prompts

---

[5]The date in Dan 1:1 may be an exception, or it may simply set the historical context for the entire book; in either case the date is curious on several scores (see Louis Hartman and Alexander A. Di Lella, *The Book of Daniel* [Garden City, N.Y.: Doubleday, 1978], pp. 128-29).

caution in extending this general pattern as an unequivocal guide to the relative dating of prophetic books.[6]

What is the significance of this pattern with regard to chronological indicators in the literary prophets? Dating with increasing precision in some[7] exilic and postexilic prophets may indicate a rising awareness of the need to preserve as much information as possible for future generations. A source for such increased historical awareness can easily be found in the destruction of Jerusalem, along with its archives, and a heightened awareness of the tenuous nature of records from the past. A focused historical sense may have been stimulated by the paucity of chronological information in the older surviving prophetic literature that seemed to have been vindicated by Jerusalem's fall. A curiosity to know more about older prophetic oracles is correlative with a self-conscious application to contemporary oracles and their preservation for the future. It is difficult to separate this phenomenon from the new interest in writing down a prophet's words as we saw in the preceding chapter, a scribal enterprise that would be accustomed instinctively to record a date when inscribing a text. The reluctance of later editors to supply missing dates is encouraging. Apart from the editorial introductions of some prophetic books that place a particular prophet in the reign of an Israelite or a Judaean king, there is no observable chronological tampering with oracles. It is this very conservatism that permits us today to confirm one more way in which the prophetic tradition changed over time. This change also isolates the exile again as the time in which prophecy underwent a significant modification, in this case closely connected with the new interest in writing down a prophet's words.

---

[6]The lack of a date in the book of Jonah is unsurprising, since it is not a collection of prophetic oracles but a short story about a prophet.
[7]We observed above that no date appears in Isaiah 40–66.

# 11

# MIRACLES

WE HAVE NOTED IN THE PRECEDING two chapters significant changes that unfolded in the actual process of writing down prophetic oracles. In particular, we saw that the time of the exile became a period of explicit transformation from an oral to a written culture for prophetic messages. The first part of Jeremiah's activity was entirely oral in contrast to the new written format that dominated the last part of his life, beginning with the Babylonian siege of Jerusalem. Ezekiel in exile, even from the beginning of his activity, became the first prophet known to have written down his messages in their entirety as a written document. Only with the period of the exile do specific dates begin to appear in prophetic texts, reinforcing the awareness of a new interest in preserving in writing for the future the chronological context in which prophetic speech took place. Collections of older oracles from earlier prophets may have been written down before this period. Of this we have no evidence. What we do know is that in the years surrounding 600 B.C. there is an explicit new focus upon writing at least some prophetic texts, a new focus that could have been extended to other prophetic oracles that may have continued to exist in an oral format up to that time. The dramatic contrast that appears at this time underscores that a new development is taking place when prophetic words are beginning to be conceived as primarily written phenomena.

There are no literary prophets associated with any period before the eighth century. At that time, Amos, Hosea, Micah and Isaiah suddenly appear and are eventually associated with texts that bear their names. Amos is the earliest of the datable literary prophets, active a century and a half before Jeremiah. Why are there no earlier literary prophetic texts? There is no book of oracles associated with the name Elijah, for example, and Elisha has left behind no collection of messages. Both of these figures appear in the ninth century. Had they, and other prophets like them, no oracles of lasting significance? Or did they have similar collections of oracles that have succumbed to the fate of most creative works of the ancient world? The Chronicler mentions several books identified with earlier prophets such as Gad, Samuel, Nathan, Ahijah, Iddo and Shemaiah (discussed above in chapter nine), but these are no longer accessible to us and we know next to nothing of their content (oracular? narrative? didactic? biographical? legenda?).

The Deuteronomistic history (Joshua, Judges, 1–2 Samuel, 1–2 Kings) preserves one perspective on a possible reason for the contrast between the literary prophets and earlier prophets whose oracles are no longer extant. The prophets who lived before the time of the literary prophets were depicted as miracle workers in the Dtr history. One horizon of this extensive work finds it of great importance that the prophets be portrayed with the ability to do extraordinary wonders: Samuel's prayers to God result in upheavals of nature (1 Sam 7:8-11; 12:17-18), a Judahite prophet's words split Jeroboam's altar from afar (1 Kings 13:5), Elijah revives the dead, provides an unending supply of oil and flour, brings fire down from heaven, and splits the Jordan (1 Kings 17:13-24; 18:30-39; 2 Kings 1:10-14; 2:8), while Elisha purifies poisoned water, provides miraculous supplies of oil and food, raises the dead, heals lepers, retrieves sunken axeheads, splits the Jordan, and strikes entire armies blind (2 Kings 2:14, 21-22; 4:1-7, 32-44; 5:10-14; 6:5-7, 18). Such phenomena are not insignificant but have evidentiary value in pointing to the unique deity of the God of Israel and the prophet as his spokeperson, as Naaman observes when healed of his leprosy, "Behold, now, I know that there is no god in all the earth except in Israel" (2 Kings 5:15; cf. 2 Kings 5:8)

Elijah and Elisha in these stories are portrayed as the last of the great miracle-working prophets. It is true that occasional miracles surface later, but there is no further sustained presentation of this spectacular dimen-. sion of a prophet's persona. In fact, the Dtr history explicitly accounts for this change with the story of Elijah's encounter at Mt. Horeb (or Mt. Sinai) in 1 Kings 19. In that account, Elijah went without food for forty days and nights (1 Kings 19:8) just as Moses was at the same mountain for the same length of time, also without food (Ex 34:28).[1] Elijah took refuge in the same cave in which Moses had received his unique revelation from God: "He [Elijah] came there to the cave, and spent the night there" (1 Kings 19:9).[2] This mountain was a crucial locus for revelation, and when God revealed himself to Moses, God was in the earthquake, wind and fire (Ex 19:16-19). Jarringly unlike other parallels between Moses and Elijah, this is no longer true for Elijah:

> Behold, Yahweh was passing by, and a great and powerful wind was splitting mountains and breaking rocks before Yahweh. Yahweh was not in the wind. After the wind there was an earthquake. Yahweh was not in the earthquake. After the earthquake there was fire. Yahweh was not in the fire. After the fire there was a sound of a light whisper.[3] (1 Kings 19:11-12)

---

[1] Robert B. Coote, "Yahweh Recalls Elijah," in *Traditions in Transformation*, ed. B. Halpern and J. Levenson (Winona Lake, Ind.: Eisenbrauns, 1981), p. 117. See George W. Savran, *Encountering the Divine: Theophany in Biblical Narrative*, JSOTSS 420 (London: T & T Clark, 2005), pp. 218-29, for a detailed analysis of the interplay between the encounters of Moses and Elijah described in these two texts.

[2] In spite of the Hebrew "the cave," most Bibles translate, "he [Elijah] came there to a cave" (1 Kings 19:9; the Elberfelder German translation is exceptional in preserving the definite article). There is only one famous recess in the mountain to which the writer could be referring, namely the place where Moses had his unparalleled revelation when he saw God pass by (Ex 33:22), a location which probably became a place of pilgrimage and was well known to Israelites (James Montgomery, *A Critical and Exegetical Commentary on the Book of Kings*, ICC [Edinburgh: T & T Clark, 1951], p. 313). Justification for translation without the article may have recourse to a grammatical peculiarity defended in GKC 126q, but this has been ably challenged by Martin Ehrensvärd, "An Unusual Use of the Definite Article in Biblical and Post-Biblical Hebrew," in *Sirach, Scrolls, and Sages: Proceedings of a Second International Symposium on the Hebrew of the Dead Sea Scrolls, Ben Sira, and the Mishnah, held at Leiden University, 15-17 December 1977*, ed. T. Muraoka and J. F. Elwolde, STDJ 33 (Leiden: Brill, 1999), pp. 68-76.

[3] It is not easy to pin down the precise meaning of this Hebrew phrase *qôl dĕmāmâ daqqâ*. The idea of a "voice" is a traditional rendering that has been widely followed from the first English Bibles (e.g., Geneva Bible, KJV, RSV, JPS). Many twentieth-century translations prefer "whisper" (e.g., Knox, Moffatt, [T]NIV) while others opt for a less committal "sound" (e.g., NRSV, NASB, NAB).

Unlike the preceding manifestations, there is no denial of God's presence in the final event. Instead, the implication points to the inconspicuous and subdued but still audible sound that marks the presence of God, not the grand displays of power in nature. What may have been true with the earlier paradigm of Moses as man of God is explicitly denied as true no more for Elijah. This event is a watershed, an apologetic for the decline of the miracle-working prophet and the rise of the literary prophet with an emphasis upon the revealed word. After Elijah and Elisha, narratives of prophets working wonders diminish in frequency. Yahweh's revelation is centered in the divine word and not in the dramatic displays of divine power.

In the literary prophets, the prophets are emphatically not depicted as miracle workers for, apart from Isaiah 36–39, there is no record in the Bible[4] of these prophets performing miraculous signs. The exceptional nature of the four chapters in Isaiah is explicable: they originate elsewhere, copied almost verbatim from the books of Kings in the Dtr history,[5] a work where—as we noted above—it was important to depict prophets as wonder-workers. The healing and miraculous dimensions of prophetic activity appear uniquely in these Isaianic chapters when Isaiah causes the shadow of the sundial to move backwards (Is 38:7-8) and when he provides the king with a poultice that prompts his recovery from an illness (Is 38:21). These are highly unusual stories in the literary prophets and only secondarily attached to the book of Isaiah, where the primary emphasis is instead upon the verbal revelation from God.

The earliest of the literary prophets insists that he is a phenomenon that does not fit in the traditional mold. In the words of Amos,

I am not a prophet *(nābî')*, and I am not a son of a prophet, for I am a

---

[4]Miracles attributed to these prophets do appear in later traditions, e.g., *The Lives of the Prophets* (D. R. A. Hare, "The Lives of the Prophets," in *The Old Testament Pseudepigrapha*, ed. James Charlesworth [Garden City, N.Y.: Doubleday, 1985], 2:379-99) where miracles not attested in the Bible are associated with Isaiah, Jeremiah, Ezekiel and others. The literary prophets shared with the prophets described in the Dtr history an outspoken use of signs as markers of events yet to unfold, but unlike the signs of the Dtr history prophets that could include both natural (e.g., 1 Sam 2:34) as well as supernatural phenomena (e.g., 1 Kings 13:3-5), the signs employed by the literary prophets were natural events (e.g., Is 7:14-15; Jer 44:29-30; cf. R. B. Y. Scott, *The Relevance of the Prophets* [New York: Macmillan, 1944], pp. 55-56).

[5]See n. 1 in chapter six.

herdsman and one who slits mulberry figs. But Yahweh took me from following the flock, and Yahweh said to me, "Go, prophesy *(hinnābēʾ)* to my people, Israel." And now, hear the word of Yahweh . . . (Amos 7:14-16)

Many have argued, and at great length, about Amos's meaning when he objected to the Bethel priest's harsh dismissal of Amos as a southern seer. Amos remarkably distances himself from the priest's assumptions about what constitutes a prophet, distinguishing himself from the institution of prophethood and the disciples ("son of a prophet") associated with it. He sees himself as breaking with the traditional understanding of what it means to be a prophet. Nevertheless, at the same time that he claims he is not a prophet, a continuity is maintained in the command from Yahweh that is unequivocal: "Prophesy!" In the popular conception, a prophet was someone who would be expected to "call upon the name of Yahweh his God and wave his hand around and remove the leprosy" (2 Kings 5:11). As Elisha backed down from that unjustified expectation, so Amos here retreats from anything more than the message that Yahweh had given him. Amos is a man with a message and no miracles in his bag.

A complete disjuncture between the prominence of the miraculous in earlier prophets and its absence in later prophets is not easily explained apart from a changing perspective on the prophetic office.[6] One expects legends about exemplary figures to develop in their lifetime and proliferate in a subsequent generation. If there were miracles associated with Amos, Hosea, or Micah, or if stories about their supernatural exploits circulated, the remarkable fact is that not a single such story entered the books that bear their names. Jeremiah and Ezekiel were either explicitly not wonder-workers or, if they were perceived to be such, this dimension of their activity was consistently screened out of the literary records now found in the Bible where their words and deeds were recorded. On either score, this view of prophecy remains at odds with that perspective depicted for the early prophets in the Dtr history.

In spite of this disjuncture, the book of Deuteronomy exhibits a notable awareness of the limited value that miracles have for prophets in general.

---

[6]See further Harry M. Orlinsky, *Ancient Israel*, 2nd ed. (Ithaca, N.Y.: Cornell University Press, 1960), pp. 125-27.

Deuteronomy 13:1-5 [13:2-6] anticipates that misleading prophets might be fully capable of performing marvels that would seem to point to divine approval. Israel is warned, however, that a prophet who successfully performs "a sign or a wonder" is not necessarily a prophet who is to be heeded. Although Elijah may use the miraculous as a litmus test on Mt. Carmel to convince gathered Israelites that Baal is impotent while Yahweh controls the forces of nature (1 Kings 18:20-39), Deuteronomy insists that the miraculous is of limited usefulness for discriminating trustworthy from untrustworthy prophets.[7]

As a result there are at least three complementary perspectives that may be distinguished in descriptions of prophetic activity. In the case of the Dtr history, one finds a general exuberance in lauding God's prophets who use uncanny powers to work God's salvation among his people, even using miracles to discriminate between reliable and unreliable prophets. A more restrained attitude toward miracles surfaces in Deuteronomy where such abilities are affirmed even as their limited usefulness is acknowledged. Finally, the literary prophets ignore the miraculous entirely.

As a postscript, it must be noted that there is a further development with regard to the miraculous that occurs at the very end of the period encompassed by the biblical canon. A different atmosphere is evident in the book of Daniel where the reader confronts a number of miraculous events. What makes these events distinctive in this context is that none of them are connected with prophetic activity. The rescue of Daniel from the lions (as with the rescue of Shadrach, Meshach and Abednego from the fire) is simply the dramatic intervention of God in human history, a feature that no prophet ever overlooked or minimized. Even here, however, the contrast with the prophets is dramatic, for the literary prophets themselves record no miraculous deliverances. Instead one finds harrowing tales of beatings and death sentences in the case of Jeremiah,[8] and later tradition records the ghastly demise of figures like Isaiah.[9] Jonah's rescue

---

[7]A helpful illustration from the Pentateuch for this mediating position is the ability of Pharaoh's magicians to duplicate only the first three of the wonders that Moses and Aaron perform (Ex 7:11, 22; 8:7, 19 [8:3, 15]). For further developments of this theme, cf. Mt 7:21-23; Rev 13:13-14.

[8]Jer 11:21; 20:1-3; 26:7-11; 32:3-8; 33:1; 36:5; 37:4, 15-16, 21; 38:4-6.

[9]M. A. Knibb, "Martyrdom and Ascension of Isaiah," in *The Old Testament Pseudepigrapha*, ed. James Charlesworth (Garden City, N.Y.: Doubleday, 1985), 2:143-76.

by the whale cannot be termed a miracle in the same sense that lions are made tame or fire does not burn, since only in Daniel, Shadrach, Meshach and Abednego's case is there the suspension or reversal of the normal course of nature.

In sum, the literary prophets do not mention the miraculous powers that a prophet might possess or be able to bring into play. One must turn to the Deuteronomistic history to discover depictions of earlier prophets as wonder-workers. On the basis of this distinction, it is possible for some to attempt to drive a wedge between the two types of prophets, highlighting one as the wonder-working prophet and the other as the prophet of the divine word.[10] However, the Dtr history itself provides a rationale in the Sinai revelation to Elijah in an attempt to bridge the divide between the two. Not only, therefore, does the exile emerge as a landmark event for the development and transformation of prophecy. According to the Dtr history and the phenomenon of the literary prophets, the ninth through eighth centuries also stand out, for they mark a decline in the perception of the miraculous in the repertoire of the prophet. A new emphasis upon the audible message itself appears, providing a rationale for the rise of the so-called literary prophets in the eighth century, and ultimately the rise of the prophetic text itself in the sixth century.

---

[10]E.g., Scott, *Relevance of the Prophets*, pp. 55-56.

# 12

# Prophets as King-Makers

We have seen in preceding chapters that the sixth century b.c., the century of Judah's exile, appears repeatedly as a time when prophecy undergoes significant transitions. It is the century when all other institutions among ancient Israelites are permanently affected. The temple was destroyed, Jerusalem was burned, and the land was devastated. For decades under Babylonian dominion, the land of Judah remained in this condition as a function of Babylonian imperial policy: what was destroyed was not rebuilt.[1] These conditions made it impossible for traditional institutions associated with temple and palace to continue. Indeed, kingship was gone, and no Jewish king would rule over the Jews for another four hundred and eighty years, until the Maccabean kings seized power.[2]

The demise of kingship in the sixth century b.c. and the simultaneous changes in prophecy are connected. As we will see, one institution could not be affected without repercussions affecting the other. It is not a coincidence that the distinctive features of the institution of prophecy appear

---

[1]Ephraim Stern, *Archaeology of the Land of the Bible: The Assyrian, Babylonian, and Persian Periods (732-332 b.c.e.)* (New York: Doubleday, 2001), pp. 348-50.

[2]The last king of Judah to sit on the throne, Zedekiah, was removed in 586 b.c., and the first member of the Hasmonean family (Maccabees) to call himself king was Aristobolus (104–103 b.c.).

primarily in the period of the Israelite and Judaean monarchies. The rise
of kingship around 1000 B.C. with Saul and David also marks the beginning of the first extensive material at our disposal that informs us of prophetic activity. This juxtaposition is not an accident.

Israelites had a love-hate relationship with kingship. Kings were capable of great good, but, as a predictable corollary, kings were also capable of
great evil. The Bible presents kingship in Israel as a secondary development, an import from neighboring cultures. As the story goes, Israel was
weary with the nadir of depravity that accompanied the erratic rule by so-
called judges. Before kingship was instituted in Israel, Israelites were killing Israelites and there was no uniform standard of justice. In words that
repeat and bring to a climax the book of Judges, "Everyone did what was
right in his own eyes" (Judg 17:6; 21:25).

A perpetually repeated cycle of depravity, repentance and rescue, which
pervades the description of this period in the book of Judges, came to a
halt when kingship came to Israel, according to the perspective presented
in the biblical texts that deal with this transition. Depravity is not eradi-
cated and may still occur, but accountability of leadership in a more stable
institution is pictured as amelioration, if not a final solution, to a complete
breakdown in moral and social stability that pervades a culture where all
is relative.

The prophetic connection with kingship begins already with the first
king of Israel. Saul becomes the first king only through the good offices
of a prophet. We are told that the prophet Samuel privately "took the flask
of oil, poured it on his (i.e., Saul's) head, kissed him and said, 'Has not
Yahweh anointed you *(mĕšāḥăkā)* a ruler *(lĕnāgîd)* over His inheritance?'"
(1 Sam 10:1). This action fulfills the mandate God had earlier given to
Samuel even before he met the one who would soon become king, for God
had said, "I will send you a man . . . and you shall anoint him to be prince
*(ûmĕšaḥtô lĕnāgîd)* over my people Israel" (1 Sam 9:16). Later the reader
learns how the prophet Samuel takes the initiative in establishing Saul's
kingship in a public ceremony when he announces to the Israelites, "Come
and let us go to Gilgal and renew the kingdom there" (1 Sam 11:14). In a
more schematic fashion it can be noted that "they (i.e., Israel) made Saul
king *(wayyamlîkû)* before Yahweh in Gilgal" (1 Sam 11:15), and from a

more theological perspective it can similarly be affirmed that "Yahweh has set a king over you" (1 Sam 12:13). But further specification repeatedly isolates the prophet Samuel as the prime human mover in the drama by which a man becomes king over Israel. In addition to his role in directing the selection of lots to confirm Saul's kingship to the people (1 Sam 11:17-25), he also notes in an address to assembled Israelites, "I have listened to your voice in all that you said to me, and I have caused a king to rule over you *(wā'amlîk . . . melek)*" (1 Sam 12:1).

This presentation of the prophet as kingmaker is not a minor concern, for it carries with it significant practical ramifications. The king is indebted to the prophet for his position, a debt which requires the king to do what the prophet asks. When Samuel approaches Saul with a command from God to exterminate the Amalekites, it is precisely Samuel's role as kingmaker that he recollects in order to motivate Saul to do what the prophet asks: "Yahweh sent me to anoint you as king *(limšāḥŏkā lĕmelek)* over His people, over Israel; now therefore listen to the words of Yahweh" (1 Sam 15:1). Kings listen to prophets not only because kings, like everyone else, are awed before a voice that claims to be speaking divine words. A prophet has a further unique claim upon a king: without the prophet, the king would not be sitting in his regal position. Even more sobering is the fact that a prophet has the authority to remove a king should the king fail to cooperate and fulfill his part of the bargain in submitting to prophetic authority.[3]

This is precisely what happens when Saul does not heed Samuel's order to exterminate the Amalekites or to wait for Samuel before going into battle:

> Samuel said, ". . . Yahweh sent you on a mission. . . . Why did you not listen to Yahweh's voice? . . . Because you rejected Yahweh's word, he has rejected you from being king. . . . You rejected Yahweh's word, and Yahweh has rejected you from being king over Israel." (1 Sam 15:17-19, 23, 26)

> He [i.e., King Saul] waited seven days for the appointed time that Samuel set, but Samuel did not come to Gilgal, and the people were dispersing.

---

[3]Abraham J. Heschel elaborates this balance of power in his chapter titled "Prophet, Priest, and King" (*The Prophets,* pp. 254-62); cf. Frank Moore Cross Jr., *Canaanite Myth and Hebrew Epic: Essays in the History of the Religion of Israel* (Cambridge, Mass.: Harvard University Press, 1973), pp. 221-29.

Saul said, "Bring me the burnt offering and the peace offerings," and he offered the burnt offering. And it happened that as he finished offering the burnt offering, behold, Samuel came. Saul went out to him to greet him. Samuel said, "What have you done?" Saul said, "Because I saw that the people were dispersing from me, and that you did not come at the appointed time. . . ." Samuel said to Saul, "You acted foolishly. You did not keep the commandment of Yahweh your God. . . . Now your kingdom will not endure . . . because you did not keep what Yahweh commanded you." (1 Sam 13:8-14)

Even though Saul continues to function as king, prophetic support for him is withdrawn. In the words of the text that follow these accounts, "Samuel did not again see Saul until the day of his death" (1 Sam 15:35). King Saul has jeopardized the legitimacy of his kingship, for the prophet who anointed him no longer endorses him. The books of Samuel present the remainder of Saul's reign as a transition period during which God waits for Saul's replacement to make his appearance as one fully qualified and capable of assuming the leadership of the people. Samuel notes the beginning of this process when he gives the bad news to Saul: "Yahweh has searched for a man for himself, according to his heart" (1 Sam 13:14). In this case, the transition will be a long process as a young David matures and develops a reputation as a warrior and a leader of men.

The prophetic removal of support for a king is not confined to Samuel, for it is a repeated feature of prophetic activity in the subsequent history of the monarchy. Just as Saul established the first dynasty over Israel and was subsequently rejected by a prophet from Shiloh as noted above, so the first king over the northern kingdom of Israel, Jeroboam, was similarly rejected by a prophet also from Shiloh, who relayed these words from God:

I raised you from among the people and made you a leader over my people Israel. . . . Behold I bring evil to the house of Jeroboam, and will cut off from Jeroboam every male. (1 Kings 14:7, 10)

Similar words mark the prophetic removal of other royal dynasties in the north such as that founded by Baasha (1 Kings 16:1-4) and the one founded by Omri (1 Kings 21:17-24).[4] The announcement of a specific

---

[4]The close verbal connection that describes the removal of these monarchs is an important feature

king's impending death is well within the prophet's job description if one can judge by the deceased Samuel's warning to King Saul of his death on the following day (1 Sam 28:19), Micaiah's prediction that King Ahab would fall in his next battle (1 Kings 22:17-23), or Elijah's words of doom upon a sick King Ahijah (2 Kings 1:16).[5]

Prophets are therefore both king-makers and king-breakers. Returning to Saul's rejection by the prophet Samuel, this same prophet selects Saul's replacement, David, and anoints him just as he had anointed Saul. God's words to the prophet Samuel are explicit:

> How long will you mourn over Saul, since I have rejected him from being king over Israel? Fill your horn with oil and go. I will send you to Jesse the Bethlehemite, for I have seen among his sons a king for me. . . . You will anoint for me the one I tell you." (1 Sam 16:1, 3)

When David appears and God informs the prophet that this young man is the next king, "Samuel took the horn of oil and anointed him" (1 Sam 16:13).

We also find explicit prophetic support when it comes time for the third king of the united monarchy, Solomon, to ascend the throne. The prophet Samuel, who had died long before David formally became king (1 Sam 25:1), had already given God's support to David's descendants as rulers of a dynasty that would last "forever" (*'ad-'ôlām*, 2 Sam 7:13, 16; cf. 2 Sam 7:15). Nevertheless, another prophet, Nathan, is present at the coronation of David's son and successor, Solomon. Even more striking is the primary role that Nathan plays as the prime mover in making sure that Solomon becomes king instead of his older brother, Adonijah:

> Nathan said to Solomon's mother, Bathsheba, the mother of Solomon, "Didn't you hear that Adonijah the son of Haggith has become king, but our lord David isn't aware? Come, now, let me advise you: save your life and the life of your son Solomon! Go, depart at once to King David and say to him, 'Did you not, my lord the king, swear to your maidservant, saying,

---

discussed in chapter fourteen below, "Continuities in History."

[5]The latter two cases only deal with the death of the king in question and not the accompanying demise of the royal family as well. One should, therefore, also include here Isaiah's oracle of death for King Hezekiah, even though the king's prayer prompted a fifteen-year postponement and his death did not mark the termination of his dynasty (2 Kings 20:1-6).

"Solomon your son will indeed rule after me, and he will sit on my throne"? Why, then, has Adonijah become king?' Behold, even as you are speaking there with the king, I will come after you and confirm your words." (1 Kings 1:11-14)

A prophet's confirmation of another's words is a very impressive confirmation indeed, of the highest sort. Nathan's plan succeeds, and he, along with other supporters of Solomon's kingship, is able to install Solomon formally as king. Nathan conducts the anointing ceremony with the priest in accord with David's orders:

> The king said, . . . "Let Zadok the priest and Nathan the prophet anoint him there as king over Israel. . . ." Zadok the priest, Nathan the prophet, and Benaiah . . . went down and seated Solomon on King David's mule and led him to Gihon. Zadok the priest took the horn of oil from the tent and anointed[6] Solomon. . . . Jonathan answered and said to Adonijah, ". . . Zadok the priest and Nathan the prophet anointed him king in Gihon." (1 Kings 1:33-34, 38-39, 43, 45)

Solomon has a prophet, Nathan, who is part of his anointing ceremony, but no prophet is mentioned for Adonijah. This absence is a notable silence, for the account mentions specific individuals (1 Kings 1:7) who support Adonijah, the alternate candidate for kingship. These individuals are a counterpart to a similar list of supporters for Solomon in his bid for the throne (1 Kings 1:8, 32, 38, 44). Although Adonijah's supporters include a priest and a general, as do Solomon's supporters, the absence of a prophet in Adonijah's camp seems to doom his bid for the throne from the beginning. Without a prophet, the candidate for kingship is illegitimate, at least from the perspective of the narrator who in this episode further develops the pattern already established: a prophet is an essential

---

[6]Of the three times that Solomon's anointing is mentioned, both the prophet and the priest are said to do it only in the first and third descriptions. The second description mentions only the priest. If the omission of the prophet in the middle description is not a scribal slip, it may reflect the institutionalizing of the process (note how the oil explicitly comes from the sanctuary) which might include the elevation of the priest in the process (the priest is always mentioned here first before the prophet). Since Israelites are said to base their kingship on foreign models (1 Sam 8:5, 20), the prominence of priests in the installation of foreign kings may account for this (cf. the role of the priest in the coronation of an Assyrian king in Karl F. Müller, *Das Assyrische Ritual*, MVAG 41.3 [Leipzig: J. C. Hinrichs, 1937]).

element in designating the next king over Israel.

After the first three kings of Israel, the actual process of choosing or installing a new king rarely appears.[7] Whether one is to assume a continuity between the brief descriptions provided for the first three kings and the actual coronation of kings of Judah and Israel is a matter of speculation—the evidence is largely lacking. Nevertheless, the fact that one of the prominent titles by which a king was identified was "the anointed one" *(māšîah)*[8] points in the direction of a continuity of tradition. What we do know is that the books of 1–2 Kings continue to assume that the prophet plays a central role. The new king who leads the civil war that splits the kingdom after Solomon's death does so with prophetic sponsorship:

> And it happened at that time, when Jeroboam departed from Jerusalem, that the prophet Ahijah the Shilonite found him on the road. Now Ahijah had covered himself with a new cloak, and both of them were by themselves in the field. Ahijah grasped the new cloak that was on him and tore it into twelve pieces. He said to Jeroboam, "Take for yourself ten pieces, for thus said Yahweh, the God of Israel, 'Behold, I am about to tear the kingdom from of the hand of Solomon and I will give you the ten tribes. . . . You I will take, and you will reign over all you wish, and you will be king over Israel.'" (1 Kings 11:29-31, 37)

Once again a prophet decrees the fate of a dynasty that is already in power, for a prophet has authority to abase as well as exalt. In this case, however, the prophet establishes two dynasties. Both dynastic houses, that of the southern kingdom of Judah and that of the northern kingdom of Israel, are legitimate according to the Dtr history because God's prophets have endorsed both: ten of the twelve pieces of the cloak go to Jeroboam, while the remainder are for David's heirs (1 Kings 11:32, 36). This

---

[7]After King Josiah dies in battle in 609 B.C., 2 Kings 23:30 records that "the people of the land took Jehoahaz the son of Josiah and anointed him and made him king in place of his father." In the exceptional installation of the seven-year-old Joash after removing Queen Athaliah in 2 Kings 11:12, a vague reference to "they" identifies those who anoint him, unlike the parallel in 2 Chron 23:11 which specifies the priest "Jehoiada and his sons" as the ones who anoint the king. Early rabbinic perspectives (*b. Kerithot* 5b) anticipated contemporary observations that anointing was essential only in founding a new dynasty or when the succession was in doubt, a phenomenon that seems to be reflected in the vocabulary of succession (Joseph Naveh, "Epigraphic Miscellanea," *Israel Exploration Journal* 52 [2002]: 240-42).

[8]E.g., 1 Sam 12:3; Ps 2:2; 18:50; 20:6 [7]; 84:9 [10]; 89:38 [39], 51 [52]; 132:10, 17; Lam 4:20; Hab 3:13.

account presents a passive candidate for kingship, much like Saul, David and Solomon, none of whom is portrayed as actively seeking the throne. Each one of these kings is instead impelled to the throne by a prophetic initiative that singles out each king in turn.

The assumption of prophetic involvement in the selection of kings surfaces again when God orders Elijah at the end of his life to "anoint Hazael as king over Syria and Jehu son of Nimshi you will anoint as king over Israel" (1 Kings 19:15-16). Although God also orders Elijah to anoint a new Israelite king (Jehu) in this same verse, the actual anointing is deferred and passed off to a later prophet, a disciple of Elisha:

> Elisha the prophet summoned one of the sons of the prophets, and said to him, "Gird up your loins, and take this flask of oil in your hand, and go to Ramoth-gilead. When you arrive there, look for Jehu, . . . have him rise from among his brothers, and lead him to an inner room. Take the flask of oil, pour it on his head, and say, 'Thus said Yahweh, "I have anointed you king over Israel."' Open the door and flee, and do not tarry." (2 Kings 9:1-3)

As one comes to expect in these stories, the future king is not presented as actively seeking the throne but is fingered by a prophet who gives him no choice but to become king in the light of a divine, and consequently irrevocable, commission.

The response of the new king's associates to the prophetic pronouncement is instructive:

> Now Jehu went out to his lord's servants, and they said to him, "Is all well? Why did this madman come to you?" And he said to them, "You know the man and his business." And they said, "That is false, please tell us." And he said, "Thus and so he said to me, 'Thus said Yahweh, "I have anointed you king over Israel."'" Then they moved quickly and each man took his clothes and placed them under him on the top of the stairs, and they blew the trumpet and said, "Jehu has become king!" (2 Kings 9:11-13)

The reaction of the men is instructive because the single item that convinces the reigning king's subjects that a usurper has the right to overthrow the king is that it is a prophet who has selected Jehu for this new role. Such a prophetic announcement is precisely the same catalyst in all earlier accounts describing a king's selection: Samuel verbally singles out

Saul and later David, Nathan confirms verbally Solomon's selection as king, and Ahijah verbally selects Jeroboam. The narrator of Jehu's anointing even binds the story more closely to the account of Saul's anointing by the use of a word (Hebrew *pak*) that appears in the Bible in only these two contexts. As the prophet Samuel took "the cruse *(pak)* of oil" (1 Sam 10:1) to anoint Saul, so the young prophet likewise takes "the cruse *(pak)* of oil" to anoint Jehu (2 Kings 9:1, 3).[9]

The crucial role of prophets as king-makers surfaces in the postexilic memoirs of Nehemiah when his enemies spread rumors that he is beginning to overstep his authority as a governor under the authority of the Persian king. The rumor that his detractors encourage is that "you (i.e., Nehemiah) are to be their (i.e., the Jews) king . . . and you have also appointed prophets to proclaim about you in Jerusalem, 'A king is in Judah!'" (Neh 6:6-7). This slander is nourished by the assumption that prophets are so essential to a legitimate king that a usurper will have to hire prophets if they will not come to him on their own initiative. The rumor deceptively presents Nehemiah here, in contrast to all other kings whose selection is recorded, as actively seeking the kingship. It is no wonder that Nehemiah vehemently denies these rumors (Neh 6:8), nor does he ever become king.

The Nehemiah memoir is particularly intriguing as a document written at a time when there were no longer native kings ruling over the Jewish people. At the time the slander is circulating that Nehemiah is hiring prophets to sponsor his kingship, the relatively insignificant province of Judah is only one part of the vast Persian Empire ruled by a Persian "king of kings." The last descendant of David to have ruled over Israel or Judah (Zedekiah) had been forcibly removed well over a century earlier. Nehemiah's experience reveals not only a persistent and long-term expectation for the return of the monarchy to Jerusalem but also the central role that prophets were assumed to play in restoring that monarchy. If the "anointed" *(māšîaḥ)* king to come is to be legitimate, any legitimation would be that

---

[9]The oil comes from a horn (Hebrew *qeren*) when David and Solomon are anointed (1 Sam 16:13; 1 Kings 1:39). Insightful rabbis, noting that the latter two were part of a long-lived dynasty in contrast to the truncated dynasties of Saul and Jehu who were anointed with oil from a small bottle, connected the oil's container with the longevity of the dynasty (*b. Megillah* 14a).

much more easily recognizable if the process were consistent with what Israelites had characteristically expected when a new king was installed.

One of the postexilic literary prophets also attests to the continued importance of the prophetic designation of Israel's leadership even after the removal of a Davidic king from Jerusalem. God tells Zechariah to make a crown[10] in order to give prophetic approval to the designated future ruler: "Make a crown and put it on the head of Joshua, son of Yehozadaq, the high priest, . . . and he will sit and rule upon his throne" (Zech 6:11-13). Regardless of the identity of the one crowned by the prophet and the elusive historical circumstances behind this oracle, Zechariah is continuing in the postexilic period a task that is explicitly prophetic in endorsing a specific individual as a future king for God's people.[11]

The dynasty of David, however, was no longer enthroned in Jerusalem. Expectations for the revival of kingship in Jerusalem were apparent, but with no successful candidates for kingship while under Persian rule, one of the central prophetic roles was now defunct. When kingship disappeared from ancient Israel, one of prophecy's major roles in ancient Israel also vanished. Without kingship, prophecy's political dimension was truncated, and consequently the rise and fall of kingship in Israel was paralleled by the rise and fall of classical prophecy.[12] Prophets made and unmade kings, and it seems that the presence of kingship also made and unmade prophecy. As we have seen, prophecy was not the same after the sixth century, and the demise of Israelite and Judaean kingship in the sixth century was yet one more aspect contributing to the modification of prophecy at this time.

The book of Malachi is both the last text among the prophetic books in the Hebrew Bible and the last book in the Old Testament in the Christian ordering of the books. The book of Malachi itself closes with God's voice affirming that at some time in the future, but before the climactic intervention of God in history, he will send a very special prophet: "Behold, I

---

[10]Although the Hebrew is vocalized as plural, there are good reasons to understand a single crown, in accord with most contemporary translations.

[11]Zechariah's contemporary, Haggai, behaves similarly in endorsing the legitimacy of Zerubbabel, a scion of the house of David, as the chosen king (Hag 2:20-23).

[12]"The institution of prophecy appeared simultaneously with kingship in Israel and fell with kingship" (Cross, *Canaanite Myth*, p. 223).

am about to send to you Elijah the prophet before the coming of the great and terrible day of Yahweh" (Mal 4:5 [3:23]). The classical literary prophets often envisaged a future ideal Davidic king,[13] and it is therefore not surprising that a monarchic expectation would imply a prophetic companion to identify, confirm and anoint this king. As of old, a future king will need a prophet to confirm his royal status. As a result of this verse in Malachi, the expectation for the prophet Elijah has remained one of the more prominent features of Jewish expectation, ritualized even now each year in Passover celebrations with an empty chair and an open door as a formal demonstration of his anticipated return. Already in the New Testament the enquiry was addressed to individuals who conceivably might fit the bill, such as Jesus or John the Baptizer:

> This is John's testimony when the Jews sent priests and Levites to him from Jerusalem in order to ask him, "Who are you?" He confessed and did not deny, and he confessed, "I am not the anointed one." And they asked him, "What then? Are you Elijah?" And he said, "I am not." "Are you the prophet?" And he answered, "No." They said then to him, "Who are you, so that we may give a reply to those who sent us? What do you say about yourself?" He said, "I am the voice of one calling out in the wilderness, 'Make straight the way of the Lord,' as Isaiah the prophet said." Now they had been sent from the Pharisees. And they asked him and said to him, "Why then are you baptizing, if you are not the anointed one, nor Elijah, nor the prophet?" (Jn 1:19-25)

> When Jesus came into the region of Caesarea Philippi, he asked his disciples, saying, "Who do people say that the son of man is?" They said, "Some say John the Baptizer, others Elijah, and yet others Jeremiah, or one of the prophets." (Mt 16:13-14)

It is noteworthy that initial appraisals of Jesus focus on his prophetic status, i.e., as one who could anoint a future king but not necessarily as the king himself.[14] After all, if Jesus were the Davidic king, he would need someone to anoint him if the pattern established in the Old Testament were to continue. As the above passage continues, Peter does make the

---

[13]Is 9:7 [6]; 11:1; 16:5; Jer 22:4; 23:5; 30:9; 33:15, 17, 21, 26; Ezek 34:23-24; 37:24-25; Hos 3:5; Mic 5:2 [1]; Zech 12:7-10.
[14]Mt 21:11, 46; Mk 6:15; Lk 7:16, 39; 13:33; 24:19; Jn 4:19; 6:14; 7:40, 52; 9:17.

further connection that actually prompts him to propose Jesus' kingship, which Peter identifies by using the term "anointed one": "You are the anointed one (Gk *ho christos;* Heb *hammāšîaḥ*), the son of the living God" (Mt 16:16).

Since the New Testament affirms Davidic ancestry and kingship in connection with Jesus, and since the Greek designation *christos* specifies "one who is anointed," is there a place where his anointing takes place? At what point does this specific description begin to fitly apply to Jesus as one who has been observably anointed for kingship? When Israel's first two kings were anointed by a prophet, it is specified that God's spirit came as a confirmation of the divine choice, in a manner similar to God's spirit coming upon a judge when he acted on God's behalf.[15] In the case of King Saul, "the Spirit of God came upon him mightily" (1 Sam 10:10; cf. 1 Sam 10:6; 11:6), just as with his successor, "the Spirit of Yahweh came mightily upon David (1 Sam 16:13). Each of these divine manifestations occurred after the prophet Samuel anointed the new king with oil, although in Saul's case a considerable amount of time elapsed between the anointing and the coming of the Spirit (1 Sam 10:1-10).

In that light, there is a necessary connection with the emphatic agreement of all canonical Gospels that the Spirit of God came upon Jesus following his baptism by the popularly acclaimed prophet[16] John (Mt 3:16; Mk 1:10; Lk 3:22; Jn 1:32-33). Each of the four Gospels connects this gift of God's spirit with the Davidic enthronement libretto found in Psalm 2 where God speaks of the newly anointed king, "You are my son" (Ps 2:7). This pronouncement is quoted as a divine voice from heaven in Matthew 3:17, Mark 1:11 and Luke 3:22, while John 1:34 records John simply affirming that as a result of what he saw, he was convinced that Jesus was God's son, i.e., the legitimately anointed king over Israel.[17]

---

[15]Othniel (Judg 3:10), Gideon (Judg 6:34), Jephthah (Judg 11:29), and Samson (Judg 13:25; 14:6, 19; 15:14).

[16]The prophetic status of John is a repeated focus of the gospels (Mt 11:9; 14:5; 21:26; Mk 11:32; Lk 1:76; 7:26; 20:6).

[17]"Son of God" reinforces the royal context here, for the specification of the king in Jerusalem as the "son of God" was a distinct aspect of Judaean royal ideology, underlining the unique relationship between the king and God (Ps 2:7; 89:26-27; 2 Sam 7:14; cf. John J. Collins, "Response: The Apocalyptic Worldview of Daniel," in *Enoch and Qumran Origins: New Light on a Forgotten Connection,* ed. Gabriele Boccaccini [Grand Rapids: Eerdmans, 2005], pp. 62-63).

When one juxtaposes in the canonical gospels the divinely sanctioned Davidic enthronement pronouncement (i.e, Ps 2:7) with both the gift of God's spirit[18] and Jesus' submission to the prophetic role of John the Baptizer, it is Jesus' baptism that marks the moment of Jesus' anointing even though no mention of an oil-rite is present. One of the emphatic agreements among all four Gospels is that John the Baptizer marks an essential introduction to Jesus' career, for John is uniformly presented as one who comes as a forerunner to Jesus.[19] The Gospel of Matthew even goes a step further in explicitly identifying John as the expected Elijah in relation to Jesus: "If you care to accept it, he himself is Elijah who was to come" (Mt 11:14).[20] The baptism by the prophet John is intended to serve as the counterpart to the prophetic anointing of kings with oil in the Old Testament.

Luke points to a similar perspective using another passage from the Old Testament. After reading the following passage from Isaiah 61:1-2 in the synagogue, Luke indicates that Jesus made a stunning concluding observation:

> "The Spirit of the Lord is upon me, because he anointed (Gk *echrisen;* Heb *māšaḥ*) me to proclaim good news to the poor. He has sent me to announce release to captives and renewed vision to the blind, to set free those who are downtrodden, to announce the favorable year of the Lord." . . . Today this scripture has been fulfilled in your hearing. (Lk 4:18-19, 21).

This synagogue reading from the prophet Isaiah preserves a claim by God's servant that God has anointed him, without further specification as to whether this is an anointing associated with royalty, the priesthood, prophethood or any other focused task. When Jesus reads this in public

---

[18]Just as anointing with oil could be done with kings, prophets, priests, brides and others (Dennis Pardee, "A New Ugaritic Letter," *Bibliotheca Orientalis* 34 [1977]: 3-20), so God's spirit could be gifted to prophets, kings and other leaders (e.g., the Israelite judges as noted above). In trying to get behind the early church's tradition about John and Jesus, for example, Joan Taylor, *The Immerser: John the Baptist within Second Temple Judaism* (Grand Rapids: Eerdmans, 1997), p. 273, argued that the spirit that came upon Jesus at the baptism by John was the spirit of prophecy identifying Jesus as a prophet. But in the Gospels as they now stand, the royal pronouncement affirming divine sonship removes any ambiguity as to which type of anointing has just taken place in the case of Jesus' baptism.

[19]Mt 3:11; Mk 1:7; Lk 3:16; Jn 3:28. This claim is made most particularly in fulfillment of Is 40:3 (Mt 3:3; Mk 1:2-3; Lk 3:4; Jn 1:23).

[20]"I say to you that Elijah already came, and they did not recognize him. . . . The disciples understood that he had spoken to them about the Baptizer" (Mt 17:12-13).

and applies it to himself, however, following as it does upon Jesus' baptism by John in the preceding chapter in Luke, there is no other event that can be construed as the "anointing" of Jesus. Indeed, this passage from Isaiah that Jesus quotes underscores that the anointing is done by God with the result that God's spirit is upon him, precisely the drama that unfolded at the baptism. It therefore becomes clear why John the Baptizer is such an essential figure in the New Testament, for he is the prophetic figure who makes it possible for Jesus to earn the appellative "Christ" / "anointed one" with reference to his kingship. This baptism by John must be the occasion to which Peter refers when he affirms of Jesus in Acts 10:38 that "God anointed him with the Holy Spirit and with power" (cf. Acts 4:26-27).

This survey of the prophet's connection with kingship throughout both the first temple period and the second temple period demonstrates that the prophet is a necessary adjunct of Israelite kingship.[21] One of the key contributions of prophecy was the institution and maintenance of kingship. When kingship disappeared from ancient Israel, prophecy could not remain unaffected.[22] The severing of kingship from the institution of prophecy in the sixth century occurred at the same time that prophecy itself was undergoing its most far-reaching transformations, as we have discussed in preceding chapters. The awareness of the intimate linkage of kingship and prophecy continued long after Israelite and Judaean kings ceased to rule. Without a prophet to identify and support a dynast, any claimant to the throne would be deprived of legitimacy.[23] Conversely, with

---

[21]"The involvement of prophets in proclaiming kings . . . is even better documented in extrabiblical sources" (Marti Nissinen, "The Dubious Image of Prophecy," in *Prophets, Prophecy, and Prophetic Texts in Second Temple Judaism*, ed. Michael H. Floyd and Robert D. Haak, LBH/OTS 427 [New York: T & T Clark, 2006], p. 31). A claim for Israelite prophetic involvement in other monarchies is made when Elijah is supposed to anoint the non-Israelite, Hazael, to be the next king of Aram (Syria). However, 2 Kings 8:7-15 makes it clear that Elijah did not do so, for Elisha is the one who reveals to Hazael that he will be the next king, a position that he seizes as a usurper by assassinating the preceding king Ben-Hadad.

[22]Cf. James Crenshaw, *Prophetic Conflict: Its Effect upon Israelite Religion*, BZAW 124 (Berlin: de Gruyter, 1977), pp. 68-69: "The existence of the monarchy was also a prerequisite of prophecy, and the prophetic movement fell into disrepute soon after the collapse of the kingship, the one great exception being Deutero-Isaiah." Other aspects of the relationship between kingship and prophecy could be elaborated, such as the sustained prophetic service rendered to the king in the temple cult and liturgy (John W. Hilber, *Cultic Prophecy in the Psalms*, BZAW 352 [Berlin: de Gruyter, 2005], p. 127).

[23]Although Saul is often identified as the first king in Israel, an earlier claimant is attested in the book of Judges when Abimelech is given a three-year reign over the city-state of Shechem.

a prophet's support, a new king was assured of divine support, and popular support could be expected to follow. So important was this aspect of prophetic activity that it was underscored in the New Testament as one of the legitimizing features of Jesus' claim to kingship, for he, too, was designated as a legitimate royal son of David by prophetic acclaim, in this case by the prophet John the Baptizer. The "anointed one" (Heb *māšiaḥ;* Gk *christos*) by definition must be preceded by a prophet, one of whose tasks is to designate the next king and confer divine approval upon him.

---

This son of Gideon installs himself as king in Judg 9 with the support of the leading citizens of Shechem, but it results in an abortive kingship that is portrayed as initiated by humans and not God, and where no prophet endorses the choice.

# 13

# The Chariots of Men
# and of God

In the preceding chapter, we discussed the intimate connection between king and prophet. Because one of the prophet's tasks was to identify, support and guide the legitimate king, the loss of kingship in ancient Israel meant a consequent diminution of the prophetic role in political life. This diminution occurred at the same time that other important changes were taking place in prophecy, and together these transformations brought a cumulative qualitative change in the prophetic office.

There is yet another distinct dimension of kingship that was intimately tied to prophecy, a dimension also affected by the sixth century catastrophe when Babylonian armies destroyed Judah and Jerusalem. This additional connection between prophecy and kingship is related to the initial explicit request that inaugurated kingship in Israel, when Israelites claimed to need an exemplary human to lead them into battle and defend them militarily against their enemies. The Israelites are pictured dialoguing with the prophet Samuel with the following words: "There will be a king over us and we also will be like all the nations, and our king will judge us and go out before us and fight our battles" (1 Sam 8:19-20). The rationale here for kingship is war. The Israelite king above all else is to be a warrior, at least as far as the people of Israel are concerned. It is this ability in leading Israel into battle that provides one of the prominent criteria for Saul's and David's evaluation as unsuccessful or successful in the performance of their obligations as kings.[1]

How does the prophet relate to the king in his role as a warrior and a leader of warriors who defend Israel? At the heart of the issue is the technology that the king uses to perform his role as the leader of Israel's armies. Not all technologies were universally recognized as legitimate for defense. One in particular that was seen as suspect was the relatively new technology of the horse-drawn battle chariot, which made its debut in the ancient Near East in the middle of the second millennium B.C. The chariot rapidly became one of the distinguishing features of the Egyptian New Kingdom, and it was one of the more dramatic pieces of visual propaganda that Pharaoh exploited to project his power and invincibility. New Kingdom Pharaohs would even have their chariots placed in their tombs, and the literati wrote hymns of praise to Pharaoh's chariot.[2] But not everyone in Israel succumbed to the media blitz. One of the most notable features of Israelite theology, a feature that remains unattested elsewhere in the ancient Near East,[3] is the complete rejection of the chariot as a legitimate means of waging war.[4]

The first references to chariots and horses that Israelites encounter in the Bible (Ex 14:6-28[5]) are, not surprisingly in light of the preceding para-

---

[1]Sam Meier, "The King as Warrior in Samuel-Kings," *Hebrew Annual Review* 13 (1991): 63-76. All critiques of Saul in the Bible indicate that he forfeited kingship in abdicating his role as a warrior and defender of Israel (Cross, *Canaanite Myth*, p. 221).

[2]Adolf Erman, *The Ancient Egyptians* (New York: Harper & Row, 1966) pp. 280-81. The king in his chariot (at war or hunting) was a frequent motif in Neo-Assyrian art contemporary with the kingdoms of Judah and Israel.

[3]Other kingdoms do mock enemies whose chariots and horses prove to be ineffective, but there is never any hint of a preference for reducing or eliminating one's own chariots. Those kings who are criticized for their use of weaponry are enemy kings who are accused of displaying an inordinate confidence in its power to bring victory (see Sam Meier, "The Sword from Saul to David," in *Saul in Story and Tradition,* ed. Carl S. Ehrlich, FAT 47 [Tübingen: Mohr Siebeck, 2006], p. 170).

[4]For the social dynamics of chariots and horses, see Walter Brueggemann, "Revelation and Violence: A Study in Contextualization," in *A Social Reading of the Old Testament: Prophetic Approaches to Israel's Communal Life,* ed. Patrick D. Miller (Minneapolis: Fortress, 1994).

[5]The chariots that appear in Gen 41:43; 46:29 are set in contexts before Israel becomes a group larger than an extended family. It is appropriate, however, that they appear with reference again to an Egyptian context where Joseph is described as having his own chariot when he is elevated to a high administrative rank, and in Gen 50:9 for Jacob's burial entourage.

graph, in the context of Egyptian warfare. When Pharaoh pursues the fleeing Israelites, God overwhelms the Egyptian chariotry and the pattern is established: chariots and horses are inadequate for protection or for giving an advantage for victory. As the Israelite victory paean affirms:

> Yahweh is a warrior, Yahweh is his name. Pharaoh's chariots and army he cast into the sea, and the elite of his officers were drowned in the Reed Sea. (Ex 15:3-4; cf. Ex 15:19; Deut 11:4)

Although Israel had no chariots at all, Egypt's six hundred chariots (Ex 14:7) were completely wiped out by God's intervention. This seminal account becomes paradigmatic for a perspective that percolates throughout the Bible: chariots and horses—the most sophisticated military technology available—actually become a liability:

> The horse is deceptive for achieving victory, and with all his strength he still may not bring deliverance. (Ps 33:17)

> He [God] breaks the bow and shatters the spear; chariots he burns in the fire. (Ps 46:9 [10])

> At your rebuke, O God of Jacob, chariot and horse are laid to rest. (Ps 76:6 [76:7])

> There are those who take pride in chariots, and those who take pride in horses, but we take pride in the name of Yahweh our God. (Ps 20:7 [8])

> He [God] does not delight in a horse's strength, he takes no pleasure in a man's legs. (Ps 147:10)

> A horse is prepared for the day of battle, but victory goes to Yahweh. (Prov 21:31)

The dramatic posture taken in such passages is breathtaking if one transports oneself back to an earlier time when the "horse-power" that propelled chariots was literal. As the poet of the book of Job describes the horse:

> Are you the one who supplies a horse's strength? Do you clothe his neck with a mane? Do you make him leap like a locust? The splendor of his snorting is frightening. He paws in the valley and rejoices, with strength he

goes out to confront weapons. He mocks fear and is not dismayed, nor does he turn back before a sword. Upon him the quiver rattles, the spear and javelin flash. . . . Whenever the trumpet sounds he says, "Aha!" and smells the battle from afar, the thunder of the commanders, and the war-cry. (Job 39:19-25)

The Bible portrays Pharaoh as one who bought into this picture and unwisely trusted in his chariots and horses, prompting him to take a course of action he would not otherwise have pursued, indeed reversing his earlier decision to let Israel leave Egypt. His unfortunate example echoes in later accounts of Israel's enemies whose chariot forces are also overwhelmed by God, such as Sisera's 900 chariots:

Yahweh routed Sisera and all his chariots and all his camp with the edge of the sword before Barak. Sisera descended from his chariot and fled on foot, but Barak pursued the chariots. (Judg 4:15-16; cf. Judg 4:3, 13)

Such accounts are instructive for Israel, for the lesson is clear: should chariots become a preferred weapon, it will lead to a misplaced confidence and defeat.

Joshua is therefore brush-stroked as a sage warrior when he overcomes enemy forces in the conquest of Canaan and burns their chariots. Rather than incorporate the captured technology into his own fighting machine, he relinquishes it in order to maintain his primary trust in Yahweh. It is so important a feature of military strategy that God himself commands the destruction of captured chariot forces:

They [i.e., a Canaanite coalition] came out, with all their forces . . . and very many horses and chariots. . . . Yahweh said to Joshua, "Do not fear them, for tomorrow at this time I will deliver all of them slain before Israel. Their horses you will hamstring, and their chariots you will burn with fire." . . . And Yahweh delivered them into the hand of Israel. . . . And Joshua did to them as Yahweh had said to him: their horses he hamstrung, and their chariots he burned with fire. (Josh 11:4, 6, 8, 9)

David, too, is portrayed as almost another Joshua in this regard when he defeats an Aramean king:

David captured from him one thousand chariots, seven thousand horsemen, and twenty thousand foot soldiers. David hamstrung all the chariot horses but retained some of them for a hundred chariots. (1 Chron 18:4; cf. 2 Sam 8:4)

This partial compromise under David was anticipated by the prophet Samuel when he acceded to Israel's request for a king but only after warning them,

> This will be the manner of the king who will rule over you: he will take and appoint your sons in his chariots and as his horsemen for his benefit, and they will run before his chariots . . . and make his instruments of war and equipment for his chariots. (1 Sam 8:11-12)

David's partial compromise becomes a complete capitulation among his offspring. David's sons, Absalom and Adonijah, will unlike their father actively pursue these military adjuncts, for each "provided for himself a chariot and horses" (2 Sam 15:1; cf. 1 Kings 1:5). Solomon pushes the boundaries even further and enters into the chariot business. He not only collects his own chariots and constructs special housing for them, but he also becomes an arms-dealer, successfully making a profit in the import-export business:

> Solomon collected chariots and horses: he had 1,400 chariots and 12,000 horses, and he placed them in the chariot cities and with the king in Jerusalem. . . . The export of horses for Solomon was from Egypt and Kue, the king's merchants receiving them at a fixed price from Kue. A chariot came up and was exported from Egypt for 600 shekels of silver, and a horse for 150, and thus they were exported by them to all the Hittite and Aramaean kings. (1 Kings 10:26, 28-29; cf. 9:19)

> Solomon had 4,000 stalls for horses and chariots, and 12,000 horsemen. (2 Chron 9:25; 1 Kings 4:26 reads 40,000 stalls)

Although this description may seem to present a neutral posture with no explicit words of commendation or condemnation, one cannot help but read it now in the light of the book of Deuteronomy that preserves only one short section devoted to regulating a monarch's behavior. Here the issue of a king's chariot force resurfaces with an emphatic rejection that seems tailored to criticize Solomon himself:

Only he [i.e., the king] will not acquire large numbers of horses, nor will he permit the people to return to Egypt in order to acquire large numbers of horses. (Deut 17:16)

As far as we can determine, the standard military posture for the kingdoms of Israel and Judah was a fully operational and extensive chariot force. Solomon's successor, Rehoboam, uses a chariot as his means of transportation (1 Kings 12:18), as do the later Davidides, King Ahaziah (2 Kings 9:27-28) and King Josiah (2 Kings 23:30; cf. 2 Chron 35:24). The Assyrian foe berates King Hezekiah for depending on horses and chariots from Egypt (2 Kings 18:24). Baasha's dynasty in Israel had such an extensive chariot force that it was divided into battalions (1 Kings 16:9), and the dynasty of Jehu—himself a former chariot commander (2 Kings 9:16)—sees its large chariot force reduced by an enemy (2 Kings 13:7; cf. 2 Kings 10:15-16). A substantial chariotry is a deciding factor in King Joram of Judah's campaign against Edom, although it is an ultimately unsuccessful venture (2 Kings 8:21-22). In addition to the biblical evidence for the use of chariots under the Omri dynasty,[6] the Assyrian king Shalmaneser III records that he fought a coalition of a dozen western kings among whom Ahab fielded more chariots (2,000) than any other king in the coalition (COS 2.263), and Assyrian records preserve evidence of equestrian officers from Samaria and a suggestion of the high regard in which the chariotry of Samaria was held.[7]

Therefore the biblical material presents a significant difference of opinion on the means by which a king should be prepared to confront an armed foe. On the one hand is a belligerent resistance to the development of a professional chariot force, on the other hand is the clear testimony that the maintenance of chariotry was standard operating procedure for both the northern and southern kingdoms. The most high profile exemplar for the latter position is Mr. Chariot, Solomon himself, the king whom the Bible depicts as setting the precedent and primarily responsible for the very existence of the two kingdoms. Where do the prophets align themselves on this debate that, on the basis of the above data, must have significantly divided ancient Israelites in at least some sectors of Israelite society?

---

[6] 1 Kings 20:33; 22:34-38; 2 Kings 7:14; 9:16, 21-24; 10:2.
[7] Stephanie Dalley, "Foreign Chariotry and Cavalry in the Armies of Tiglath-Pileser III and Sargon II," *Iraq* 47 (1985): 31-48.

## CHARIOTS AND HORSES AND THE PROPHETS

In the literary prophets, the message is unanimous, widespread and un-equivocal. For the literary prophets, it is a certain sign of infidelity to God to militarize with chariots and horses. It was God who had promised to protect Israel and Judah, and they did not need an additional insurance policy. From the perspective of the preexilic literary prophets, God's promise should suffice without recourse to lavish expenditures on armaments that in the final analysis are not determinative in deciding the outcome of a battle. The literary prophets repeatedly berate their fellow countrymen for capitulating to the business-as-usual mentality of royal ideology that opts for the latest technology for defense. Indeed, the literary prophets provide additional evidence to supplement the evidence noted above that Judaean and Israelite kings made chariots a high priority. It appears among the indictments Isaiah levels against the kingdom of Judah:

> His [i.e., Jacob's] land is filled with silver and gold,
>     And there is no end to his treasures.
> His land is filled with horses,
>     And there is no end to his chariots.
> His land is filled with idols. (Is 2:7-8)

The juxtaposition here of idolatry with sophisticated armaments hints at the intensity of opposition directed at the latter. This hyperbole of border-to-border horses and chariots is reinforced elsewhere in Isaiah when the second most powerful man in the kingdom is condemned for the misuse of office, his doom including God's violently exiling him abroad where "there you will die, along with your glorious chariots, you shame of your master's house" (Is 22:18). In the same chapter, Hezekiah's arms build-up in Jerusalem is condemned in retrospect because it represented a misplaced confidence:

> You looked in that day to the weapons of the Forest House, . . . and you tore down the houses to fortify the wall, and you made a reservoir between the two walls for the waters of the old pool, but you did not look to the one who made it. (Is 22:8, 10-11)

Although chariots and horses are not the specific issue in this passage, the rationale for an intense investment in armaments is that it takes one's eyes off God as the source of Judah's defense. However, this perspective is applied elsewhere explicitly to chariots and horses that Hezekiah hoped to receive from Egypt:

> Woe to those who go down to Egypt for help! They rely on horses! They trusted in chariots because they are numerous, and in horsemen because they are very strong. But they did not look to the Israel's Holy One, they did not seek Yahweh. (Is 31:1)

Isaiah is a contemporary of Hezekiah about whom much biblical and extrabiblical material is available. Specifically for our purposes, biblical records of his extensive preparations for rebellion against Assyria are supplemented with inscriptional and archaeological data.[8] Hezekiah's reliance on a treaty of mutual military assistance with Egypt is attested elsewhere not only when Egypt makes a brief and ineffective appearance on the battlefield (2 Kings 19:8-9) but also when his foes mock him: "You trusted in Egypt for chariots and horsemen!" (2 Kings 18:24). The words recorded in the book of Isaiah, however, leave no room for doubt: Hezekiah's trust in Egyptian chariotry was a mistake. As Isaiah continues, "Egypt is human and not divine, and their horses are flesh and not spirit" (Is 31:3).

Isaiah's contemporary, Micah, has similar problems with Judah's long-standing commitment to sophisticated military technology, and he looks forward to a day when divine intervention will result in a chariot-free zone in Judah: "And it will be in that day, says Yahweh, that I will cut off your horses from your midst, and I will destroy your chariots" (Mic 5:10 [9]). Perhaps Micah's opening chapter of poetic mockery of assorted cities in Judah assumes a similar problem, although the laconic allusions are difficult to pin down. Lachish, however, was one of the most prominent fortified cities in Judah after Jerusalem, and Micah mockingly singles out one feature of this defense:[9]

---

[8]2 Kings 20:20 records Hezekiah's diversion of the water supply to the city from outside. 2 Chron 32:2-5, 27-31 records the construction of cities and storehouses along with the redirection of the Gihon spring to the city and the strengthening of Jerusalem's defenses. For discussion of Hezekiah's water tunnel, the massive city wall on the west of Jerusalem, archaeological activity in Judah, and the ceramic evidence of the *lmlk* jar handles, see conveniently Gösta Ahlström, *History of Ancient Palestine* (Minneapolis: Fortress, 1993), pp. 697-701.

[9]It is not clear to what the feminine singular "it" refers (the city Lachish? the action just described?

Harness the chariot to the swift steed *(rekeš),* you who live in Lachish *(lākîš).* It is the beginning of sin for the daughter of Zion, for in you were found Israel's transgressions. (Mic 1:13)

Also from the same century, Amos speaks of Israel's certain doom, coupling with it the hopelessness of depending upon any kind of military superiority:

Flight will elude the swift,
And the strong will be unable to get a second wind.
The warrior will be unable to save himself,
And the one who grasps the bow will not stand his ground.
The swift-footed will not escape,
And the one who rides a horse will not save himself.
The most stout-hearted warrior will flee naked in that day, says Yahweh.
(Amos 2:14-16)

It is not simply that Israelites and Judaeans are warned against, or castigated for, thinking that military might gives them security independent of God. The chariots and horses of Israel's enemies are also taken down a notch by the prophets in order to assuage Israel's fear that this technology brings any advantage to its sponsors. In his oracles against Babylon, Jeremiah notes how God uses Babylon as a tool, specifically when "I shatter horse and rider by means of you, I shatter chariot and rider by means of you" (Jer 51:21-22). But *mirabile dictu,* Jeremiah notes how Babylon's own horses and chariots are subject to the same decimation at God's hands: "a sword against his [i.e., Babylon's] horses and against his chariots" (Jer 50:37). The first millennium B.C. war-machine that was Assyria, whose might was predicated upon solicitous care for their horses and chariots, is also a target for Nahum: "Behold, I am against you, says Yahweh of hosts, and I will burn up her chariots in smoke" (Nah 2:13 [2:14]). According to Ezekiel, God anticipates scavenging birds and animals who will clean up the battlefield on which Gog lies defeated, saying to the scavengers, "You will be satiated at my table with horse and charioteer, with warrior and every man of war, says the Lord Yahweh" (Ezek 39:20).

---

the chariot [feminine]?). See Francis I. Andersen and David Noel Freedman, *Micah* (New York: Doubleday, 2000), pp. 200-249, for the context and options.

This portrait of chariots and horses remains a stable feature of prophecy that does not change from the preexilic to the postexilic period. When the small Persian province of Judah is in its infancy and at its most vulnerable, there is no option for the Jews to even consider self-defense. Without a king and with no standing army whatsoever, they are completely dependent upon divine intervention. The postexilic prophet Haggai finds this a comfortable position for the Jews, and picks up the old theme of his predecessors when he records God's encouraging words to the Jewish governor of this vulnerable polity: "I will overthrow the thrones of kingdoms and destroy the strength of the kingdoms of the nations, and I will overthrow chariots and their riders. Horses will go down along with their riders, each felled by his companion's sword" (Hag 2:22).[10]

When one moves from the literary prophets to stories about prophets in the books of Kings, a similar perspective emerges but with a new component. The peculiar relationship of the prophet to the king takes on a new dimension beyond the prophet as king-maker and king-breaker. According to some of these prophetic stories, there is an excellent reason why chariots and horses should be absent from Israel's arsenal: the prophet functions as Israel's chariots and horsemen all merged into one person. As the prophet Elisha lies dying, for example, the king of Israel makes one last sorrowful visit, crying out, "My father, my father, the chariots of Israel and its horsemen!" (2 Kings 13:14). In identifying the prophet as his "father," King Joash—actually the biological son of the preceding king, Jehoahaz (2 Kings 13:10)—is simply affirming that the prophet is his mentor and counselor, just as Joseph was identified as a "father" to Pharaoh (Gen 45:8). But the king in this outburst of sorrow proceeds to further identify the source of his sadness, which results not only from the loss of a valued counselor but from the loss of the true defenses of his kingdom, "the chariots of Israel and its horsemen." With Elisha dead, Israel's true chariots and horses will no longer be protecting the land. The prophet is the real defense of Israel against military aggression.

---

[10]In Zech 9:10 God speaks of his intentions in an oracle that is difficult to date: "I will cut off chariot from Ephraim and horse from Jerusalem; battle-bow will be cut off, and he [i.e., the future king] will speak peace to the nations." The ambiguity is unresolved: are the weapons ones that Judeans are using or are they weapons being used against them? In either case, the point remains that military technology is not the determining factor for the conflict.

This same cry of grief was heard when Elijah ascended in the chariot of fire. The last words that his replacement, Elisha, spoke as he saw Elijah vanish were, "My father, my father, the chariots of Israel and its horsemen!" (2 Kings 2:12). Elisha, too, sees his mentor leave and affirms as did King Joash that Israel's real source of power is no longer on earth. In this case, however, Elisha's exclamation accompanies an actual appearance of a divine chariot drawn by supernatural horses, "a chariot of fire and horses of fire" (2 Kings 2:11). There is a hint in this account that the description of the prophet is more than mere metaphor, for the prophet is here actually in the presence of chariotry that surpasses anything that could be produced in the forges of the ancient world, and this chariot is present to render him service.

This hint becomes explicit in the story of Elisha's pursuit by a Syrian army. The king of Syria was frustrated that the Israelites always managed to circumvent his battlefield strategies:

> Now the king of Syria was waging war against Israel, and he took counsel with his servants, saying, "My camp will be in such and such a place." The man of God [later identified as Elisha] sent to the king of Israel, saying, "Take heed lest you pass this place, for the Syrians are going down there." And the king of Israel sent to the place about which the man of God told him and warned him, and he was protected there, not just once or twice. The Syrian king's heart was in turmoil over this matter, and he summoned his servants and said to them, "Will you not tell me who among us is for the king of Israel?" One of his servants said, "No, my lord the king, but Elisha, the prophet that is in Israel, tells Israel's king the words you speak in your bedroom." He said, "Go and see where he is, so that I may send and take him." It was told him, saying, "Behold, he is in Dothan," so he sent there horses, chariots and a great army, and they came by night and surrounded the city. (2 Kings 6:8-14)

This story provides a fine demonstration of the way that the prophet was Israel's "chariots and horses," for his inside information made it possible for Israel's armies to avoid any confrontations with the enemy. By heeding the prophet's advice, the king could dispense with chariotry since in this case he was always in a position to avoid a battle. Because the prophet stood on the divine council (as discussed earlier), he was privy to the deliberations that took place there about the affairs of human kingdoms, even the deliberations of a king in his bedroom.

But there is more to the prophet as Israel's chariots and horses in this story. Elisha has at this point in the plot become the lightning rod instead of the king of Israel, and the focus of attack now shifts to target the prophet. The Syrian strategy is precise: take out the prophet—Israel's best defense—and Israel will be vulnerable. Consequently, one morning the prophet wakes up to find his city surrounded by Syrian forces waiting for him, with the author placing a repeated stress upon their armaments:

> He [i.e., the king of Syria] sent there horses, chariots, and a great army. . . .
> An army encircled the city with chariots and horses. (2 Kings 6:14-15)

At this point, the prophet can no longer use the avoidance strategy he counseled Israel's king to follow. When Elisha's servant panics ("Alas, my master! What shall we do?" 2 Kings 6:15), Elisha nevertheless remains unruffled. One can almost hear him yawn at what is presented as business as usual in his response:

> He said, "Don't be afraid, for those who are with us are more than those who are with them." Elisha prayed and said, "Yahweh, please open his eyes that he may see." Yahweh opened the young man's eyes, and he saw, and behold, the mountain was full of horses and chariots of fire surrounding Elisha. (2 Kings 6:16-17)

Wherever the prophet is, this account makes explicit that that place is where the chariots and horses of God's army can be found as well. Since Elisha is a seer, one who sees what escapes normal human vision, Elisha can see something that can only come as a special revelation to his less gifted servant. What was briefly glimpsed in Elijah's ascent to heaven is now seen to be unexceptional: horses and chariots of fire accompany the prophet, and one may even speculate that they are presumably at his command.

As the story moves toward its finale, the servant's eyes are not the only eyes affected. Elisha successfully petitions God to in turn blind the entire Syrian army, a feat that enables Elisha to lead the foreign foe to the very heart of Israel where they are placed in the hands of Israel's king (2 Kings 6:18-22). Elisha is a formidable asset who does not even need to exert himself as he directs an enemy chariot force wherever he wishes. Furthermore, if the prophet were a chariot force *in nuce* that behaved like any other standing army, one could at best hope for victory with carnage, but Elisha demonstrates in the conclusion of the story that God's economy is quite different. When the king of Israel asks the prophet if he can massacre the captive Syrians, Elisha responds that the enemy should be fed and released. The king behaves as an obedient son, commensurate with the title by which he just addressed the prophet ("my father," 2 Kings 6:21). Because he provides the foe with a feast, as this wise counselor advised, a remarkable conclusion wraps up the story:

> He [i.e., the king of Israel] prepared for them a lavish feast,[11] and they ate and drank. He then sent them off, and they went to their lord. Aramean troops no more came into the land of Israel. (2 Kings 6:23)

This story is replete with counterintuitive behavior that is characteristic of the prophets. Provide ample food and water for an enemy, and then let them go? One man can subdue an army? But it is precisely this prophetic guidance that results in a lasting peace for Israel, a peace that could not have been achieved by conventional means.[12]

The books of Kings contain numerous stories where the prophets demonstrate repeatedly their role as the "chariots and horses" of Israel. It is to the prophets that a king turns when he considers a military expedition: does the prophet endorse or discourage the enterprise? "The king of Israel gathered the prophets, about four hundred men, and said to them, "Should I go into battle against Ramoth-Gilead, or shall I refrain?" (1 Kings 22:6). On another occasion, Rehoboam mustered an army to conquer the northern secessionists, but he terminated the enterprise when a prophet gave the divine ultimatum: "Do not go up and do not fight with your brothers, the Israelites. Return, each one to his home" (1 Kings 12:24).[13] On the other hand, when prophetic approval comes for an anticipated battle, the prophet

---

[11]The terms used in this phrase appear no elsewhere in the Bible, but a possible Akkadian cognate *qerītu* "banquet, festival" lends credence to the NJPS translation "lavish feast."

[12]This conclusion is quite different from the outcome that a prophet desires in the Aramean war of 1 Kings 20:30-43.

[13]On this occasion, a prophet takes the initiative to approach the king about military ventures, an initiative that reappears elsewhere (e.g., 1 Kings 20:22, 28).

may even provide a few specific details of strategy (1 Kings 20:13-14):

Prophet:     Thus said Yahweh, "Do you see this great multitude?
                Behold, I am about to give it today into your hand, and you
                will know that I am Yahweh."

King Ahab:  By whom?

Prophet:     Thus said Yahweh, "By the young men of the provincial
                commanders."

King Ahab:  Who will begin the battle?

Prophet:     You.

When the king follows prophetic guidance, it is appropriate for the story to close with the comment, as in this case, that the Israelites "struck the horses and the chariots" of the enemy (1 Kings 20:21).

## GOD'S CHARIOT AND HORSES

The connection of the prophet to the king, therefore, goes far beyond the initial act of anointing. The king, whose role is to defend Israel from its enemies, depends throughout his reign upon the prophet for that very defense that cannot be found in military technology. A final connection binds the prophet to the king, perhaps the most important connection of all, one that encourages an outspoken attention to chariots and horses in the literary prophets and the prophetic stories of the Deuteronomistic history. One of the most pervasive themes of the Bible is that God himself is a warrior who personally goes into combat against the forces that are opposed to his rule.[14] Among the first texts discussed above was the poem that celebrated the successful passage of the Reed Sea, a poem attributed to that paragon of prophets (Moses), with an antiphonal response led by a prophetess (Miriam):

Yahweh is a warrior, Yahweh is his name. Pharaoh's chariots and army he

---

[14]The subject has received a considerable amount of attention. Among significant and helpful treatments one may consult Sa-Moon Kang, *Divine War in the Old Testament and in the Ancient Near East*, BZAW 177 (Berlin: de Gruyter, 1989); Martin Klingbeil, *Yahweh Fighting from Heaven: God As Warrior and As God of Heaven in the Hebrew Psalter and Ancient Near Eastern Iconography*, OBO 169 (Göttingen: Vandenhock & Ruprecht, 1999); Tremper Longman III and Daniel G. Reid, *God Is a Warrior: Studies in Old Testament Biblical Theology* (Grand Rapids: Zondervan, 1995); and Patrick D. Miller Jr., *The Divine Warrior in Early Israel* (Cambridge, Mass.: Harvard University Press, 1973).

cast into the sea, and the elite of his officers were drowned in the Reed Sea. (Ex 15:3-4)

Because God is a warrior, the armies in Israel's employ are more than of passing interest to him. Because God is a warrior, the way that Israel defends itself is a focus of his attention. Because God is a warrior, there can be no wiser counsel than to follow the directives of the most successful warrior in the cosmos. And as we have seen above, the biblical material throughout affirms that prophets have direct access to God and the supernatural armies in his employ.

This is, after all, the significance of the title, "Yahweh of hosts," where the word "hosts" is a reference to the supernatural armies at his command. The Hebrew term *ṣābā'*, translated "host," means simply "army."[15] In the same way that *ṣĕbā' yiśrā'ēl* means "the army of Israel" (2 Chron 25:7), so *yhwh ṣĕbā'ôt* is a military designation signifying "Yahweh of armies."[16] Based upon the above discussion, it is appropriate for a prophet such as Micaiah to stand comfortably among these "armies of heaven" as he listens to them debate strategy about an upcoming military encounter (1 Kings 22:19-20). These heavenly armies are composed, according to a variety of texts, of the heavenly bodies (sun, moon or stars) or angels, and many texts equate the two.[17] When the prophetess Deborah recounts the

---

[15]Thus Israel's warriors mustered for battle are so identified by this word (Num 1:3), as is Gideon's army (Judg 8:6), Abimelech's army (Judg 9:29), David's army (2 Sam 10:7), and the like. The verb form of this root means "to wage war" (e.g., Is 29:7-8; Zech 14:12).

[16]The inertia of the entrenched English rendering "host," which did mean "army" to the original readers of the King James Bible, along with perhaps a reluctance to jettison the ambiguity of the phrase "Lord of hosts" for the stark reality of its militant intent, has resulted in few modern translations that bother to clarify this word for readers when it refers to God. Among rare exceptions are the NLT(se) and the NCV, the latter of which commendably renders "heavenly army" to describe the members of the divine council that Micaiah observes in debate (1 Kings 22:19), or "armies of heaven" (Ps 148:2), but unfortunately it typically renders "Lord of hosts" as Lord All-Powerful" (e.g., 2 Kings 3:14).

[17]The "host of heaven" are specifically identified as the sun, moon or stars (Deut 4:19; 17:3; 2 Kings 23:5; Jer 8:2), something that humans are quite capable of seeing (Is 40:26). The connection between astral bodies and angels is apparent in poetry (Job 38:7; Ps 148:2-3), and an angel with a drawn sword identifies himself to Joshua before the conquest of Canaan as "commander of the host of Yahweh" (Josh 5:13-15). Even the New Testament employs the Greek word for "army" *(stratia)* in a phrase referring to angels that is commonly rendered, "multitude of the heavenly host *(stratias)* praising God" (Lk 2:13). The connection of supernatural divine beings with stars is a very old one, attested already at the dawn of writing: the sign for god in cuneiform (Sumerian DINGIR) is a star.

victory over Sisera's army, she speaks of how "the stars fought from heaven, they fought Sisera from their courses" (Judg 5:20).

At God's command, therefore, are the supernatural chariots and horses of the divine armies. Zechariah records how God entrusts the patrolling of the earth to supernatural beings who ride in chariots and horses, and apparently use their power to calm a potentially boisterous planet:

> Four chariots were coming out from between the two mountains, and the mountains were mountains of brass. With the first chariot were red horses, with the second chariot black horses, with the third chariot white horses and in the fourth chariot strong dappled horses. . . . These are the four winds of heaven going out from standing before the Lord of all the earth, the one with the black horses going out to the north country, and the white ones went out after them, and the dappled went out to the south country. . . . Those who go out to the north country appeased my spirit in the north country. (Zech 6:1-3, 5-6, 8)

It is acceptable for God to have chariots, for it is the technology that reverberates as the most compelling military display of force. Since God is superlative in his power, it is appropriate to borrow the language of the military to point toward God's unbeatable strength as one who can muster far more powerful and far more numerous comparable resources. The prophets are using descriptive language that is not confined to the prophets, for hymns attest the same conviction that God is "the one who appoints clouds to be his chariots" (Ps 104:3). The psalmists already knew that all the chariots of the heavens are at his command, employing the highest possible numbers imaginable to describe them: "God's chariots are twenty thousand" (Ps 68:17 [18]).

The prophet, then, is supremely qualified to reveal God's military projects to humans. Since the prophet has participated in the military strategy sessions where the heavenly armies debate their objectives (the divine council), and since the prophet is recognized as the single best military resource available to Israel as "the chariots and horses of Israel" as discussed above, and since the prophet is speaking on behalf of a warrior God, it is not surprising that the prophet's words are heavily weighted with military subjects. Many contemporary readers with (post)modern sensitivities agonize with perplexity over the prophetic fixation on doom and destruction. But this militant perspective is the inextricable heart of the prophetic role. When kings and disciples epitomize the prophet as "the chariots and horses of Israel," they are capturing precisely the prophetic role as God's spokesman for the combat that takes place between the forces of good and evil. The prophet who is in touch with the divine plan, who sees a world in strife with God's eyes, and who has participated in the divine council where all problems must be resolved, is by definition going to have a message of conflict. One should as soon expect a prophet to be conciliatory as to expect doctors and cancer to learn to get along with each other.

It is with good cause that researchers have suggested that the prophetic oracles of doom against foreign nations represent core concerns of early prophets.[18] And in these oracles, and their later successors, God is characteristically dramatized as the warrior who comes in battle array to personally engage his enemies. In these dramatizations, a basic template undergirds the storyline: God arms himself for battle and descends from his holy mountain (variously identified as Mt. Paran, Mt. Sinai, Mt. Teman, Mt. Zion) to the battlefield where he encounters the foe oppressing his people. After God destroys his enemy, he returns with his rescued people to his sacred mountain where rejoicing, banqueting and restoration climax the narrative. Each prophet elaborates various aspects of this generalized scenario to suit his purpose. One of the most detailed and extended treatments in the literary prophets appears in the two successive chapters of Isaiah 34–35.[19]

We will select below, however, not from this passage but from a variety of isolated texts examples of how various prophets develop particular pieces of the whole. Habakkuk's book, for example, closes with an extended exemplary account that stresses God's departure and the battle

---

[18]Duane L. Christensen, *Transformations of the War Oracle in Old Testament Prophecy* (Missoula, Mont.: Scholars, 1975). One finds many of these war oracles against foreign nations clustered in discrete sections in the prophetic books, such as the clusters in Isaiah 13–24, Jeremiah 46–51, Ezekiel 25–32, Amos 1:3–2:3, Zeph 2:4-15 (Alexander Rofé, *Introduction to Prophetic Literature*, trans. Judith H. Seeligmann, The Biblical Seminar 21 [Sheffield: Sheffield Academic, 1997], pp. 41-43). Some of the literary prophets are in their entirety war oracles against a foreign kingdom (Nahum against Assyria, Obadiah against Edom).

[19]For the imagery in these chapters in particular and their connection with a variety of traditions in the Bible, see Cross, *Canaanite Myth*, pp. 170-74.

itself. The action begins with God's departure from his holy mountain, accompanied by a retinue of accompanying supernatural beings and cataclysms of nature:[20]

> God came from Teman,
> And the Holy One from Mount Paran. . . .
> Before him went Pestilence,
> And at his feet Plague went out. . . .
> The ancient mountains broke apart,
> The primeval hills sank down. (Hab 3:3, 5-6)

The enemy is soon identified in this case as the rebellious primordial waters (rivers, the sea, the deep)[21] that refuse to cooperate with God. God's weapons are itemized as chariots and horses, bows and arrows, and finally a spear, weapons against which the waters of the deep are unable to contend. On the basis of such imagery, it becomes evident that any chariots and horses that humans might manufacture would be but sorry competition for the chariots and horses that God himself uses against his opponents. God's chariots and horses trivialize any human counterpart:

> Was Yahweh enraged against the rivers?
> Was your anger against the rivers?
> Was your wrath against the sea?
> For you mounted your horses,
> Your chariots of victory.
> You uncovered your bow . . .

---

[20]These descriptions of cataclysms in nature accompanying God's presence are traditional both in and outside of Israel, and are found in both prophetic (e.g., Is 24:18-20; 64:1-12 [63:19–64:11]; Hag 2:6; Nah 1:5) and hymnic (e.g., Job 9:6; Ps 29:3-9; 77:16-19 [17-20]; 99:1) literature. The imagery is predicated upon, and is an integral part of, the description of the divine warrior (Samuel E. Loewenstamm, "The Trembling of Nature during the Theophany," in *Comparative Studies in Biblical and Ancient Oriental Literatures*, AOAT 204 [Neukirchen-Vluyn: Neukirchener Verlag, 1980], pp. 173-89).

[21]The single most powerful symbol of evil in the Hebrew Bible is the Sea (cf. John Day, *God's Conflict with the Dragon and the Sea: Echoes of Canaanite Myth in the Old Testament* [Cambridge: Cambridge University Press, 1985]). In addition to the morally charged description of the origins of the primeval Sea in Job 38:8-11, in Genesis 1 it is associated with darkness and God must split it to allow the dry land to appear so that life may germinate. The crossing of the Reed Sea (Ex 14–15) is a replay of God's creation activity where God again splits the waters that prevent his people from escaping death at Pharaoh's hands. The motif of the subduing of the Sea is exploited by the prophets (e.g., Is 27:1; 51:9-11; Nah 1:4) and the imagery is broadly attested (e.g., Dan 7:2-3). Note how the Sea is banished from the creation of the new heavens and earth (Rev 21:1).

You split the earth with rivers.
The mountains saw you and writhed,
A surge of water passed by,
The deep roared,
The sun lifted high his hands.
The moon stood on his dais.
Your arrows went glistening,
Your lightning spear flashing. (Hab 3:8-11[22])

Finally, the reason for the battle and God's unappeasable anger is specified: God must rescue his people and their king (the "anointed one") from the forces of evil that refuse to submit to God's dominion.

In indignation you marched though the earth,
You threshed the nations in anger.
You went forth for the salvation of your people,
For the salvation of your anointed one.
You smashed, . . . you laid bare . . .
You pierced his head with his own shafts. . . .
You made your way through the sea with your horses,
The surge of many waters. (Hab 3:12-15)

This scenario can be summarized in the prophets by the succinct phrase, "the Day of Yahweh,"[23] along with variations such as, "the Day of Yahweh's Wrath," (Zeph 2:2, 3) or "the Day of Vengeance for Yahweh" (Is 34:8). Other prophets elaborate on God's preparation of his armor and war apparel whenever God makes ready to do battle on such a day. This aspect of preparation is singled out for detailed treatment in Isaiah 59:15-20 where, curiously, all manner of defensive armor is inventoried without a single piece of offensive gear being noted. Nothing is mentioned with regard to departure from the sacred mountain, nor are there clues as to who the enemy might be, but the final victory march in the return to Zion closes the description:

---

[22]See also Theodore Hiebert, *The God of My Victory: The Ancient Hymn in Habakkuk 3*, Harvard Semitic Monographs 38 [Atlanta: Scholars, 1986].

[23]Is 13:6, 9; Joel 2:31 [3:4]; 3:14 [4:14]; Obad 15; Mal 4:5 [3:23]. See James D. Nogalski, "The Day(s) of YHWH in the Book of the Twelve," in *SBL Seminar Papers 1999* (Atlanta: Society of Biblical Literature, 1999), pp. 617-42, for the pervasiveness of the concept even apart from the specific phrase and its unifying effect in the Minor Prophets.

Yahweh saw, and it displeased him that there was no justice.
He saw that there was no one and was appalled that there was
    no intercessor.
His own arm achieved victory for him,
And it was his own righteousness that supported him.
He donned righteousness as a breastplate,
And the helmet of victory was on his head.
He donned garments of vengeance as his clothing,
And was covered with zeal as a mantle.
He will repay them according to their deeds,
Wrath to his enemies, recompense to his foes. . . .
A redeemer comes to Zion,
To those who turn from transgression in Jacob. (Is 59:15-20)

On other occasions, the aspect of the drama that a prophet may choose
to elaborate is the immediate aftermath of battle. God's return from
bloody combat is not a pretty picture, but it stunningly rivets the reader's
attention to the life and death dimensions of the issues that are at stake.
One prophet poses this return from battle as a dialogue that begins with
a question, the interrogator inquiring as a watchman on a battlement in
order to identify the initially unrecognizable figure who approaches covered with blood that masks his identity:

| | |
|---|---|
| Prophet: | Who is this coming from Edom, from Bozrah with dyed garments, this one splendid in his apparel, marching with extraordinary strength? |
| God: | I, the one speaking in righteousness, the one strong enough for victory. |
| Prophet: | Why are your clothes red, and your garments like one who treads in the winevat? |
| God: | I trod the winepress alone, and from the peoples there was no one with me. I trod them in my anger and trampled them in my rage. Their lifeblood is sprinkled on my clothes, and I have stained all my clothing. For the day of vengeance was in my heart, and the year of the one I was to redeem came. I looked and there was none to help, and I was appalled that there was none to give support. So my own arm achieved victory for me, and it was my own |

> wrath that supported me. I trod down the peoples in my
> anger, made them drunk with my wrath and drained their
> lifeblood to the earth. (Is 63:1-6)

Another prophet may choose to provide additional details about the celebratory banqueting and abundance that accompanies the establishment of peace and God's kingdom. After detailing the summoning of hostile armies to Jerusalem for a final conflict and the resulting upheavals that accompany God's onslaught, the prophet dwells upon the exuberant fertility that will characterize the new land under God's direct jurisdiction:

> Come quickly, all you surrounding nations, gather together. . . . The sun
> and the moon grow dark, and the stars constrict their brilliance. Yahweh
> roars from Zion and bellows from Jerusalem, and heaven and earth tremble, but Yahweh is a refuge for his people, a stronghold for Israelites. You
> will know that I, Yahweh, am your God, the one who dwells in Zion, my
> holy mountain. Jerusalem will be holy, and strangers will pass through her
> no more. It will be in that day that the mountains will drip sweet wine and
> the hills will flow with milk. All Judah's streams will flow with water, and
> a spring will gush forth from Yahweh's temple and will water the valley of
> Shittim. (Joel 3:11, 15-18 [4:11, 15-18])

The whole panorama that unfolds throughout the literary prophets finds a prophet developing a piece here and another prophet contributing a piece there.[24] The important point for our purposes at present is that the entire package is predicated upon God's personal involvement as a warrior who will in the last analysis not delegate to others the task of vindicating his people. He may wait for the strategic moment, which for the battered among his people may seem to be too long a wait. But they will be vindicated:

> Yahweh goes out like a warrior, he rallies his zeal like a man of war. He
> gives a war cry, even a loud shout: against his enemies he plays the part of
> a fighter. "I have long kept silent, kept quiet and restrained myself. But

---

[24]Is 51:9-11 stresses the battle itself and the foe (the Sea), along with the return of the rescued people to the sacred mountain. The process of mustering God's army is often elaborated (Is 13:2-5; Jer 51:27-28), while Joel 2:1-11 stresses the devastating army itself that comes at God's command. The dismay of those attacked is the focus of Jer 51:30-32, and the devastation that results can also be developed at some length (Is 13:19-22; 34:9-15). The final rejoicing and restoration is the focus of Is 35:1-10 (cf. the final victory banquet in Is 25:6-10).

now like a woman in labor I will cry out, gasp and pant all at once. I will devastate mountains and hills and dry up all their vegetation. I will turn rivers into islands and dry up the pools. I will lead the blind in a way they do not know, and I will guide them in unfamiliar paths. I will transform darkness into light before them and make twisted ways straight. These things I will do and will not abandon them. (Is 42:13-16)

One of the unfortunate developments in this picture is that a time comes when God's patience over his own people's recalcitrance reaches a limit. The march of the divine warrior against his enemies now becomes a march against his own people who have, by opposing God, aligned themselves with God's enemies. The "Day of Yahweh" which Israelites instinctively associated with judgment upon other nations has boomeranged: God now comes against Israel in judgment.[25] God's justice has no place for favoritism, and to the contrary he actually requires a higher standard for his own people (Amos 3:2). Consequently, already in the earliest literary prophets the war oracle against other nations is turned by the prophets into an oracle of war against God's own people if they refuse to keep their covenant obligations with God. A surprise is in store for those Israelites who could not wait for the Day of Yahweh in order to see their enemies judged, according to Amos:

Woe to you who look forward to the Day of Yahweh! Why is the Day of Yahweh something you want? It is darkness, not light. . . . Is not the Day of Yahweh darkness, not light, even deeply dark, without illumination? (Amos 5:18, 20)

Amos begins his book with a cluster of oracles against foreign nations (Amos 1:3–2:3), but the climax is an oracle of war against his own rebellious people (Amos 2:4-5). Zephaniah also caps off God's plans of judgment against the nations in general (Zeph 2:4-15) with a finale addressed to Judah as one who will not be exempt (Zeph 3:1-7). In all these cases, the Day of Yahweh continues to have the dimension of rescue, but this time it means only a few, a remnant within the larger polity of the people who will be judged:

Hate evil and love good. Establish justice in the gate. Perhaps Yahweh, the God of armies, will be gracious to the remnant of Joseph. (Amos 5:15)

---

[25]The phrase "Day of Yahweh" is applied to God's march against Israel in Ezek 13:5; Amos 5:18, 20; Joel 1:15; 2:1, 11; Zeph 1:7, 14.

Seek Yahweh, all you meek of the earth who have carried out his judgements. Seek righteousness, seek meekness. Perhaps you will be hidden in the day of Yahweh's anger. (Zeph 2:3)

"A redeemer will come to Zion and to those that turn from transgression in Jacob," said Yahweh. (Is 59:20)

The matter of chariots and horses was therefore hardly a peripheral concern of the prophets, for it went to the very heart of their message. Since God is a warrior, there can be no enemy forces that can overcome God's people, if Israel and Judah do as God orders. The prophets are united on this subject, whether they be the literary prophets or the stories about the prophets related in the Deuteronomistic history. According to 1 Samuel 8, Israel had initiated kingship with the explicit rationale that they wanted to imitate other nations in military protocol: "There will be a king over us and we also will be like all the nations, and our king will judge us and go out before us and fight our battles" (1 Sam 8:19-20). It was that very mimicry that eventually marked the parting of ways in the conduct of war, for modeling kingship upon surrounding kingdoms resulted in copying the technology of war. As far as the prophets were concerned, the chariots in which humans invested could not help but prove inadequate and, as a false hope, ultimately self-destructive in the face of the divine reality of God's chariots, a force mediated by the prophet himself if the king would only be willing to listen:

Yahweh comes with fire,
And his chariots are like the whirlwind,
To bring back his anger with wrath,
And his rebuke with flames of fire. (Is 66:15)

Nevertheless, when Israelite and Judean kingship passed from history, so too did the special role of the prophet as a king's military guide, the "chariots and horses of Israel," to whom the king could turn for assistance in defending God's people. The awareness of God as the divine warrior never passes, but the day of the prophet as the human in touch with God's heavenly armies was no more. One of the more prominent features of the Israelite prophet diminishes to the point where it is notable by its absence.

# 14

# CONTINUITIES IN HISTORY

WE HAVE ARGUED UP TO THIS POINT for a number of major prophetic transitions. We discussed the importance of the ninth century as a transition point in the Deuteronomistic history for the beginning of a decline in the miraculous dimension of prophetic identity. We have also observed how the sixth century B.C., in which the Babylonian exile takes place, has repeatedly surfaced as the most prominent landmark, a time when a number of transitions occur or begin to make their appearance in the presentation of prophecy. These transformations include the prophet's increasingly questionable relationship to the divine council and his waning ability to see what God is doing in history. A metamorphosis appears in the way in which God is presented as revealing himself, accompanied by a changing role for angelic beings. We have seen how the abolition of kingship at this time prompted the loss of one of prophecy's key political and military connections. Even the process of writing down prophetic oracles crystallizes explicitly in the sixth century.

In the midst of such developments, it is advisable to pause in order to inquire how the prophets might have envisioned such transformations. An informative parenthetical comment jumps out at the reader in the Dtr history in describing the prophet Samuel, observing that "the prophet *(nābî̕ )* today was formerly called the seer *(rō'eh)*" (1 Sam 9:9). Embedded in such a comment is the awareness of historical development in this institution, at least the recognition of a name-change over time. We have already noted (chap. 4) how after the exile, Zechariah nostalgically distinguishes himself from the preexilic prophets by the designation "the former prophets" (Zech 1:4). And we have seen the candid self-presentation of those prophets who do not rise to the same level of insight or performance as their predecessors, part of a notable decline in prophetic ability and intimacy with God that sets in with the exilic period. What is the larger view of prophetic texts toward history and these prophetic transformations? Can we uncover prophetic attitudes toward change and God's dealing with humans under congruent but nevertheless modified circumstances?

There is a conviction throughout biblical literature that patterns appear in the unfolding of change in history. One prominent paradigm that surfaces in several prophets is the primal corruption and subsequent destruction of Sodom and Gomorrah. The pervasiveness of this paradigm is underscored by the cliché, "as when God overthrew Sodom and Gomorrah," applied at different times by different prophets to different national entities. Amos uses the phrase to speak of God's destruction of parts of Israel, Isaiah employs it to speak of Babylon's uncompromising destruction and Jeremiah repeats it on two different occasions to describe the complete overthrow of Edom and the overthrow of Babylon:

> I overthrew you as God overthrew Sodom and Gomorrah. (Amos 4:11)

> Babylon . . . will be as when God overthrew Sodom and Gomorrah. (Is 13:19)

> Like the overthrow of Sodom and Gomorrah . . . no man will live there. (Jer 49:18)

> As when God overthrew Sodom and Gomorrah . . . no man will live there. (Jer 50:40)

One does not even need the cliché to appreciate the paradigmatic nature of Sodom and Gomorrah for the prophetic vision, for elsewhere in the prophets the imagery of Sodom pops up with creative applications that transcend any frozen phrase. Zephaniah exploits the imagery of the destruction of Sodom and Gomorrah, eloquently elaborating what that imagery means for Moab and Ammon who will suffer a similar fate: "Moab will be like Sodom, and the Ammonites like Gomorrah, a place of weeds and salt pits, a desolation forever" (Zeph 2:9). Jeremiah asserts that Jerusalem's population reminds him of Sodom and Gomorrah (Jer 23:14), but Isaiah goes a step further in more dramatically addressing his own people as "you rulers of Sodom, . . . you people of Gomorrah" (Is 1:10). He can speak like this because the people of Judah and Jerusalem are as shameless as the former inhabitants of Sodom: "They tell of their sin like Sodom, they don't hide it" (Is 3:9).

Ezekiel jarringly proposes that there must be some family connection to account for the continuity in depravity, as if there is some genetic condition that predisposes siblings to act alike: "Like mother, like daughter" (Ezek 16:44). For Ezekiel, Jerusalem can be described as Sodom's older sister. Unlike Isaiah's perspective that the citizens of Jerusalem behave just like Sodom, Ezekiel insists that Jerusalemites are worse. To press his case, Ezekiel elaborates a list of specific offenses where he claims Jerusalem is more despicable than even reprehensible Sodom: arrogance, surplus food and a failure to care for the poor in spite of luxurious living (Ezek 16:49). In these areas, and others, Jerusalem makes Sodom look righteous by comparison (Ezek 16:52). Although separated by time and geography, and although two different nationalities are in view, Jerusalem's doom is as certain as Sodom's. Be patient, for time will demonstrate the cause-and-effect nexus that is a part of history. As Ezekiel crisply summarizes: "This was the sin of your sister Sodom, . . . therefore I removed them" (Ezek 16:49-50).

Ezekiel also introduces yet a further novelty. The paradigm of historical development will also play out with respect to national recovery. Will Jerusalem be rebuilt? Yes. Will Sodom as well? Indeed. All the restorations are bundled together in a stunning affirmation of the continuity of destiny among the world's populations:

> I will restore their fortunes—the fortunes of Sodom and her daughters, the fortunes of Samaria and her daughters—and along with them your fortunes. . . . And your sisters, Sodom with her daughters and Samaria with her daughters, will return to their former state, and you with your daughters will return to your former state. (Ezek 16:53, 55)

The cause and effect continuum between Sodom's rebellious behavior and God's destructive judgment is a mirror in which one can see the history of one's own nation and other nations. Reciprocally, the way that God deals with Judah and Israel reflects the way God deals with other nations that are outside the covenant that was made with Israel. Will God restore Judah? Yes. Will God restore Sodom? Yes.

It must be underscored that history does not repeat itself as a lithograph repeats with undetectable precision a master copy. "Paradigm" is a preferred word to describe general contours that have a way of recurring even though the details vary. This is because one does not detect in the literary prophets any sense of inevitable destiny that cannot be affected by the choice of a person or a group of individuals. This awareness can be seen even with respect to the Sodom and Gomorrah paradigm, for once Isaiah exploits it to point out a contrast where—surprisingly—Judah had a different fate from those two cities: "If Yahweh of hosts had not left for us some survivors, we would have been like Sodom, we would have resembled Gomorrah" (Is 1:9). All else being equal, Jerusalem should have been wiped out in the light of previous experience. In this case, Isaiah can explain the aberration by divine intervention. But how does one know when the paradigm will play out or when it will be modified? Detecting the difference in advance is the special gift of the prophet.

The motif of Sodom and Gomorrah as a pattern that recycles in the prophets can be supplemented with another example from a single prophet who persistently applies a single set of historical consequences to a variety of kingdoms. Although Amos primarily addresses Israel in the book that bears his name, in Amos 1–2 his target is doom upon Israel's neighbors: Damascus to the northeast, Gaza to the southwest, Tyre to the northwest, Edom to the southeast, Ammon and Moab to the east, and finally Judah in the south. Each kingdom merits catastrophe for different reasons, ranging from covenant betrayal (Edom) to mistreatment of the dead (Moab), from deporting a population (Gaza) to extreme abuse of a civilian population for the sake of *Lebensraum* (Ammon). Although the crimes are different, Amos nevertheless sees continuity in identical punishments once a critical stage of unrelieved rebellion has been reached:

For three transgressions of **Damascus** and for four I will not revoke it, . . . and I will send fire upon **the house of Hazael** and it will devour the strongholds of **Ben-Hadad**. (Amos 1:3-4)

For three transgressions of **Gaza** and for four I will not revoke it, . . . and I will send fire upon **the wall of Gaza** and it will devour its strongholds. (Amos 1:6-7)

For three transgressions of **Tyre** and for four I will not revoke it, . . . and I will send fire upon **the wall of Tyre** and it will devour its strongholds. (Amos 1:9-10)

For three transgressions of **Edom** and for four I will not revoke it, . . . and I will send fire upon **Teman** and it will devour the strongholds of **Bozrah**. (Amos 1:11-12)

For three transgressions of **the Ammonites** and for four I will not revoke it, . . . and I will **kindle** a fire upon **the wall of Rabbah** and it will devour its strongholds. (Amos 1:13-14)

For three transgressions of **Moab** and for four I will not revoke it, . . . and I will send fire upon **Moab** and it will devour the strongholds of **Kerioth**. (Amos 2:1-2)

For three transgressions of **Judah** and for four I will not revoke it, . . . and I will send fire upon **Judah** and it will devour the strongholds of **Jerusalem**. (Amos 2:4-5)

Amos wants his audience to experience déjà-vu.[1] This is not a minor matter for Amos, for his persistence requires careful attention to detail in precisely quoting the same words seven times. This is more than poetry, for Amos exploits a pattern of cause and effect in history that he sees applying cross-culturally. The consequences of transgressions may have id-

---

[1] It has been observed (e.g., James Luther Mays, *Amos*, OTL [Philadelphia: Fortress, 1969], p. 24) that other verses elsewhere are so similar that one can speak of a formula that Amos is using: Hos 8:14 ("And I will send fire upon **its cities** and it will devour its strongholds"), Jer 17:27 ("And I will kindle a fire upon **its gates** and it will devour the strongholds of **Jerusalem**"), Jer 21:14 // 50:32 ("And I will kindle a fire upon **its forest/cities** and it will devour **all its environs**"); for Jer 49:27 see below. This may be so, but the phrase appears clearly only in two other literary prophets, namely Amos's contemporary to Israel (Hosea) and a prophet (Jeremiah) who is heavily dependent on earlier prophetic material. It is thus not necessarily a poetic formula, and even if it were, Amos is the only one to deliberately use the phrase as a structuring principle linking varied offenses with a common consequence.

iosyncratic results that he acknowledges with variations linked to only one kingdom or city-state: only of Damascus does he say that God will break its gate-bars (Amos 1:5), only of Gaza does he speak of God's hand turned against a city (Amos 1:8), of the Ammonites only do we hear of an exiled king and the storming chaos of battle (Amos 1:14-15), and only of Moab is there a report of a kingdom's death and slain judges and princes (Amos 2:2-3). But beyond the peculiarities of each kingdom's sin and punishment is a common thread that a common oracle links. Like a jazz musician who has internalized the basic theme, he is able better to highlight the individuality of each player.

A paradigmatic way of looking at history, where patterns repeat with variations but with consistency, is one of the sinews that hold together the grand history that stretches from Joshua through 2 Kings. This Deuteronomistic history depends upon a paradigmatic view of history, and it is precisely prophets who are most visible in focusing this subject. When the northern kingdom of Israel witnessed a succession of dynasties, one replacing another in a series of bloody coups, the prophets articulated a common theme that bound these events together. According to the book of 1 Kings, each of the dynasties founded by Jeroboam, Baasha and Omri provoked a prophetic reaction that was formulated with similar words in each case. The reader of the Dtr history consequently hears an echo through time, as events unfold with a clear affirmation of déjà-vu. (See table 14.1; items in bold show where the oracles differ, word in italics represent only a minor variation.)

According to the book of 1 Kings in the light of these parallel passages, the prophet Ahijah delivered the oracle against Jeroboam's dynasty (the first column of the table) during the reign of the dynastic founder himself, even though it was not until his son's reign that the royal family was wiped out (1 Kings 15:29). Similarly, another prophet identified as Jehu delivered the same, and often verbatim, oracle to the founder of the next dynasty, Baasha (the second column of the table), whose family was again exterminated during the reign of his son (1 Kings 16:11). The third frequently verbatim oracle against an Israelite dynasty (last column above) was not delivered to the dynastic founder, Omri, but instead to his son Ahab by the prophet Elijah. Although Ahab had one son succeed him briefly, it was during the reign of

Table 14.1.

| Dynasty of Jeroboam 1 Kings 14:7-11 | Dynasty of Baasha 1 Kings 16:2-4 | Dynasty of Omri 1 Kings 21:21-24 |
|---|---|---|
| Because I have raised you from **among** the **people** and made you a leader over my people Israel. . . . | Because I have raised you from the **dust** and made you a leader over my people Israel. . . . | |
| Behold I bring evil to **the house of Jeroboam** | | Behold I bring evil to **you,** |
| | | And I will consume **you,** |
| and I will cut off from **Jeroboam** those who piss against a wall, bound and free in Israel. And I will consume the house of **Jeroboam.** . . . | **Behold** I *consume* **Baasha and his** house. | and I will cut off from **Ahab** those who piss against a wall, bound and free in Israel. (see above) |
| | And I will make your house like the house of Jeroboam son of Nebat. | And I will make your house like the house of Jeroboam son of Nebat. . . . |
| The one who dies of **Jeroboam** in the city the dogs will eat, and the one who dies in the field the birds of the sky will eat. | The one who dies of **Baasha** in the city the dogs will eat, and the one who dies in the field the birds of the sky will eat. | The one who dies of **Ahab** in the city the dogs will eat, and the one who dies in the field the birds of the sky will eat. |

his second son that his family, too, was wiped out (2 Kings 10:11).

This repetition—with variations—of a basic oracle spoken by different prophets to different dynasties is one of the devices that the editors of the Dtr history use to present to the reader not only a continuity of perspective but a conviction that there are patterns in history and God's dealing with humans.[2] Each of these kings had violated the covenant that God had

---

[2]For our purposes it is irrelevant whether the pattern is original with the editor or a prior prophetic source (e.g., Campbell, *Of Prophets and Kings*). Von Rad's ("Deuteronomic Theology of History," p. 159) observation that the Dtr editor of these prophetic oracles did not have abundant sources "or he would not have quoted three times over, and against three different kings," is a fundamental misunderstanding of the phenomenon that we are correcting here. Rabbinic perspectives on this matter are more comprehensive in addressing the similarity between Obad 3 and Jer 49:16, articulating the principle that prophets often shared oracles but never completely in precisely the same words (*b. Sanhedrin* 89a).

made with Israel, and each had—as Israel's leader—"caused Israel to sin" (1 Kings 14:16; 16:2; 21:22). Similar consequences therefore come upon each for not only breaking the covenant but causing others to violate it.

In the light of such explicit emphasis upon duplicated oracles for similar events, it should come as no surprise that similar and even verbatim oracles resurface in the literary prophets. One oracle that appears in Isaiah is also found essentially verbatim in Micah. (See table 14.2.)

**Table 14.2.**

| Is 2:2-4 | Mic 4:1-3 |
| --- | --- |
| And it will be at the end of days, that the mountain of the house of Yahweh *established will be* as the highest of mountains, raised above the hills. All **nations** will stream to it, and many **peoples** will come and say, "Come, let us ascend to the mountain of Yahweh, to the house of the God of Jacob, that he may teach us of his ways and that we may walk in his paths. For instruction will go forth from Zion, and the word of Yahweh from Jerusalem. And he will judge among **the nations**, and he will arbitrate for **many peoples**. They shall beat their swords into plowshares, and their spears into pruning hooks. Nation will not lift up the sword against nation, and they will no longer learn war. | And it will be at the end of days, that the mountain of the house of Yahweh *will be established* as the highest of mountains, raised above the hills. All **peoples** will stream to it, and many **nations** will come and say, "Come, let us ascend to the mountain of Yahweh, **and** to the house of the God of Jacob, that he may teach us of his ways and that we may walk in his paths. For instruction will go forth from Zion, and the word of Yahweh from Jerusalem. And he will judge among **many peoples**, and he will arbitrate for **mighty nations afar**. They shall beat their swords into plowshares, and their spears into pruning hooks. Nation will not lift up the sword against nation, and they will no longer learn war. |

Moving from the portrayal of prophets in the Dtr history, who repeated oracles found in the mouths of others, such shared words between two literary prophets should be predictable. From a twentieth century Western perspective where plagiarism is a major concern in protecting intellectual property, such unattributed copying is problematic to a degree that obviously was not an issue in ancient Israel, or in the ancient Near East for that matter. The fact that scholars debate whether Isaiah copied from Micah, or whether Micah copied from Isaiah, or whether there is yet another source behind both of these contemporary prophets, highlights the lack of concern in the text to provide substantive clues that would permit tracking the direction of borrowing.[3]

The situation is similar when the book of Obadiah begins with an oracle against Edom that also appears in the book of Jeremiah with only minor variations. (See table 14.3.)

**Table 14.3.**

| **Obadiah 1-4** | **Jer 49:14-16** |
|---|---|
| **We** have heard a report from Yahweh and an envoy is sent among the nations. *Arise* **so that we may rise** against her to war. Behold I make you small among the nations, **you are very** despised. The arrogance of your heart has deceived you, you who dwell in the clefts of **a** rock, in the height of **his abode.** . . . **If** you make high like an eagle **and if you place among the stars** your nest, from there I will bring you down, said Yahweh. | **I** have heard a report from Yahweh and an envoy is sent among the nations. **Gather together and come** against her, and *arise* to war. **For** behold I make you small among the nations, **among men** despised. **As for your horror,** deceived you has the arrogance of your heart, you who dwell in the clefts of **the** rock, **who occupy** the height of a **hill.** **Though** you make high like an eagle your nest, from there I will bring you down, said Yahweh. |

| **Obadiah 5-6** | **Jer 49:9-10** |
|---|---|
| If grape-gatherers came to you, *would* they not leave gleanings? **How** *exposed is* Esau. | If grape-gatherers came to you, would they not leave gleanings? . . . **For** *I exposed* Esau. |

Unlike the passage duplicated in Isaiah and Micah, which was a general oracle of the climax of history, here the oracle is addressed to a specific national entity. As with Micah and Isaiah, scholars wrestle with the elusive ultimate source, although most at present argue for the priority of Obadiah.[4]

This phenomenon is connected with the seven-fold oracle that Amos applied to seven different kingdoms or city-states, discussed above. Part of

---

[3]For discussion, see Andersen and Freedman (*Micah,* pp. 413-27), who indicate that, although they lean toward Micah's priority, the present consensus is that Isaiah's oracle has priority.

[4]Josef Wehrle, *Prophetie und Textanalyse—Die Komposition Obadja 1-21 interpretiert auf der Basis textlinguistischer und semiotischer Konzeptionen,* Arbeiten zu Text und Sprache im Alten Testament 28 (St. Ottilien: Eos, 1987), pp. 12-13. Geoffrey H. Parke-Taylor dedicated a monograph (*Formation of the Book of Jeremiah: Doublets and Recurring Phrases,* SBLMS 51 [Atlanta: Society of Biblical Literature, 2000]) entirely to the phenomenon of repeated oracles in order to investigate the process by which the book of Jeremiah came to be and concluded that in this passage neither Obadiah nor Jeremiah depends on the other, but both are utilizing a common oral source (pp. 147-51).

Amos's repeated oracle was seen as not only applicable to eighth-century political realities but as equally relevant over a century later to one of the same kingdoms that Amos had in his sights. This time, however, it appears in an oracle collection against nations found in the book of Jeremiah. (See table 14.4.)

**Table 14.4.**

| **Amos 1:4** | **Jer 49:27** |
|---|---|
| And I will *send* fire upon the **house** of Hazael and it will devour the strongholds of Ben-Hadad. | And I will *kindle*[a] a fire upon the **wall** of Damascus and it will devour the strongholds of Ben-Hadad. |

[a]The term here translated "kindle" does appear in one of Amos's seven oracles as a variant (Amos 1:14) for the word translated "send" in the other six appearances in Amos 1–2. Some (e.g., Hans Walter Wolff, *Joel and Amos* [Philadelphia: Fortress, 1977], p. 161) wish to see Amos 1:14 as a scribal modification influenced by Jer 49:27. The text of Jer 49:27 is quite close to the oracular pattern established in Amos, and in any case there is no question of a connection between the two (see discussion above in n. 1).

What Amos saw as a synchronic pattern equally applicable to many kingdoms in his own day becomes by comparison with its use in Jeremiah a diachronic pattern that resurfaces from one generation to the next.

One can also find an oracle copied to some extent verbatim, but also modified to a significant degree. Isaiah 15–16 is a single unit that has been unfortunately separated into two chapters, for these twenty-three verses are entwined as one long oracle against Israel's neighbor to the east, Moab. Much of the material in this extended oracle is duplicated in Jeremiah's even longer single chapter directed against Moab (with forty-seven verses, i.e., twice as many; see table 14.5).

One can also find within a single literary prophet an oracle excerpted largely verbatim against two different entities, similar to Amos's sevenfold repetition discussed above. A self-conscious awareness of such connections is explicitly affirmed apart from the repeated oracles themselves when one hears God's voice underscoring the principle: "I am about to punish the King of Babylon and his land just as I punished the King of Assyria" (Jer 50:18). In the examples below (see table 14.6), the book of Jeremiah applies the same oracle both to Edom and Babylon, another similar oracle to both Moab and Edom, another single oracle targets both Damascus and Babylon, and finally a single oracle against Babylon

**Table 14.5.**

| | |
|---|---|
| **Is 15:2-3** | **Jer 48:37-38** |
| Every head **of his** is bald, every beard cut off. **In his streets they gird with** sackcloth. On **her** roofs and in her streets everyone **wails.** | Every head is bald, **and** every beard cut off, **on all hands gashes and on the loins** sackcloth. On **all** the roofs **of Moab** and in her streets everyone **laments.** |
| **Is 15:4-6** | **Jer 48:34** |
| **And** *cries* Heshbon **and** Elealeh, even to Jahaz their voice **is heard.** . . . **His fugitives up to** Zoar, Eglath-Shalishah. . . . For even the waters of Nimrim will be desolate. | **From** *a cry of* Heshbon **to** Elealeh, even to Jahaz **they raise** their voice, **from** Zoar **to Horonaim**, Eglath-Shalishah, for even the waters of Nimrim will **be** desolate. |
| **Is 15:5** | **Jer 48:5** |
| For he ascends the ascent of Luhith with weeping *on it*, for the **way** to Horonaim they **hear** an *out*cry of destruction. | For he ascends the ascent of Luhith with weeping, *weeping*, for **in** the **descent** to Horonaim they **raise distresses of** a cry of destruction. |
| **Is 16:6-11** | **Jer 48:29-33, 36** |
| We have heard of the pride of Moab, an excessive pride, his arrogance, his haughtiness, his **wrath**. His boasts are not so. . . . Therefore **Moab** will wail for Moab, every one will wail. For the **raisin cakes** of Kir-hareseth **you** will moan. . . . | We have heard of the pride of Moab, an excessive pride, his **superciliousness**, his haughtiness, his arrogance. . . . His boasts are not so. Therefore **I** will wail for Moab, **I will cry out** for every one of Moab. For the **men** of Kir-hareseth **he** will moan. **More than** the tears for Jazer I weep for **you**, vine of Sibmah. They have passed over the sea. |
| They have reached even to Jazer. . . . They have passed over the sea. **Therefore** I weep with tears for Jazer, for the vine of Sibmah. . . . Upon your summer fruits and upon your harvest a *shout (hêdād)* has fallen, and joy and gladness are taken away from the fruitful field. . . . Wine in the presses no **treader** treads, I have brought to a halt shouting. . . . | They have reached even to **the Sea of** Jazer. Upon your summer fruits and upon your harvest a *ravager (sōdēd)* has fallen, and joy and gladness are taken away from the fruitful field. . . . Wine in the presses I have brought to a halt. No one treads with shouting. . . . |
| Therefore my **insides** murmur like **harp**, and my **soul** for Kir-Hares. | Therefore my **heart** murmurs like **flutes**, and my **heart** for **the men of** Kir-Hares. |

**Table 14.6.**

| | |
|---|---|
| **Jer 49:19-21** | **Jer 50:44-46** |
| Behold, he will come up like a lion from the jungle of the Jordan to a perennially watered pasture, for I will suddenly make **him** run away from it. And who is a chosen one whom I may appoint over it? For who is like me? And who will appoint me as a witness? And who is this shepherd who can stand before me? Therefore listen to the counsel of Yahweh that he counseled against **Edom**; and his thoughts that he thought against the **inhabitants of Teman**. They will certainly drag off the youngest of the flock, he will certainly desolate their pastures on their account. At the sound **of their fall** the earth shake**s**, an **out**cry is heard in the **Red Sea**. | Behold, he will come up like a lion from the jungle of the Jordan to a perennially watered pasture, for I will suddenly make **them** run away from it. And who is a chosen one whom I may appoint over it? For who is like me? And who will appoint me as a witness? And who is this shepherd who can stand before me? Therefore listen to the counsel of Yahweh that he counseled against **Babylon**; and his thoughts that he thought against **the land of the Chaldeans**. They will certainly drag off the youngest of the flock, he will certainly desolate their pastures on their account. At the sound, **"Babylon is taken!"** the earth **is** shaken, **and** a cry is heard in the **nations**. |
| **Jer 48:40-41** | **Jer 49:22** |
| Behold he will soar like an eagle, and he will spread his wings over **Moab**. . . . And the heart of the mighty men of **Moab** will be in that day like the heart of a woman in labor. | Behold he will **ascend and** soar like an eagle, and he will spread his wings over **Bozrah**. And the heart of the mighty men of **Edom** will be in that day like the heart of a woman in labor. |
| **Jer 49:26** | **Jer 50:30** |
| Therefore her (i.e., **Damascus**) young men will will fall in her streets, and all **the** men of war will be stilled in that day, oracle of Yahweh **of hosts**. | Therefore her (i.e., **Babylon**) young men will will fall in her streets, and all **her** men of war will be stilled in that day, oracle of Yahweh. |
| **Jer 6:22-24** | **Jer 50:41-43** |
| Behold, a people is coming from **the land of** the north, and a great nation **is** aroused from the ends of the earth. They grasp bow and spear, they are cruel and show no mercy. Their sound roars like the sea, and they ride on horses. Prepared as a man for battle against you, daughter of **Zion**. **We** heard **his** report, **our** hands go limp. Anguish seizes **us**, pain as a woman in childbirth. | Behold, a people is coming from the north, and a great nation **and many kings are** aroused from the ends of the earth. They grasp bow and spear, they are cruel and show no mercy. Their sound roars like the sea, and they ride on horses. Prepared as a man for battle against you, daughter of **Babylon. The king of Babylon** heard **their** report, **and his** hands go limp. Anguish seizes **him**, pain as a woman in childbirth. |

reappears as words that can equally well be applied to Judah.[5]

One can even find an essentially verbatim oracle applied in one prophet to three different addressees. (See table 14.7.)

**Table 14.7.**

| Jer 19:8 | Jer 49:17 | Jer 50:13 |
|---|---|---|
| **And I will make this** **city [Jerusalem]** a desolation, **and an object of hissing**; | And **Edom** will be a desolation; | And it will be **completely** *desolate*; |
| everyone who passes by her will be horrified and will hiss at all her wounds. | everyone who passes by her will be horrified and will hiss at all her wounds. | everyone who passes by **Babylon** will be horrified and will hiss at all her wounds. |

Above we began by noting that in the Deuteronomistic history, different prophets over time reapplied the same oracle to different doomed Israelite dynasties. One can also find in the literary prophets a similar phenomenon, where a prophet adapts another prophet's oracle that is addressed to a specific addressee, but in adapting it essentially verbatim, it is applied to another addressee. (See table 14.8.)

What began with Amos's hammering blows of a single refrain directed to a number of different nations has now become in other literary prophets an aggressive application of one intricate template to multiple entities. As Amos did not shrink from applying his refrain against the nations also to the Israelites, neither do other literary prophets have a problem in treating

**Table 14.8.**

| Is 24:17-18 | Jer 48:43-44 |
|---|---|
| Terror and pit and snare are upon you, O inhabitant of **the earth. And it will be** **that** the one who flees from the **sound of** the terror will fall into the pit, and the one who ascends from **within** the pit will be caught in the snare, for . . . | Terror and pit and snare are upon you, O inhabitant of **Moab, says Yahweh.** The one who flees from **before** the terror will fall into the pit, and the one who ascends from the pit will be caught in the snare, for . . . |

---

[5]So fundamental is this perspective that Rofé noted (*Introduction to Prophetic Literature,* p. 76) in affirming Christensen's work (*Transformations of the War Oracle*), "This is the ground on which classical prophecy came into existence, reworking traditional material, manipulating it to suit new trends. Oracles formerly spoken against Edom are now turned against Israel as well."

Israel as one of the nations, subject to the same historical realities. The inevitable conclusion from recyclable oracles, interchangeable with Israelites or non-Israelites, the kingdom of Judah or the kingdom of Israel, is that there is a continuity in history that transcends the special place of Israel as God's covenant people. Whether one prophet reapplies his own oracles to different addressees, or whether many prophets exploit one another's oracles to the same or different groups, the assumption is that both God and humans have characteristic behavior with characteristic consequences. This generalization must not be taken to mean that God and humans are predictable or are chained by some inevitability that overrides individual idiosyncracies. If that were true, there would be no sense to the prophetic calls for repentance.

Explicit statements in prophetic texts affirm that God deals with Israel as he deals with other nations. The perceptive eye of the prophet can discern such patterns of continuity. The foundational event for Israel's origin, the exodus from Egypt, may seem to be a uniquely magnificent display of God's special relationship with Israel. Although Amos does not deny God's special relationship with Israel, he points out to his people that Israel was not the only nation to have experienced an exodus. He provides as parallel examples God's care for Israel's traditional enemies, the Philistines and the Aramaeans:

> "Are you not as the Ethiopians to me, O Israelites?" declares Yahweh. Did I not bring Israel up from the land of Egypt, and the Philistines from Caphtor, and the Arameans from Kir?" (Amos 9:7)

We saw earlier that the destiny yet to unfold for despicable Sodom is connected with Jerusalem's future. In this passage in Amos, we now see that the past as well as the future is congruent for both Israel and the nations. Whether the patterns be for judgment or for redemption, both unfold for Israelites and non-Israelites with remarkable parallels. The historical contexts will vary, the accusations may vacillate and the consequences can fluctuate, but an underlying grid provides continuity for shared experiences. It is this perspective that makes sense of oracles that can be adapted, recycled, modified and reapplied from one group to another and from one time to another.

We have been investigating the transformations that prophecy experienced in the first millennium B.C. In the process, we have seen that the prophets presented such changes with an awareness of contrasts between earlier prophets and later prophets, exhibiting a self-consciousness that prophecy was a fluid gift that did not remain the same. Zechariah does not see with the same perspicacity as his predecessors, but the humiliating contrast is preserved nonetheless. Angelic messengers become the medium of revelation to later prophets, a transparent diminution of the prophet's status from an earlier presentation of the prophet in intimate dialogue with God himself. In this chapter we have moved a step further in observing within the phenomena of prophetic oracles themselves an awareness of historical development as oracles have a life of their own that may not stop with an initial articulation. Adaptations of oracles are predicated, however, upon an underlying continuity that endures from one generation to the next and from one culture to another. This raises the question: What are some of the essential features of prophecy that did not change regardless of the changes that took place in the first millennium B.C.? Are there features of prophecy that form a template that cannot change?

## 15

# RELIABLE PROPHETS IN
# THE CONTEXT OF CHANGE

THE VACILLATING FEATURES OF PROPHECY over half a millennium prompt an inevitable question. Are some of these changes so significant that the very integrity of prophecy itself is undermined? Are there features of prophecy that are non-negotiable and that must remain untouched? Can prophecy undergo so much of a metamorphosis that it really is no longer prophecy at all? Is it possible for the tree to bend so far that it breaks?

In order to confront these questions, one can more pointedly ask about the degree to which people living with the prophets as contemporaries might have been confused about some of these transformations. Any confusion about whom to heed as a legitimate spokesperson for God, especially when there are competing voices, is of course always an issue. But the problem becomes more acute when an institution with credibility, such as ancient Israelite prophecy, changes so dramatically that one can justifiably ask whether the new face it presents exhibits appropriate maturing or if it is really a new identity that is irreconcilably at odds with what has gone before. Since not all change is for the better, how would ancient Israelites have perceived the transformations of prophecy?

Biblical texts provide us with explicit categories that many Israelites found helpful in navigating among prophets, some of whom were found to be reliable and others who were seen to be suspect.[1] Many contemporary researchers despair of ever finding reliable criteria that successfully assisted ancient Israelites in this task, and it must be admitted there are no criteria that guarantee certain results. But neither is there any infallible guide to discriminating between the fiancé(e) who marries a wealthy spouse for love or who marries for the money, but there are individuals who do fall into each category. Since there is no category of human relationships where criteria exist that permit decisive and irrefutable judgments of behavior for all observers, it is asking too much to expect such criteria in the case of prophets. One speaks of juries that convict individuals in capital cases "beyond all reasonable doubt," but even here in this most intricately scrutinized domain of human decision-making, mistakes are made. In the case of jury decisions, the presence of the adjective "reasonable" points to the full awareness of the lack of any such thing as the removal of all doubt. As with discernment in all human activities, certainty of judgment with respect to prophets is usually unrealistic and not a privilege readily available to all. Simply put, all certifications in human affairs can be persuasively falsified to some degree.

There were morally charged choices that the prophets presented to ancient Israelites with consequences that demanded a high price. In the following pages we will address some of the themes that appear in the

---

[1]One often finds the problem posed as a conflict between "true" and "false" prophets, designations that are never used in the Hebrew Bible. Translations that do use the phrase "false prophets" (e.g., CEV in Is 44:25; Jer 23:16) are interpretive and not precisely translating the Hebrew, assimilating like the Septuagint (e.g., Jer 6:13; Zech 13:2) toward the culture represented in the New Testament where the designation is quite at home (e.g., Mt 7:15; Mk 13:22; Lk 6:26; 2 Pet 2:1; 1 Jn 4:1). Consequently there is a tendency to speak today of "prophetic conflict" rather than of true versus false prophecy (e.g., Lester L. Grabbe, *Priests, Prophets, Diviners, Sages: A Socio-Historical Study of Religious Specialists in Ancient Israel* [Valley Forge, Penn.: Trinity Press International, 1995], pp. 113-18). An on-going discussion in discriminating between such prophets has generated a prodigious bibliography. For works that provide an orientation to the diversity of perspectives on the subject, one may consult with profit Mowinckel, "The 'Spirit' and the 'Word'"; Edward F. Siegman, *The False Prophets of the Old Testament* (Washington, D.C.: Catholic University of America, 1939); Rowley, "The Nature of Prophecy"; Crenshaw, *Prophetic Conflict;* and Robert R. Wilson, "Interpreting Israel's Religion: An Anthropological Perspective on the Problem of False Prophecy," in *"The Place is Too Small for Us": The Israelite Prophets in Recent Scholarship*, ed. Robert P. Gordon, Sources for Biblical and Theological Study 5 (Winona Lake, Ind.: Eisenbrauns, 1995), pp. 333-44.

prophets in order to pinpoint the degree to which prophetic mutations in the first millennium B.C. were tolerated, accepted or rejected by the society in which they occurred. We will discover that a constellation of factors unfolds to help an observer deliberate whether or not any given prophet is to be seen as a reliable prophet of Yahweh. Even when all these factors merge, however, we will also see that confidence always remains elusive. No single aspect of a prophet's performance is always sufficient to assist one to know: is this prophet for real? Has the prophet gone too far? The subject casts its shadow over much of the Bible, for biblical texts are constantly presenting the dilemmas that Israelites must navigate in discerning who is qualified to speak for God, a problem compounded when prophecy itself mutates.

### Paying the Prophet

The means by which a prophet earned his livelihood was one of the most widespread criteria by which prophecy maintained its credibility over time. The overriding conviction that prophets brought God's message to humans carried an important corollary: God would provide for the needs of his prophets. Indeed, prophets even had a special privilege in being able to depend upon God's support when other Israelites found God's grace withdrawn. During years of drought and famine, for example, God told Elijah to leave Israel in order to reside by a wadi, or dry river bed (Hebrew *naḥal*) for there "you will drink from the wadi, and I have commanded the ravens to feed you there" (1 Kings 17:4 NJPS). While Israelites are starving and while God's people may be undergoing divine discipline, the prophet, as a specially delegated servant of God, has a special status as one enjoying God's focused care. God can use other agents in creation to provide for his prophets, as the ravens in the account just noted: "The ravens brought him bread and meat every morning and every evening, and he drank from the wadi" (1 Kings 17:6 NJPS). Supernatural beings can also be enlisted for this purpose, as in the case of the angel who brings provisions to Elijah when he fearfully runs from Jezebel:

> He [i.e., Elijah] lay down and slept under a certain broom tree, and behold, there was an angel nudging him. He said to him, "Get up, eat." He looked and behold, at his head was a bread cake baked on stones and a jar of water.

He ate, drank and again lay down. Yahweh's angel returned a second time and nudged him and said, "Get up, eat, because the way ahead is daunting." He arose, ate and drank, and went in the strength of that food forty days and forty nights to Horeb, the mountain of God. (1 Kings 19:5-8)

More frequently, God uses other humans to provide for a prophet's basic needs. When the ravens are no longer capable of finding food to bring to Elijah in the story noted above, God eventually informs Elijah of his backup plan to care for him: "Arise, go to Zarephath, which belongs to Sidon, and remain there. Behold, I have commanded a widow there to care for you" (1 Kings 17:9). Along similar lines, Elijah's successor, Elisha, is invited in for a meal by a well-to-do woman, an extension of hospitality that soon expands to providing him with his own room and furniture which he can use whenever he is in the neighborhood (2 Kings 4:8-11). She expects nothing in return, and even when Elisha asks if there is anything he can do for her, she declines the offer (2 Kings 4:12-13).

Such narratives point to a ready willingness on the part of people to care for a prophet whenever able. The prophet was apparently someone that the rest of the community cared for simply because Israelites saw the prophet as a valuable person who had access to the divine in a unique way. Consequently, individuals are portrayed making provision for the prophet whenever they were in a position to assist him. One finds a prophet supervising a large community of disciples who need to be fed, apparently a community of some one hundred people (2 Kings 4:43). To feed this community, an individual residing in a neighboring area "brought to the man of God bread of the first fruits *(bikkûrîm)*, twenty loaves of barley and fresh grain in his sack" (2 Kings 4:42), food which is then distributed to the prophet's disciples for them to eat. The specification that this food is from the first barley harvested in the spring seems to be a deliberate emphasis in order to draw attention to a remarkable fact: this gift of food to the prophet parallels gifts to God that one makes to the priests at the sanctuary. Both come from the firstfruits of the harvest.[2] One provides for the prophet in the same way one provides for the priest. Most notably this

---

[2]The term *bikkûrîm* reappears in Ex 23:16 and prefixed with the word "first of" *(rē'šît bikkûrîm)* in Ex 34:26; the term "first of" *rē'šît* stands alone in Lev 23:10; Deut 18:4; 26:10.

means that one gives to such individuals from the first part of the harvest and not from what might remain when the harvest is over.

There is also another dimension to such a gift. More specifically, this gift made by individual Israelites to prophets sounds very much like similar contexts describing firstfruits and tithes that were to be used to help the needy in society. In proximity to the brief, almost creedal, statement that an Israelite is to say upon surrendering the first part of the harvest to the priest, mention is made of the care for the legally and economically marginal members of the community:

> You will take some of the first of all the produce of the ground that you will bring in from your land, which Yahweh your God gives you, and you will put it in a basket and go to the place where Yahweh your God will choose to have his name reside. . . . The priest will take the basket from your hand and place it before the altar of Yahweh your God. You will respond and say before Yahweh your God, "My father was a perishing Aramean, and he went down to Egypt and took up temporary residence there, few in number. . . . The Egyptians abused us. . . . We cried to Yahweh, the God of our Fathers, and Yahweh heard our voice and saw our affliction, our labor, and our oppression. . . . He brought us to this place and gave us this land, a land flowing with milk and honey. Now I hereby bring the first of the produce of the ground. . . ." When you finish paying the tithe of your produce in the third year, the year of tithing, then you will give it to the Levite, the resident alien, the fatherless and the widow that they may eat in your gates and be satisfied. You will say before Yahweh your God, "I removed what is holy from my house and gave it to the Levite, the resident alien, the fatherless and the widow according to all your commands." (Deut 26:2, 4-7, 9-10, 12-13)

The Israelite in this confession before the priest stresses the history of the Israelites as a people with a past marked by a precarious existence and even oppression. As a result of this history, an Israelite is to learn that he or she should in turn assist those who are in need with the gifts God has provided to the Israelites. The particular persons singled out for assistance in the immediately following context are orphans, widows, strangers and Levites (the latter having no property and apparently dependent upon the gifts of the community). Prophets, too, belonged in this category of peripheral and marginal elements of society for whom one is to make provision even if no services are returned to the giver.

Prophets were not, however, entirely dependent on the voluntary gifts of the communities they encountered. A prophet often made his living from payments that people would make when they used his services. When consulting a prophet about lost animals, personal illness or insight into the future, it was customary to reimburse the prophet for these services that he rendered. Payment typically took the form of food that the prophet could eat. Thus, when Saul's servant advises Saul to consult the prophet Samuel about the lost donkeys, Saul's first excuse in support of his counterclaim that they should not consult the prophet is that he does not have any food to give the prophet:

> Saul said to his servant, "Behold, should we go, what would we bring the man? For the bread is gone from our sack, and there is no present *(tĕśûrâ)* to bring to the man of God. What do we have?" (1 Sam 9:7)

The first notion that comes to Saul's mind is that food is the appropriate and presumed first choice to give to a prophet who assists someone. As a backup plan, the servant indicates that a small amount of silver will suffice in the absence of food:

> The servant answered Saul again and said, "Behold, I have in my hand a fourth of a shekel of silver, so I can give it to the man of God and he will tell us our way." (1 Sam 9:8)

Several items are of significance in this brief dialogue. First is the presumption on Saul's part that a prophet's services are not free. Secondly, the preferred means of payment is food, specifically bread. Thirdly, when some type of monetary payment is considered, the amount is quite small. A fourth of a shekel is approximately one-tenth of an ounce. Such a fee is hardly extravagant, and if it were used to purchase food would only provide a small amount that would suffice a single individual for a few days at best.[3]

These observations taken together provide crucial perspectives into the social standing of the prophet. It was not an occupation that would lead to

---

[3] In 2 Kings 7:1, 16, 18 set in the ninth century B.C., food prices when grain is abundant and prices low (in contrast to famine prices in 2 Kings 6:25) indicate that a fourth of a shekel might purchase some 2 liters (a fourth of a seah) of fine flour or some 4 liters of barley.

surplus wealth under such circumstances. Other narratives confirm this general perception of the prophet's social standing, as in the case of the queen who disguises herself as a commoner in order to find out if a young prince's illness will prove fatal or not. As part of the disguise, and thus what one would expect of an inquiry about a child's malady, her husband, king Jeroboam, tells her to "take ten loaves with you, some cakes, and a jar of honey" (1 Kings 14:3). Once again, the prophet is provisioned with perishables, food items that must be consumed and will not permit long term storage. God's provision of manna in the wilderness presents a close analogue, for Israelites were forbidden to store the food that God provided each day, and any attempt to save the manna was frustrated by its decomposition (Ex 16:16-30). It is even possible that the parallel ways God cared for both his prophets and Israel in the wilderness provide the context for part of the prayer that Jesus taught his disciples: "Give us this day our daily bread" (Mt 6:11).

One discovers in biblical narrative that prophets learn to expect bread and water and little more as their due. Consequently there is no room for complaint when bread and water is the fare they receive for being Yahweh's faithful servants. One may suspect nothing remarkable when Elijah arrives in Zarephath and is eventually granted what he asks from a poor widow, "Please bring me a piece of bread in your hand" (1 Kings 17:11). But even the well-to-do woman of Shunem invites Elisha simply to eat "bread" (2 Kings 4:8). A prophet sent on a round-trip mission from Judah to Israel is given a divine commission neither to "eat bread nor drink water" until he completes the mission (1 Kings 13:9, 17), and he is waylaid by an offer from another prophet who invites him to "eat bread and drink water" with him (1 Kings 13:18). In contrast to the hundreds of prophets of Baal and Asherah "who eat at Jezebel's table" (1 Kings 18:19), the royal steward Obadiah risked his life for a hundred prophets of Yahweh—in hiding from Ahab and Jezebel—and "provided them with bread and water" (1 Kings 18:4). If one were to judge success by the quality of one's diet and the place where one dined, the relative prosperity of these prophets supported by the palace would prejudice an observer in favor of the more attractive ambience—and presumably higher quality fare—of the palace. But it is clear that a respected prophet lives day-to-day, dependent on the food that is sufficient for each day. Indeed, during the same reign, Ahab incarcerates the prophet Micaiah pending his return from battle and promises the jailed prophet "bread of affliction and water of affliction"[4] (1 Kings 22:27). The irony is that bread and water is precisely what the prophet would have expected whether jailed or otherwise, no matter how miserable the king might think the fare. The irony is compounded with the hostile king providing even for God's prophet whom he disdains. Ezekiel's later diet of water and bread—made from a mixture of assorted grains—is similarly not far from what a prophet expects (Ezek 4:9-17). In Ezekiel's case, the key element is the small quantity (eight ounces per day) that he is allowed in order to dramatize what siege conditions will be like when Jerusalem is under attack.

The intimate connection between a prophet and his reimbursement by food for services rendered is a repeated and assumed feature of Israelite prophecy. When a hostile priest in Bethel dismisses the prophet Amos because he does not like Amos's message of doom, the priest tries to send him packing with advice to earn his living elsewhere: "Go, you seer, scurry off to the land of Judah and there eat bread and there do your prophesying!" (Amos 7:12). Not only do prophesying and eating go hand in hand here, but Ezekiel also makes the connection when he berates the prophetesses who are off target:

> As for you, son of man, set your face against the daughters of your people who are prophesying from their own hearts. Prophesy against them and say, ". . . For handfuls of barley and pieces of bread you profaned me to my people in order to put to death some who should not die and to preserve others who should not live, by your lying to my people who listen to lies." (Ezek 13:17-19)

As all social institutions are subject to abuse, so even here one finds corruption infecting the prophet's role in society. These prophetesses were modifying their oracles based upon whether or not they were given food to eat. The paltry diet for which the prophetesses sell out is underscored

---

[4]The Hebrew phrase *(lehem lahas ûmayim lahas)* has been variously rendered: "with bread of affliction and with water of affliction" (KJV), "scant bread and scant water" (NJPS), "sparingly with bread and water" (NASB).

by the inferior nature of the grain (barley, not wheat)[5] and the minimal amounts which they receive (mere handfuls and fragments), perhaps a function of the tenuous existence in Jerusalem for most of the populace between the first (597 B.C.) and second (586 B.C.) deportations by Nebuchadnezzar. The prophet Micah records a similar manipulation of prophetic oracles over a century earlier:

> Thus said Yahweh concerning the prophets who cause my people to stray, who bite with their teeth and cry, "Peace!" but who declare war against the one who puts nothing in their mouths. (Mic 3:5)

An even more insidious corruption is evident when prophets are not satisfied with their daily bread, provided by a community of people whom they assist in daily affairs. An easy temptation was to agree to sign on to the payroll of a wealthy benefactor. Some four hundred prophets vouch for King Ahab's certain victory in 1 Kings 22, a striking unanimity which a fellow king Jehoshaphat finds peculiar. This unanimity is not surprising, however, if the narrator or editor of the story wants the reader to make a connection with an earlier dialogue in which Elijah asked Ahab for a showdown with the "four hundred and fifty prophets of Baal and four hundred prophets of the Asherah, who eat at Jezebel's table" (1 Kings 18:19). These prophets are not receiving their meals by the good graces of the people of Israel, nor does their food come from the providential care of the God they serve. Instead, they are hired hands, whose temptation is to tell the king what he wants to hear: if one wants to eat at the royal mess, don't rock the boat.[6] This notion is simply an extension of the indictments of Ezekiel and Micah against prophets who adjust their oracles depending upon who feeds them. In this case, however, they have a regular provider—not God—whom they would wish to keep in good spirits. As Ahab later says about the lone prophet who dissents from the unanimous

---

[5]Barley was a quite legitimate gift given to the prophet and distributed to his disciples in the story noted above from 2 Kings 4:42-43, underscoring that the prophetic life style was not an attractive one.

[6]The description of Gad as "David's seer" and not "Yahweh's seer" in 2 Sam 24:11 (//1 Chron 21:9) in this regard is curious, even though the narrative unequivocally sets Gad in opposition to David as Yahweh's spokesman. It is to David's credit that although priests appear in a brief list of officials in David's administration, no prophets appear (2 Sam 8:16-18; the same is true of Solomon's administration in 1 Kings 4:2-19).

voice of the four hundred, "I hate him, because he does not prophesy good concerning me, but evil. . . . Did I not tell you that he would not prophesy good concerning me, only evil?" (1 Kings 22:8, 18). Ahab is presented as a king who insists on good news, not the truth. Consequently, several hundred prophets on his daily palace ration lists know how best to remain there. Appropriately this lone prophet is placed in prison and given only bread and water (1 Kings 22:27). Ahab sees this as a punishment, but this fare is precisely what the prophet would have otherwise expected to receive from the God of Israel. The prophet is vindicated who does not try to maneuver outside God's directives.

There are other related ways that are equally suspect for prophets to bypass the precarious existence that the God of Israel prefers for his spokesmen. One way is to take large non-edible gifts such as silver and valuable commodities. Such benevolences violate the basic strategy of prophetic sustenance: the prophet is not to accumulate a supply of commodities which would undermine his daily dependence upon God's provision. When Saul's servant offered to give Samuel a quarter of a shekel (one-tenth of an ounce) for helping them locate their lost donkeys, we noted above that this amount of silver would buy provisions for one person that would last for only a few days at most. Contrast this quarter shekel with a gift hundreds of thousands of times larger that the Syrian general, Naaman, offered to Elisha when he healed him of his skin disease: "ten talents of silver and six thousand shekels of gold and ten changes of clothes" (2 Kings 5:5). Where the slave proposed a quarter shekel of silver, an extravagant 36,000 shekels of silver alone are being offered here.[7] This phenomenal, indeed exorbitant, amount of silver does not even include the far more precious 6,000 shekels of gold. Naaman does not understand how Israelite prophets work when it comes to reimbursing them for services rendered:

> He [i.e., Naaman], along with all his entourage, returned to the man of God and came and stood before him. He said, "Behold now, I know that there is no God in all the earth except in Israel. Now, please take a present from your servant." He [i.e., Elisha] said, "As Yahweh lives, before whom I

---

[7]A single talent is some sixty to seventy pounds, each talent being the equivalent of 3,600 shekels.

stand, I will take nothing." He [i.e., Naaman] urged him to take it, but he
refused. (2 Kings 5:15-16)

No reason is given for Elisha's declining to accept the payment in the
passage, but the larger context of prophetic activity that we have been investigating above makes his refusal entirely predictable.[8] Elisha is on no
one's payroll. Elisha cannot be bought at any price. He has learned the
prophetic way of life, dependence upon God's daily provision. If Elisha
had taken the extravagant gift from Naaman, Elisha would have found a
new source of security that would have disqualified him from serving as a
genuine mouthpiece for God.

The story of Elisha's refusal to accept Naaman's gift has an additional,
and surprising, conclusion. A final twist underscores that one of the primary purposes of the story is precisely to single out this non-negotiable
feature of the prophetic lifestyle. Elisha's servant, Gehazi, finds it difficult
to subscribe to his master's abstemious behavior. He surreptitiously runs
after Naaman, concocting a lie in order to cash in on some of the items
that, from his perspective, his master gave up too quickly:

> He said, "All is well. My master sent me, saying, 'Behold, just now two
> young men of the sons of the prophets came to me from Ephraim's hill
> country. Please give them a talent of silver and two changes of clothes.'"
> Naaman said, "Please take two talents!" (2 Kings 5:22-23)

When the servant takes and hides these items, he tragi-comically seems
to have forgotten that he works for a prophet who sees hidden things.
Elisha asks a pointed question when the servant once again stands in his
presence:

> Elisha said to him, "Where have you been, Gehazi?" He said, "Your ser-
> vant went nowhere." He (i.e., Elisha) said to him, "Did not my heart go

---

[8]D. P. O'Brien differs but overlooks this larger context, an oversight most apparent in his claim
("'Is This the Time to Accept . . . ?' [2 Kings V 26b]: Simply Moralizing [LXX] or an Ominous
Foreboding of Yahweh's Rejection of Israel [MT]?" *VT* 46 [1996]: 449) that Elisha accepts the gifts
from Ben-Hadad in 2 Kings 8, a transaction that is however never noted (see below). Overlook-
ing the larger context and the distinction between gifts of food and non-perishables is frequently
repeated (e.g., W. Brian Aucker, "A Prophet in King's Clothes: Kingly and Divine Re-Presentation
in 2 Kings 4 and 5," in *Reflection and Refraction: Studies in Biblical Historiography in Honour of A.
Graeme Auld*, ed. Robert Rezetko, Timothy H. Lim and W. Brian Aucker, VTS 113 [Leiden: Brill,
2007], p. 17).

with you when the man turned from his chariot to meet you? Is this the time to take silver and to take clothes, oliveyards, vineyards, sheep, oxen, and male and female servants? Naaman's skin disease will cling to you and your descendants forever." He went out from his presence a leper as white as snow. (2 Kings 5:25-27)

Elisha's summary statement has the clarity of crystal in defining the prophetic lifestyle: accumulation of silver and property is an obstacle to all that a prophet stands for. It may be acceptable for other Israelites to whom God has given the land as an inheritance, but not for prophets. It is not a mild offense to accept such payment, for the consequences could hardly be more disastrous for the prophet's servant who tried to live in both worlds. His leprosy now separates him permanently from both the prophetic community and the community of his fellow Israelites.

The indictment of the prophet Micah reverberates in the light of this story when he observes that "her [i.e., Israel's] leaders pronounce judgment for a bribe, her priests instruct for a price and her prophets divine for silver" (Mic 3:11).[9] When Nehemiah writes of opposition to his governorship and his projects in the fifth century B.C., the opposition is fueled by a prophet "hired" by his political enemies (Neh 6:12-14), although it is not specifically stated what form the bribe took. Compromising an oracle on the basis of any expected reward undermines the entire prophetic enterprise. It is precisely hard cash that is the least compatible with the prophetic lifestyle, even though Micah's contemporaries find this a preferred method of payment. Legitimate prophets who were not in the business for personal profit could be identified as those who, like Elisha, turned down payments that were extravagant and not in the form of food. As one prophet replied to King Jeroboam's offer of a "gift" (1 Kings 13:7):

If you would give me half of your estate, I would not go with you, nor would I eat bread or drink water in this place. (1 Kings 13:8)

For this reason, it is not difficult to anticipate the conclusion of a story about Elisha when Hazael brings a gift of "all the best of Damascus, a load

---

[9]It is not clear that Zech 11:12 refers to payment for a prophetic oracle, but Carol L. Meyers and Eric M. Meyers, *Zechariah 9-14* (Garden City, N.Y.: Doubleday, 1993), make a case for it, specifically as something that "probably reflects ongoing tension between true and false prophecy (p. 273).

of forty camels" (2 Kings 8:9). No mention is made about Elisha's response to this gift after he successfully provides Hazael with the information that he is after. Nevertheless, readers of the biblical text have come to expect that such a gift would be turned down.

The continuity of this practice exists long after evidence for Israelite prophets diminishes in the first millennium B.C. When prophetic activity becomes one of the distinguishing features of the early church, for example, the old standards for reimbursement are still in effect. The *Didache*, an early second century document that sets standards of conduct in many areas of early church life, is quite specific about this very matter:

> Concerning the apostles and prophets, do as follows according to the decree of the Good News: every apostle who comes to you is to be received as the Lord, but he will not remain beyond one day. If there is an exigency[10] an additional (day is permitted), but if he should stay three days, he is a false prophet. The apostle who goes out is to take nothing but bread until he reaches the night's lodging, and if he asks for money, he is a false prophet. (*Didache* 11.3-6).

This passage assumes a problem that needs attention, a problem demonstrable elsewhere in the Mediterranean world, as in Creon's outburst against the seer Tiresias in Sophocles' *Antigone:* "The entire prophetic breed are lovers of money!" (l.1055). The repeated details discussed above that surface in prophetic texts with respect to the maintenance of the prophet highlight the persistent problem that must have plagued Israelite society. The temptation to buy favorable prophetic oracles on the one hand was encouraged on the other hand by the temptation for a prophet to turn oracles into a money-making enterprise. The only antidotes for resisting the twin temptations would be the prophet's fidelity and commitment to his or her call from Yahweh, balanced with the ordinary Israelite's perception of prosperous prophets as an oxymoron, a contradiction in terms.

This feature of prophecy was an immovable bedrock that remained stable throughout the history of prophetic transformations.[11] One might

---

[10]E.g., travel on the Sabbath or injury, and see the Mishnah (*m. Pe'ah* 8.7) for similar concerns (Aaron Milavec, "Distinguishing True and False Prophets," *Journal of Early Christian Studies* 2 [1994]: 117-36).

[11]There are dissenters. Crenshaw (*Prophetic Conflict*, p. 56), for example, finds this criterion inad-

wonder why any one would bother to trust a wealthy prophet,[12] or pay a high price to buy a favorable oracle. After all, such a prophet could be in the oracle business for the money, a scam artist the likes of which plague every society. The psychology of those who patronize the high-priced and affluent prophets, however, is not difficult to unravel. If there is an individual who makes claims to access to the divine, a persistent human desire to manipulate the divine lures the gullible to hope to buy what cannot be bought. Every generation has its suckers for the easy sell, those who will pay for the self-delusion of good news when that is all they want to hear. The peripheral prophet who turns his back on prestige and possessions is not an attractive figure to the many who prefer appearances to substance, especially when he is blunt and abrasive in his lack of concern for the opinions of men.[13] Although such a prophet is clearly not in the oracle business for personal gain, most who speak words that are not welcome experience as their fate the disregard of their fellows.

## THE PROPHET AS BEARER OF BAD NEWS

In the light of the many transformations that characterize prophecy in the first millennium B.C., we have just seen one aspect of the prophetic lifestyle that remained a touchstone for identifying a prophet regardless of any features that might have changed over time. In fact, the prophetic

---

equate, but the two brief paragraphs he dedicates to a rebuttal are insufficient to make his case. He provides no evidence to support an internally contradictory claim that actually undermines his presentation, namely, that "while it may be true that the free charismatic prophet was *more faithful* to the Word of Yahweh, there is no reason to deny that *exceptional* cultic prophets achieved the same degree of freedom to declare the word of the Lord" (emphasis mine in order to underscore that he affirms a qualitative difference among such prophets). His denial of the relevance of 1 Kings 22 to the issue (where the "royal prophets acted in good faith") begs the question, for sincerity is not the issue. His dismissal of Amos's reply (Amos 7:12-17) as ambiguous and isolated— "the fact that one prophet . . . scorns institutionalism does not mean that this criterion may be applied to all prophets"—unfortunately overlooks the numerous references discussed here.

[12]It is hardly surprising that one can make a plausible, albeit not decisive, case that a prophet such as Isaiah came from the upper class (Rainer Albertz, *A History of Israelite Religion in the Old Testament Period. Volume One: From the Beginnings to the End of the Monarchy* [Louisville, Ky.: Westminster John Knox, 1994], pp. 163, 325). The point remains intact that, regardless of a prophet's background, there is no evidence that any reliable prophet used his office to elevate himself socially, or, already being in the upper class, exploited his prophetic status for personal gain.

[13]Albert Jay Nock's classic article, "Isaiah's Job," in *Free Speech and Plain Language* (New York: William Morrow, 1937), pp. 248-65, readily available on the Internet, encapsulates well the human condition that perennially results in this divide.

relinquishing of wealth and property singularly prepared prophets for the destructions that marred Israel's and Judah's histories in the eighth and sixth centuries. Those prophets who did not prioritize wealth and personal prosperity were not disoriented with the collapse of Israelite society. Not only did they anticipate the dissolution of society, they had been living apart from that society as a matter of course.

A second unchanging feature of prophecy that encouraged contemporaries to discern a reliable spokesperson for God was related to this prophetic disdain for personal wealth. As we noted at the close of the preceding discussion, an important attitude accompanied the refusal to accumulate wealth and the commitment to live on the gifts that God and man provided. The prophetic disdain for popular opinion gave the prophet the freedom to speak objectionable truths.[14] Since he was not an oracle dealer for his own benefit, it mattered little if he went unrewarded for speaking bitter truths. When the prophet Jeremiah spars verbally with the adversarial prophet Hananiah in Jeremiah 28, the single feature that Jeremiah finds disturbing about Hananiah's content is that it is good news that people would want to hear in contrast to Jeremiah's dismal forecast that echoes the messages of earlier prophets. In Jeremiah's words, "As for the prophet who prophesies peace, the prophet whom Yahweh has truly sent will be known when the word of the prophet comes to pass" (Jer 28:9). Jeremiah here posits a presumption that a prophet's words are supposed to be foreboding, for the claim is not that bad news needs to be confirmed by waiting. It is good news that is suspicious and needs to be waited out. Indeed, Jeremiah presumes bad news to be the typical burden

---

[14]One often hears that prophets "speak truth to power," but this is both a severe limitation on the prophetic task and hardly unique to the prophet. Prophets were supposed to simply speak the truth, regardless of its harshness or the audience, which could include the marginal (e.g., 1 Kings 17:8-16; 20:35-36; 2 Kings 8:1-2). Nor is one expected to be a prophet in order to speak the truth at all times. Indeed the only time that speaking the truth becomes virtuous is when any relatively social inferior speaks the truth to those with greater authority (e.g., Gen 38:25-26; 2 Sam 14:1-20; 2 Kings 5:3; Esther 8:3), but this does not make such a one a prophet. Since figures other than prophets "speak truth to power," this feature is not enough to identify a prophet. Claims that individuals such as Reinhold Niebuhr or Martin Luther King Jr. are prophets are defensible only as rhetorical flourishes that otherwise dilute the meaning of the world "prophet." In the Second Temple period when the definition of a prophet expanded beyond its original significance (Kugel 1990), at least a privileged access to supernatural knowledge continued to be a fundamental *sine qua non* (e.g., Lk 7:39; Jn 4:16-19).

of prophets from time immemorial, something hardly extraordinary but quite predictable: "As for the prophets of old who were before me and you, they prophesied war, calamity, and plague against many lands and great kingdoms" (Jer 28:8). According to Jeremiah, what requires special attention is the prophet who prophesies good news. Behind such a message always lurks the suspicion that the prophet is telling people only what they want to hear.

This principle is often employed in the Bible as a powerful sieve that is useful in separating reliable prophets from counterfeits.[15] In the Deuteronomistic history, for example, King Ahab finds the solitary dissenting voice of the prophet Micaiah an irritant that he prefers to ignore, claiming, "I hate him because he prophesies not good but evil about me" (1 Kings 22:8). In contrast to the four hundred prophets who are depicted as a chorus of echoes affirming what the king wants to hear—victory over Syria!—Micaiah's pronouncement of death to the king evokes Ahab's I-told-you-so response: "Didn't I tell you he prophesies not good but evil about me?" (1 Kings 22:18). Even a lower-level bureaucrat sent to summon Micaiah endorses the deceptive culture of cooperation when he advises Micaiah, "The prophets' words are uniformly positive for the king, so please let your word be like their unanimous message and speak favorably" (1 Kings 22:13). When Ahab dies of wounds received in the very battle in which he engages with the blessing of the four hundred, it appears that the prophet of doom has a purchase on reality denied to his more numerous crowd-pleasers.

There is an element of insightful psychology at work that can easily be overlooked by the myopic or the self-satisfied: be wary of advisors who tell you what you want to hear. There does not seem to be any substantial gain for one who relays bad news to someone hoping for a bright future. Delivering bad news instead may sour a relationship and bring little reward for the messenger. Micah observes that good news is predictable for the high-

---

[15]Prophets "characteristically perceive their time and place as a circumstance of crisis, a context in which dangers are great. . . . The prophets not only respond to crisis, but by their abrupt utterance, they generate crisis" (Brueggemann, *Theology of the Old Testament,* p. 624). So prominent is this feature that early literary-critical scholarship argued that the preexilic prophets could only have been prophets of judgment, a position that was first seriously challenged by H. Gressman who argued that there was no intrinsic contradiction between threat and promise.

bidder whom a prophet wants to please:

> Thus said Yahweh concerning the prophets who cause my people to stray, who bite with their teeth and cry, "Peace!" but who declare war against the one who puts nothing in their mouths. (Mic 3:5)

Oracles tailored to the audience is what the bona fide prophet of Yahweh is to avoid, and therefore if one hears bad news from such a prophet, the likelihood is that the prophet is making no profit in the words of God. The reasoning is that only a prophet with a genuine oracle would be stupid enough to make enemies unless he was under compulsion and accountable to a higher authority.

As a result, the refrain reverberates in more than one prophetic indictment against false prophets:

> They led my people astray by saying, "Peace!" but there is no peace. (Ezek 13:10)

> Saying, "Peace! Peace!" but there is no peace. (Jer 6:14; 8:11).

> The prophets are saying to them, "You will see no sword, nor will you have famine, for I will give you lasting peace in this place." (Jer 14:13; cf. Jer 14:15).

> Do not listen to the words of the prophets. . . . They continually say to those who despise me, "Yahweh said, 'You will have peace, . . . calamity will not come upon you.'" (Jer 23:16-17).

Ezekiel exploits word-pictures to wake his people up to what it means to give good news when the reality is otherwise. Because a prophet of good news can be like a building inspector who grants a permit to a house that is ready to collapse, Ezekiel elaborates the image of a run-down wall needing repair that is simply white-washed so that it looks good (Ezek 13:10-16). Such men do not have the best interests of their audience at heart, aiming for short-term gain—prestige, monetary support, notoriety, friendship—at the expense of inevitable long-term disaster, especially if an audience is not inclined to hear about the latter. The prophets of good news tapped into and mined a rich vein of human nature.

This pervasive and distinguishing feature of reliable Yahwistic prophets as bearers of bad news may partially explain resistance to the prophetic call from God that surfaces in some prophetic call narratives. When God commissions Jeremiah (Jer 1:4-9) and Moses (Ex 3:11, 13; 4:1, 10, 13), for example, each offers distinctive but transparent excuses, hoping to avoid the task thrust upon them. It is no surprise that Isaiah responds, "How long?" when God informs him in his commissioning,

> Go and say to this people, "Listen attentively but do not understand, look long and hard but do not comprehend." Fatten this people's heart, make their ears heavy, and paste over their eyes, lest they see with their eyes and hear with their ears, and their heart understand and repent and be healed. (Is 6:9-10)

Because the prophet's burden was essentially that of the doctor before a sick patient, by definition the genuine prophet was one who brought the bad news, diagnosing what is wrong. In his encounter with Hananiah, Jeremiah touched upon an essential component of prophecy that remained unchanged by the very nature of human society that is always in need of correction.

It might be tempting to affirm that "Jeremiah maintains that the prophet of disaster is the normal prophet who needs no further credentials."[16] But Jeremiah does indicate elsewhere that there are other requirements for a genuine prophet of Yahweh: for example, Jeremiah's insistence that the prophet be one who has stood in the divine council (see the earlier discussion in chapter two). This criterion, as with other criteria that we are looking at, cannot stand alone as an ultimate and singular test of a legitimate prophet. After all, even the prophets who most object to cries of "Peace!" are the same prophets who do envision peace someday for God's people:

> And I will make with them a covenant of peace. (Ezek 34:25; cf. Ezek 34:26)

> Behold, I will bring it health and healing, and I will heal them, and I will reveal to them abundance of peace and stability. (Jer 33:6)

> "In this place I will give peace," said Yahweh of hosts. (Hag 2:9)

---

[16]Mowinckel, "The 'Spirit' and the 'Word,'" p. 222.

> How beautiful upon the mountains are the feet of the one who brings good news, who proclaims peace, who brings excellent news, who proclaims salvation, who says to Zion, "Your God reigns!" (Is 52:7)

> "Peace, peace, to one who is distant and to one who is near," said Yahweh, "and I will heal him." (Is 57:19)

In general such texts are explicable as the relaying of good news that can come only after God has dealt with the very real and present sin problem, a sign of hope for those who must endure the pruning before the vine can be fruitful again. In all of these, the prophet affirms an intervening judgment as the prelude, the good news that makes the bad news palatable, the good news of health that a physician can hold out to the sick patient who will take his medicine.[17]

The prophet Haggai is a classic example of good news coming appropriately from a prophet of Yahweh. This postexilic prophet seems to be unusually encouraging to a devastated community, for he speaks of how God is supporting the leaders of the community:

> "I am with you," declares Yahweh. (Hag 1:13; cf. Hag 2:4)

> "Be strong, Zerubbabel," declares Yahweh, "be strong also, Joshua son of Jehozadak, the high priest, and all you people of the land be strong." (Hag 2:4)

> "From this day on I will bless." (Hag 2:19)

This exuberant optimism would seem at first glance to catapult Haggai into the category of the misleading prophets noted above who proclaim peace when there is no peace. But Haggai's words of hope are grounded in a brutal analysis of the community's misplaced priorities. The Jews who survived the Babylonian destruction and exile had with self-absorption pushed God to the margins of their lives. Haggai verbally scourges them for their warped priorities:

> "Is it time for you yourselves to live in your paneled houses while this temple is desolate? . . . You sowed much but harvested little, you eat without

---

[17]This is the same significance that the word "gospel" (literally "good news") carries in the New Testament, for the gospel is good news only for those who have recognized and dealt with the bad news of the sin problem.

satiety. . . . Consider your ways! . . . You anticipate much but it comes to little, and I blow it away when you bring it home. Why?" declares Yahweh of hosts. "Because of my temple which is desolate, while each of you runs to his own house. Therefore, because of you the sky has withheld the dew and the earth has withheld its produce." (Hag 1:4, 6-7, 9-10)

Haggai is no crowd-pleaser. These words require but one acceptable response from his audience: an admission that they were wrong. Haggai's trenchant criticism expects a change of behavior, an admission that present habits are destructive and repentance for selfish choices. This message is neither an easy one to deliver nor an easy one to hear. As with all the literary prophets in the Bible, the bad news has to come first before any hope of God's blessing can be offered.[18]

In many ways, then, misleading prophets were those who behaved like cheerleaders on the sidelines of a game, shouting to the team that they are great, that they can win, that no matter how many points they are behind they are still number one. The prophets to whom one should pay heed, however, are more like coaches on the sidelines who single out players who are not doing their job, who point out mistakes so that they are not repeated, who pull players out of the game when they are not doing their job. In a lament over the fall of Jerusalem, this very issue is pinpointed as an indictment of prophetic failure and a sign of abdication of duty: "Your prophets saw vain and foolish visions for you, and they did not expose your iniquity" (Lam 2:14). Where the cheerleading prophets delude the team into a false hope for victory based on good feelings, the prophets who behave like coaches slap the players into a reality which, if dealt with properly, can lead to victory. This fundamental contrast remained an unshaken feature of prophecy throughout its transformations. In spite of the existence of prophets in Israel who lulled people into a stupor with feel-

---

[18]Horst Dietrich Preuss, *Old Testament Theology*, trans. Leo G. Perdue (Edinburgh: T & T Clark, 1992), 2:85, observed, "If the prophecy of salvation was or is principally false, then Deutero-Isaiah was for this reason also a false prophet." On the contrary, like Haggai, Israel's sin is very much in the forefront with a repeated insistence on a minimum level of conduct that must be maintained for the good news to materialize (cf. Is 42:18-25; 43:22-28; 50:1-3). As Paul Ricoeur, *Figuring the Sacred: Religion, Narrative, and Imagination* (Minneapolis: Fortress, 1995), pp. 266-67, noted, "It is, at first, in a situation of distress that the prophet is called. . . . The prophet is the figure of crisis. . . . Next, his words . . . presuppose an instruction . . . that has been transgressed." Second Isaiah is unintelligible without the recognition of Israel's sin issues.

good messages that were easy to peddle, never were the reliable prophets ever seen as an institution whose task was to make God's people feel good just for the sake of maintaining a positive attitude.

In conclusion, one should note that there are other contexts where reliable prophets render a tangible service on a regular basis to the community in meeting social needs. The good news that they provide in such contexts is easily explicable. Samuel, for example, can give good news to Saul that his father's lost donkeys have been found (1 Sam 9:20). Naaman can receive good news that he can be healed of his leprosy (2 Kings 5:10). A hapless builder who has lost a neighbor's ax can hear the good news that it is retrievable from the water in which it sank (2 Kings 6:5-7). In all these and similar cases, a member of the community comes to the prophet for guidance and the prophet provides the service of providing a supernatural perspective otherwise unavailable to ordinary folk. There is no presumption of whether the news will be good or bad in such cases of solicited information. Here the question is simply can the prophet see the solution to the problem. In contrast, when the prophet comes unsolicited to the king, to a priest, to Israel's leader, and to the wealthy, the presumption is that the prophet would not be making an unbidden appearance unless there was a problem. A prophet does not speak to give an approving pat on the back. When a prophet speaks unbidden, there is a problem that needs to be addressed. This is the context of the bad news that characterizes the literary prophets who have no choice:

> As often as I speak, I cry out! I cry, "Violence and destruction!" For the word of Yahweh has turned into reproach and derision for me all day long. I said, "I will neither remember him nor speak any more in his name," but in my heart it became like a burning fire, smothered within my bones, and I grew weary holding it in, and could not endure. (Jer 20:8-9)

The prophet does not enjoy conveying his message, but he has no choice when the one who commissions him is God. As Aldous Huxley ironically observed, "The most distressing thing that can happen to a prophet is to be proved wrong; the next most distressing thing is to be proved right."[19]

---

[19]With this sentence he opens his essay "Brave New World Revisited" (1956), an analysis of his own insightful vision of humanity's dystopic future twenty-five years earlier in *Brave New World* (1932).

## Minority Status

Up to this point, we have seen that the changing face of prophecy during the first millennium B.C. did not extend to the lifestyle of the prophets, nor did it affect their essential message that good news can only come once the bad news has been addressed. A third non-negotiable dimension of prophecy that seems to have remained stable and permitted contemporaries to discern a prophet who was not a con artist was the tendency for prophets to represent a minority voice. When four hundred prophets of Yahweh in 1 Kings 22, for example, give King Ahab the thumbs-up sign for a battle looming on the horizon, a disagreeable dissent from a single voice may strike the reader as a minor irritant. This is particularly true in a twenty-first-century democratic context where the will of the majority is idealized as the sanest way to resolve political quarrels. But one of the lessons of the histories of democracies, from Athens to the present, is that the will of the majority is quite frequently wrong, selfish, short-sighted and self-destructive. Mobs are notoriously mindless and the will of the majority is often oppressive, facts that prompted the founders of the American Republic to seek ways to protect the rights of political minorities who are often right. And when King Ahab followed the advice of the four hundred and disregarded the solitary dissenter, he fell into the easy trap that lures victims with the comfort of numbers. Nowhere in biblical literature is ethical behavior determined by a show of hands.

Quite the contrary, biblical texts repeatedly emphasize that the minority, often identified as "the remnant," tends to be in the right more frequently than the majority. Humanity typically behaves like wayward sheep: "All of us have wandered like sheep, each has turned to his own way" (Is 53:6), echoing Micaiah's solitary voice observing to the overwhelming majority of the four hundred noted above, "I saw all Israel scattered on the mountains like sheep that have no shepherd" (1 Kings 22:17). When twelve spies reconnoiter the land that God wants to give to Israel, only two endorse God's perspective while the Israelites resoundingly accept the more shortsighted verdict of the ten (Num 13–14). Disaster results when the minority report is discarded. The legal texts of the Torah warn of this reality: "You must not be led into wrongdoing by the majority, nor, when you give evidence in a lawsuit, should you side with the majority to pervert justice" (Ex 23:2 REB). The psalmists typically perceive themselves as overwhelmed by crowds of opposition: "Yahweh, how my opponents have increased! Many are those who rise up against me" (Ps 3:1 [2]).[20] It is Noah alone among all humanity who is righteous and able to survive the Deluge with his family (Gen 6:5-8), just as Lot with his family are the only righteous ones to be delivered from Sodom (Gen 18–19). Such precedents provide the evidence to back up Jesus' assertion that "the gate is wide and the way is broad that leads to destruction, and many are those who enter by it, for the gate is small and the way is narrow that leads to life, and few are those who find it" (Mt 7:13-14).

The prophets repeatedly play out this message so persistently that it is easy to generalize that a reliable prophet of Yahweh is likely to represent a minority voice. An echo of Micaiah's experience above appears when Elijah on Mt. Carmel delineates to the gathered crowd the difference between himself and his opponents: "I alone am left a prophet of Yahweh, but Baal's prophets are 450 men" (1 Kings 18:22). This oppositional stance of one against many becomes a badge that Elijah here sports with honor. Even earlier when Israel wanted to experiment with a king, the narrative presents the prophet Samuel as the sole dissenter who elaborates accurately what will happen when the people get what they want. The majority vote, however, overrides the solitary prophet, for "the people refused to listen to Samuel's voice, and they said, 'No, but there shall be a king over us'" (1 Sam 8:19). The book of Jonah presents the reluctant prophet as the only voice of rebuke against the excessively sprawling urban population of the condemned city of Nineveh, which in this case listens to Jonah's message unlike Israel's callous response to Samuel (Jon 3:3-10).

The literary prophet Micah gives voice to the prophet's awareness of his isolation when he groans,

> Woe is me! For I am like those who gather the summer fruit and pick the grapes: there is not a cluster to eat, or a first-ripe fig that I look for. The godly person has perished from the land, and there is none upright among men. (Mic 7:1-2)

---

[20]Cf. also Ps 22:12 [13]; 25:19; 56:2 [3]; 119:157. Jeremiah's frequent resonances with the Psalter are reflected in this matter, for an identical phrase reappears in both Ps 31:13 [14] and Jer 20:10: "For I have heard the whispering of many, terror on every side."

But it is Jeremiah who provides the most extended account in the literary prophets of one who, with few or no allies,[21] repeatedly stands opposed to far more numerous prophets. In Jeremiah 26 he is on trial for his life because of the message of doom that he publicly and indiscriminately proclaims to all. In the light of this principle of the minority voice, it should be no surprise that the prophets (plural) along with the priests are the ones who clamor for the death penalty (Jer 26:11) in contrast to the general populace, bureaucrats and elders who defend him (Jer 26:16-17). But elsewhere, Jeremiah notes how the crowd can be expected to follow most of the misleading prophets: "The prophets prophesy falsely, and the priests rule on their own authority, and my people love it so" (Jer 5:31). An inescapable leitmotif of the book of Jeremiah is that the prophets as a whole proclaim a distinctly different message from Jeremiah and are lumped together as a group that is disturbingly misguided:

The prophets are wind, and the word is not in them. (Jer 5:13)

Yahweh said to me, "The prophets prophesy lies in my name." (Jer 14:14)

My heart within me is broken because of the prophets. (Jer 23:9)

Do not listen to the words of the prophets who prophesy to you. (Jer 23:16)

I did not send the prophets, but they ran; I did not speak to them but they prophesied. (Jer 23:21)

I heard what the prophets said who prophesy falsely in my name. (Jer 23:25)

I am against the prophets, declares Yahweh. (Jer 23:30)[22]

The fact the Jeremiah feels comfortable in branding all the prophets as a group opposed to his message has prompted some to suggest that Jeremiah so emphatically distances himself from them that it is not even ap-

---

[21]Cf. individuals who save Jeremiah's life when in jeopardy from powerful foes, such as Ebed-melech (Jer 38:7-13) and Ahikam (Jer 26:24).

[22]The prophets who prophecy peace, no submission to Babylon, and the return of exiles are most notably grouped together as opponents of Jeremiah and Yahweh's plan (cf. Jer 14:13, 15; 27:9, 14, 16; cf. Mic 3:5).

propriate to call Jeremiah a prophet.[23] This is going too far, for not only is Jeremiah repeatedly identified as a prophet in narrative portions of the book that bears his name, there is also no alternative designation that is presented for him in the text. As it is quite understandable for a politician to berate politicians and a lawyer to condemn lawyers, so a prophet can castigate his fellows. The point is clear, nevertheless, that Jeremiah stands essentially alone against the majority of prophets. Other prophetic books to a lesser degree also echo this theme:

> The sun will go down on the prophets, and the day will be dark over them. (Mic 3:6)

> Yahweh poured over you a spirit of deep sleep, and closed your eyes, the prophets. (Is 29:10)

> Her [i.e., Jerusalem's] prophets are reckless, treacherous men. (Zeph 3:4)

> O Israel, your prophets are like foxes among the ruins. (Ezek 13:4)

> There is a conspiracy of her prophets within her, like a roaring lion tearing the prey. They devoured lives, they took treasure and valuables, they have made many widows within her. (Ezek 22:25)

Even a poetic lament over Jerusalem's fall preserved in the book of Lamentations takes this same view that a mass of prophets betrayed Jerusalem to her doom: "Your prophets saw false and foolish visions for you, and they did not expose your iniquity, to turn away your captivity, but they envisioned for you false and misleading oracles" (Lam 2:14).

Such prophets are given the rubric "false prophets" in the New Testament.[24] It is not surprising that there are so many when substantial financial remuneration is a reward and when the message is a popular one that appeals to a broad audience. But these prophets have pushed the profile of prophet so far that it breaks. They may still bear the title "prophet," but there is a qualitative difference. Those prophets easily proliferate who make a good living from their status as prophets, often because they tell people

---

[23]E.g., Bruce Vawter, "Were the Prophets *nābî*'s?" *Biblica* 66 (1985): 206-20, and Graeme Auld, "Word of God and Word of Man: Prophets and Canon," in *Ascribe to the Lord: Biblical and Other Studies in Memory of Peter C. Craigie*, ed. Lyle Eslinger and Glen Taylor, JSOTSS 67 (Sheffield: JSOT Press, 1988), pp. 237-51.

[24]Mt 7:15; 24:11, 24; Lk 6:26; Acts 13:6; 2 Pet 2:1; 1 Jn 4:1; Rev 16:13; 19:20; 20:10.

agreeable messages from God. But the very nature of prophecy is compromised by such individuals. Is this a new development? Hardly. Indeed, it is one of the characteristic features of prophecy that alongside the many who exploit prophetic status for personal gain there will subsist the few with a painful message of correction that will not be easy to communicate. Both can be called "prophet," but only one bears the epithet with justification, spanning all the transformations that prophecy experienced.

The disruptive minority status of many prophets such as Jeremiah often resulted in their persecution, resulting over time in a stereotypical perception that trustworthy prophets tend to be persecuted: "The characteristic fate of the prophets . . . is to be killed."[25] The seeds for this perception are planted early, for already the first literary prophet experiences the determined opposition and rebuke of those in control. The priest supervising the Bethel sanctuary orders Amos to leave the country as well as the sanctuary, claiming "it is a royal sanctuary and a dynastic temple" (Amos 7:13). God tells Ezekiel not to fear when he is rebuffed by his audience, warning him to expect an encounter with them that will be as pleasant as sitting among thistles, thorns and scorpions (Ezek 2:6). Ezekiel knows like Isaiah (Is 6:9-10) that he will not be successful in persuading the people, and for that reason God makes his "face as hard as their faces" and his "forehead as hard as their foreheads" (Ezek 3:7-9). Two irreconcilable worldviews will collide and the prophet will take the onslaught. Jeremiah's ex-

---

[25]Brueggemann, *Theology of the Old Testament*, p. 632; cf. Crenshaw, *Prophetic Conflict*, pp. 94-95. E.g., "They killed your prophets who admonished them" (Neh 9:26); "Which one of the prophets did your fathers not persecute" (Acts 7:52); "Thus they persecuted the prophets who were before you" (Mt 5:12); "You are sons of the ones who killed the prophets" (Mt 23:31); "Jerusalem who kills the prophets" (Mt 23:37); "As an example of suffering and patience take the prophets who spoke in the name of the Lord" (Jas 5:10). Although the Bible does not record many deaths of prophets, several are mentioned who do die because of persecution (1 Kings 18:4, 13; 2 Chron 24:20-22; Jer 26:20-23; cf. the threat in 1 Kings 19:1-2), to be supplemented with later traditions recording the martyrdoms of Isaiah, Jeremiah, Ezekiel, Micah, Amos and others recorded in works such *The Lives of the Prophets* (Hare, "Lives of the Prophets") and the *Ascension of Isaiah* (cf. J. Rendel Harris, *The Rest of the Words of Baruch: A Christian Apocalypse of the Year 136 A.D.* (London: C. J. Clay & Sons, 1889), pp. 23-24, for Jeremiah's demise). J. J. M. Roberts, "Prophets and Kings: A New Look at the Royal Persecution of Prophets against Its Near Eastern Background," in *A God So Near: Essays on Old Testament Theology in Honor of Patrick D. Miller*, ed. Brent A. Strawn and Nancy R. Bowen (Winona Lake, Ind.: Eisenbrauns, 2003), pp. 341-54, explores the broader context of this phenomenon in the ancient Near East. The persecuted prophet is never presented as necessarily reliable, for the legitimacy of killing false prophets is embedded in multiple traditions (Deut 13:5; 1 Kings 18:40; 2 Kings 10:18-28).

perience is similar when God forewarns him that his experience will resemble an armed conflict with his own people:

> As for me, I hereby transform you into a fortified city, an iron pillar and walls of bronze against the entire land, against kings of Judah, against its princes, against its priests and against the people of the land. They will wage war against you but will not succeed against you, because I am with you. (Jer 1:18-19; cf. Jer 15:20)

God's promised presence makes sense precisely because of the minority status of the prophet who would otherwise be overwhelmed by the resistance he encounters.

It should be underscored again that none of these enduring features of prophecy that we are addressing can stand alone as an isolated criterion to determine if any given prophet stands in a long tradition and consequently represents a reliable resource for ancient Israelites. Simply because a prophet is poor and depends upon God for his daily bread does not mean in and of itself that anything he has to say is venerable. Bringing stinging words of criticism does not by itself exonerate a prophet. One can conceive of conditions where these behaviors could be facades exploited by charlatans. As with these other criteria for sifting prophets, the common prophetic stance of standing alone against a sizable opposition is likewise not always helpful as an infallible guide to discriminating between prophets. This principle does not guarantee that all minority positions taken by prophets are legitimate, nor does it indicate that every majority decision that sides with a prophet is wrongheaded. This principle would render the prophet Haggai suspect, for example, for he was able to persuade the majority—the governor, priests, bureaucrats and the people in general—to mobilize and finish building the temple without any recorded opposition (Hag 1:12-14).[26] As a general principle, however, there is a marked tendency for trustworthy Yahwistic prophets

---

[26]One could supplement Haggai's example with that of Deborah who seems to have had a broad and favorable reception among the people, as did the exemplary figures Samuel and Moses. But even these cases prove the rule, for Moses is often pictured as a minority dissenting voice opposed to the Israelite mob's momentum (e.g., Ex 14:10-14; 16:2-12; 17:2-7; 32:19-29; Num 14:1-45), just as Samuel is memorable as the conscience of the people to which the people refuse to give heed (1 Sam 8:4-22).

to expect to be in a minority, tendencies that are equally true of the other themes discussed above.[27]

### DOES A PROPHET'S PREDICTION COME TO PASS?

We have observed so far three themes that remain stable throughout prophetic literature. Ancient Israelites were on firm ground if they listened to individuals who claimed to be prophets if such prophets refused to accumulate wealth as a function of their prophetic gift, if their message was critical and not a crowd-pleaser and if they were a minority voice. These themes repeat throughout biblical literature and are easily explicable as generally successful in unmasking individuals who donned the prophetic persona for motives different from those who spoke with the conviction that they were speaking the words of God.[28]

A fourth theme surfaces when we see the prophets making statements about future events and when we observe their ability to anticipate future realities with precision. This feature undergirds the Deuteronomistic history where repeatedly events are depicted as unfolding in accord with prophetic predictions. The prophet Jehu foretells the demise and complete eradication of King Baasha's dynasty (1 Kings 16:1-4), and when it comes to pass we are told that it happened "according to the word of Yahweh that he spoke against Baasha through Jehu the prophet" (1 Kings 16:12). Elijah predicts an extended drought that devastates the land, providing the context for several stories about Elijah (1 Kings 17:1). Micaiah accurately predicts King Ahab's demise in his next battle, affirming beforehand, "If you indeed return safely, Yahweh has not spoken by me" (1 Kings 22:28). Elijah correctly informs King Ahaziah that his physical injury will be fatal (2 Kings 1:16-17), in contrast to King Hezekiah's illness that Isaiah claims

---

[27]"I submit that the prophetic word of God is the unending, resilient minority insistence" (Walter Brueggemann, *Like Fire in the Bones: Listening for the Prophetic Word in Jeremiah* [Minneapolis: Fortress, 2006], p. 85). "The common focus of all these prophets [i.e., Israel's literary prophets] is that their messages did not agree with the messages expected by their targeted audiences" (Armin Lange, "Literary Prophecy and Oracle Collection: A Comparison Between Judah and Greece in Persian Times," in *Prophets, Prophecy, and Prophetic Texts in Second Temple Judaism*, ed. Michael H. Floyd and Robert D. Haak, LBH/OTS 427 [New York: T & T Clark, 2006], p. 256). The classic exposition of this principle is, again, Nock, "Isaiah's Job."

[28]Authenticating the experience behind such a conviction is, of course, impossible. For this conviction as a fundamental feature of the prophet see Heschel, *The Prophets*, pp. 206-26.

will not take his life (2 Kings 20:5). Elisha anticipates fluctuating commodity prices despite all indicators to the contrary (2 Kings 7:1-2, 16). Jonah's oracle that the territory of Israel would expand is connected with Jeroboam's northern exploits (2 Kings 14:25). Observers confirm that they are witnesses to events that had long before been predicted by a prophet (2 Kings 9:36; 23:17). The writer is impressed that a prophetic oracle anticipating a longevity of four generations for Jehu's dynasty literally unfolds when the fourth successor is assassinated: "This is Yahweh's word that he spoke to Jehu, saying, 'Your sons to the fourth generation will sit on the throne of Israel,' and so it was" (2 Kings 15:12). These instances, and many more in the Dtr history, endorse the undisputed recognition that prophecy and fulfillment is part of the backbone of this extended work.[29]

The literary prophets consistently take a similar stance. Their entire orientation is toward the future consequences of present behavior, and they regularly describe the future for their audiences. Habakkuk, for example, anticipates that conditions in preexilic Judah will deteriorate, and Yahweh's word is:

> The vision is yet for the appointed time. It hastens toward the end, and it will not deceive. Should it be slow, wait for it, for it will certainly come. It will not delay. (Hab 2:3)

Unlike the Dtr history that presents the big picture of prophecy along with its fulfillment, the literary prophets are characteristically written from the standpoint of anticipation, without including the fulfillment. Habakkuk's contemporary, Zephaniah, takes a similar perspective in his uncompromising depiction of the judgment of God that is to come to a recalcitrant Judah:

> Yahweh's great day is near, near and quickly coming. The sound of Yahweh's day is bitter, the warrior cries out. That day is a day of wrath, a day of trouble and distress, a day of destruction and desolation, a day of darkness and gloom, a day of clouds and deep darkness, a day of trumpet and battle cry against fortified cities and high corner towers. (Zeph 1:14-16)

---

[29]Similar passages appear in 1 Kings 14:7-18; 20:13-21, 28-29; 2 Kings 3:16-20; 4:16-17; 8:1-3. For a survey of the fulfillment notations in Joshua through 2 Kings, see Campbell, *Of Prophets and Kings*.

Every literary prophet makes specific observations about the future that are related to present behavior, observations that can be tested as to their veracity when events unfold.[30]

It is crucial to underscore this aspect of prophecy, for there has been in the past century an unfortunate emphasis upon the prophet as primarily a "forthteller" (i.e., a preacher) with a concomitant minimizing of the prophet as "foreteller" (i.e., one who makes predictions about the future). Such a recalibration of emphasis has more to do with a post-Enlightenment humanistic vision than with the biblical data. Many might like to see the prophets as social reformers, but the simple fact is that they were not.[31] One of the core elements of prophets was their supernatural access to knowledge that other humans did not have, knowledge that by definition would encompass knowledge of the future. As God told Ezekiel with respect to his prognostications about the future, "When it comes to pass, and it will come, they will know that a prophet was among them" (Ezek 33:33). How did Israel know that Samuel was a prophet? God vindicated all Samuel's revelations, or in the words of 1 Samuel 3:19-20, "Yahweh . . . let none of his [i.e., Samuel's] words fall to the ground, and all Israel knew from Dan to Beersheba that Samuel was confirmed as a prophet for Yahweh."[32] A prophet who did not have reliable knowledge beyond what other humans had, especially about the future, was simply not a prophet no matter how great an orator he might be. The prophet was a foreteller.[33]

This aspect of prophecy presents a deceptive simplicity when viewed in retrospect. When a prophet's vision of the future was first articulated to his fellow Israelites, however, on what basis would an audience be able to adjudicate the likelihood that it was a trustworthy vision? How should one react when a prophet approached with the advice, "Arise and go, you and your household, and take up temporary residence wherever you can, for Yahweh has called for a famine, and it will even last seven years in the

---

[30]A sampling: Is 20:1-6; Jer 24:1-10; Ezek 24:1-7; Hos 8:13-14; Joel 2:11-20; Amos 3:11-4:3; Obad 6-9; Mic 2:3-4; Nahum 3:1-7; Hag 2:14-19; Zech 1:3-6; Mal 2:1-4.

[31]Grabbe, *Priests, Prophets, Diviners, Sages*, pp. 99-107.

[32]For the image of "words not falling" to indicate complete vindication of one's statements, cf. 1 Kings 8:56.

[33]See Grabbe, *Priests, Prophets, Diviners, Sages*, p. 104; Rowley, "The Nature of Prophecy," pp. 35-36. Note the poetic parallelism of Ps 74:9, and cf. Jn 4:17-19.

land"? Was this fellow who offered this order crazy? What if he is wrong? On what basis did one decide to listen to such advice? It is not enough to say that since this advice came from Elisha to a widow in 2 Kings 8:1 it must be heeded, for we are looking with the luxury of hindsight. How did one know at that time that Elisha was reliable, particularly if this was one's first exposure to Elisha? If one decided to wait for the famine to come to see if Elisha was right, this postponement would have branded the decision as one of distrust.

The classic standoff between two opposing prophets, Jeremiah and Hananiah, frames this problem well in Jeremiah 28. Hananiah presents the marvelous news that within two years Babylon will be defeated and Judah's exiles will return along with the plundered temple treasures. Jeremiah retorts, however, that on the contrary Babylon's oppressive presence will endure. We observed above that the very nature of Hananiah's attractive message, good news that people in Judah would want to hear, makes it suspect. But if one is relying exclusively upon a prophet's ability to anticipate the future accurately, how will that criterion assist an individual in the audience to decide which of the two men is to be trusted? One does not have the luxury of waiting two years to see if Hananiah's vision unfolds as he predicted. Decisions have to be made immediately by the king and his counselors with respect to foreign alliances, military preparations and the conduct of the kingdom. History showed that Hananiah was wrong, but his audience did not yet know that. In this impasse between the two prophets, Jeremiah provides no alternative but to wait and see. Jeremiah simply suggested the following consideration: "As for the prophet who prophesies peace, the prophet whom Yahweh has truly sent will be known when the word of the prophet comes to pass" (Jer 28:9). Wait and see.

Perhaps the single greatest problem with this criterion is that it provides no help in the crisis that is being debated. If one has to wait until the crisis is resolved, the criterion is unhelpful for the present problem. Postponing a decision about a prophet's veracity is not an option in matters of life and death. Jeremiah and Hananiah disagreed over the issue of surrendering to the Babylonians or continuing to rebel. Since the revolt had already started, to simply wait would be to continue to revolt, following the counsel of Hananiah. A failure to make a decision prompts a default decision. Any decision to wait and see typically favors one side of a disagreement. To wait and see who is right is actually the abdication of responsibility.

Since this criterion for identifying a trustworthy prophet is initially problematic, it is possible that Jeremiah does not intend his words to be taken in this fashion, as some sort of broadly applicable criterion for discovering prophets that can be trusted. His words are more likely intended to express a conviction that is best summarized by the skeptic's common response, "I'll believe it when I see it." In other words, although Jeremiah would vastly prefer a peaceful resolution to Jerusalem's woes, he knows that Jerusalem has earned God's judgment. For this reason, he does not provide a general truism about how to tell the difference between reliable and unreliable prophets. Rather, he skeptically addresses only those prophets who prophesy about peace: "As for the prophet who prophesies peace, the prophet whom Yahweh has truly sent will be known when the word of the prophet comes to pass" (Jer 28:9). In other words, I will believe Hananiah's prophesy of peace only when I see it happen. Of course, his skepticism was later remedied when Jeremiah received a clear oracle from Yahweh that Hananiah was wrong (Jer 28:12-16).

One reason for understanding Jeremiah's words in this fashion is the fact that other biblical texts affirm an awareness that misleading prophets can make accurate forecasts. It would make no sense for Jeremiah to propose that a single fulfilled prophecy qualifies its speaker as a trustworthy prophet if elsewhere this very principle is denied. In the book of Deuteronomy, which shares so many common themes and emphases with the book of Jeremiah, prophetic prescience is highlighted as an inadequate indicator of a true prophet:

> If a prophet or a dreamer of dreams arises among you and gives you a sign
> or a wonder, and the sign or the wonder comes to pass, about which he
> spoke to you, saying, "Let us go after other gods that you have not known,
> and let us serve them," you shall not listen to the words of that prophet or
> that dreamer of dreams. (Deut 13:1-2 [2-3])

A moment's reflection will be sufficient to recall the old truism that even a broken clock reflects the correct time twice a day. It is not impressive if self-indulgent prophets can produce a prognostication that comes to pass, for the law of averages affirms that the luck of the draw will periodically favor even the most inept of fortunetellers. In light of the perspective of Deuteronomy 13, then, Jeremiah is not so much providing a criterion for discerning a reliable prophet as he is posing his own skepticism. To paraphrase Jeremiah: "When it comes to forecasts of peace, although it's hard for me to believe Yahweh would do such a thing counter to all prior prophets, if it happens I will concede that Yahweh is behind it."

The book of Deuteronomy is particularly attuned to the problem of discerning between competing prophetic visions about the future, for another passage addresses with great precision the issue of prophecies coming true, but from a significantly different viewpoint:

> If you say in your heart, "How will we know the word that Yahweh has not spoken?" The word that the prophet speaks in the name of Yahweh that does not happen and does not come to pass, that is the word that Yahweh has not spoken. The prophet has spoken it presumptuously. Do not fear it.[34] (Deut 18:21-22)

This test for a prophet is less helpful than it might appear at first glance, and it differs notably from Jeremiah's statement. Of first importance is the fact that it is emphatically not a criterion for identifying prophets who are to be heeded. The text only weeds out some—not all—who are charlatans. The question asked is not, "How shall we know the word which Yahweh *has* spoken?"[35] Instead it focuses on the "word which Yahweh has

---

[34]With NRSV (contrast most translations that read "him"). Although in Deut 18:21-22 the noun "word" (Hebrew *dābār*) appears thrice and the noun "prophet" appears twice, all but this one of the five appearances of a third masculine singular pronoun refer unequivocally to "the word" and not the prophet. Since the question began with the query, "How will we know the word?" it is best to continue the emphatic reference of all other pronouns to the primary subject of the passage, namely the "word" and not the prophet.

[35]This is the question, for example, that is incorrectly posed in *Sifre* 178 in discussing this passage, and frequently repeated since (e.g., "In Deuteronomy 18, it says the way you can tell a true prophet is whether what the person says comes true" [Brueggemann, *Like Fire in the Bones*, p. 209]; "According to Deut 18:20 . . . a person is a true prophet whose announcement is fulfilled" [Preuss, *Old Testament Theology*, p. 85]). Once one sees this distinction, it is apparent that there is no dissonance between the standard proposed in this chapter and the standard proposed in Deut 13:1-6 as some maintain (e.g., Brueggemann, *Theology of the Old Testament*, p. 634). Similarly there is no dissonance between the criteria of non-fulfillment of woe oracles in Deut 18:21-22 ("Do not fear") and the explicit fulfillment of prosperity oracles in Jer 28:9.

*not* spoken." As Deuteronomy noted above (Deut 13:1-2), misleading prophets can make predictions that come to pass. Here we are told something entirely different and of only limited applicability: one has good reason to ignore the message of a prophet whose prediction for the future fails to materialize. Once again, however, waiting until after the fact does not solve the problem as to which prophet to heed in the interim.

Nor does this test address the problem of genuine prophets whose oracles do not come to pass because God has changed his mind. This issue was addressed in an earlier chapter (chap. 3) where we saw that individuals such as Isaiah, Nathan, Jonah and Ezekiel rank among prophets who are presented as making oracles about a future that does not unfold as they claim. This does not disqualify the prophet from ever again being trusted, for God makes it clear that he can rescind oracles of doom or blessing for a variety of reasons. If, for example, human behavior changes, God reserves the right to recall an oracle that was based on their former behavior:

> At one moment I might speak about a nation or a kingdom to pluck up and to break down and to destroy. Should that nation about which I have spoken turn from its evil, I will relent about the evil that I intended to do to it. At one moment I might speak about a nation or a kingdom to build and to plant. Should it do what is evil in my sight, without listening to my voice, I will relent about the good that I had said I would to it. (Jer 18:7-10)

Deuteronomy 18 does not disqualify genuine prophets simply because they make such announcements that God rescinds.

The limited applicability of Deuteronomy 18:21-22 is therefore apparent at every turn. It is helpful only after the fact, separates out only some of the charlatans, cannot be used to disqualify a legitimate prophet from making oracles that are later revised, and is applied specifically only to an isolated oracle of a specific prophet. The passage itself underscores the latter point by repetition:

> "How shall we know *the word (singular)* . . . ?" If *the word (singular)* does not come about, . . . that is *the word (singular)* which Yahweh has not spoken. The prophet has spoken *it (singular)* presumptuously. (Deut 18:21-22)

This focus upon the isolated prophetic oracle is what permits a legitimate prophet to avoid the opprobrium of being labeled a deceptive prophet when Yahweh's decrees change. One snowflake does not mean it is winter, and one failed prediction means no more than that the message that accompanies it can be ignored.

The problem can be ameliorated, then, if one couples a single statement about the future with an entire series of successful predictions. When this happens, biblical texts affirm the likelihood that the prophet in question is one who can be trusted. This is, of course, nothing more startling than common sense or received wisdom, and is observable outside the Bible. Indeed, the principle is found in other cultures in the ancient world. The aged Halitherses, for example, described in the Odyssey as "far beyond the men of his generation in understanding the meaning of birds and reading their portents" (2.158-159), addresses the men of Ithaca with a prediction of the future accompanied by a reminder that he is not a novice but has proven his ability in the past: "I who foretell this am not untried" (2.170). It seems that an inventory of successful, testable prognostications was behind the attribution of the title "prophet" to an individual. That is, one did not simply give oneself the title and have instant credibility. The biblical "sons of the prophets"[36] may have been just such a social mechanism by which gifted individuals could be screened in a communal context, much like a guild preserves its credibility by standing behind those individuals who have demonstrated their ability to those who best know.

Thus, when Deborah is introduced to the reader in the book of Judges, she is not only given the title "prophetess" (Judg 4:4), but she is further specified as someone who "used to sit under Deborah's palm tree, between Ramah and Bethel in the hill country of Ephraim, and the Israelites came up to her for judgment" (Judg 4:5). In other words, the community over time has a chance to observe publicly her performance in her role as prophetess. We have no idea by what standards the community evaluated her, but according to the book of Judges, she passed muster. Of course, many self-serving prophets also succeeded in passing community standards, and it is precisely this acceptance that frustrates the literary prophets in the Bible. In such cases, the community has been swindled with low expectations, duped by con artists, or self-deluded in seeing what they want to see.

---

[36]E.g., 2 Kings 2:3; 4:1, 38; 5:22; 6:1; 9:1.

When the community, however, can evaluate the prognostications of a prophet over an extended period of time, the problem presented by a single, isolated accurate or wrong forecast about the future recedes into the background. The young prodigy Samuel is evaluated on just such a scale when it is related that as he grew up, "Yahweh was with him and let none of his words fall to the ground, and all Israel knew from Dan to Beersheba that Samuel was confirmed as a prophet of Yahweh" (1 Sam 3:19-20). The colorful idiom that speaks of "words not falling to the ground" identifies promises, predictions or statements about the future that unfold as stated. For example, Solomon spoke of God fulfilling his promise to Israel where "not one word fell to the ground of all his good word which he spoke" (1 Kings 8:56), and King Jehu affirmed that all of Elijah's prophetic statements would come to pass: "There will fall to the earth nothing of Yahweh's word that Yahweh spoke about Ahab's house" (2 Kings 10:10). When this phrase is applied to Samuel's prophetic pronouncements, it is apparent that he already has such a backlog of identifiable successes even as a youth, verified statements that "all Israel" has been able to scrutinize in order to come to a conclusion that he is a prophet indeed. As Saul's servant later observes about Samuel in support of his reliability, "Everything he says certainly comes to pass" (1 Sam 9:6).

A helpful contrast between two prophets underscores the leverage that a portfolio of prophetic successes could provide a prophet. One of the stories of Elisha presents him early in his career when he is not yet known to all of the kings who have set out on a campaign and who need a prophet's advice. When a search is made for a prophet, "one of the Israelite king's servants answered and said, 'Elisha son of Shaphat is here, who poured water on Elijah's hands'" (2 Kings 3:11). The names of Elisha's biological father and his prophetic mentor are both needed to introduce him to royalty, much like recommendation letters in a resume, information that would be unnecessary if his credibility were already established by confirmed prophetic activity, of which the servant presents none. In contrast, another prophet, Micaiah, needs no introduction to the king of Israel simply because he has a long trail of prophecies that permits the king to profile him easily: "I hate him because he does not prophesy good about me, but evil" (1 Kings 22:8).

As with the other themes that we have discussed that pervaded the depiction of reliable prophets in biblical literature, it must be underscored that this theme of accurate foretelling is also insufficient on its own to identify a prophet who legitimately stands in the long tradition of Israelite prophecy. This awareness applies, of course, to the prophets of Yahweh that we have discussed earlier who had a history of successful prognostications but who at some point proclaimed publicly an oracle that Yahweh reversed. The community somehow had to integrate the failed prediction with the rest of the prophet's career. This caveat also applies to prophets who could be labeled deceptive prophets, such as the four hundred prophets of Yahweh who unanimously voiced approval of Ahab's campaign (1 Kings 22:6). These prophets were wrong when it came to giving advice about what turned out to be Ahab's last campaign. The narrative seems to assume that this group of prophets, like other sizable prophetic groups sustained by the palace (1 Kings 18:19, 22), could be a ready source for royal consultation, much like the well-documented astrologers and diviners in the Neo-Assyrian court of the seventh century B.C.[37] In order to exist, such groups must have met, or were perceived as meeting, whatever standards for success the community or their patrons implicitly or explicitly set. This group of four hundred is depicted as missing the mark. Would such failures be factored in when future consultations were considered? Was a degree of failure tolerated, a toleration that could vary from time to time and person to person? Could the prophets conjure up mitigating circumstances that compromised only temporarily their effectiveness? All of these are conceivable means by which a poor track record could be exonerated.

The two most common criteria that surface in the Bible by which prophets are identifiable are an ability to perform miracles and access to special knowledge beyond that of normal humans, especially knowledge about the future.[38] We discussed in chapter eleven the changing role that miracles played. There we concluded that the role of miracles in authenti-

---

[37]Thorough discussion of the material appears in Simo Parpola, *Letters from Assyrian Scholars to the Kings Esarhaddon and Ashurbanipal*, vol. 2, AOAT 5/2 (Neukirchen: Neukirchener-Vluyn, 1983), with texts available in Parpola, vol. 1 (1970), and Herman Hunger, *Astrological Reports to Assyrian Kings*, SAA 8 (Helsinki: Helsinki University Press, 1992).

[38]Both of these activities are said to provide grounds for observers to "know that there is a prophet" (2 Kings 5:8; Ezek 33:33).

cating prophets was presented as significant at certain times, but problematic and often equivocal. Likewise in this discussion about knowledge of the future, it is apparent that there are popular perceptions of a prophet's ability to peer into the future that are overstated when compared to the presentation of prophets in the Bible itself. Both criteria have their self-imposed limitations that are readily conceded by the texts themselves.

In conclusion, there is unanimity among the prophets that accurate visions of the future are essential for a prophet to be trusted. This feature never varied as an essential component of the prophetic office. Whenever the community is presented as accepting the credibility of a prophet based on prior performance, the implication is that this public accountability was seen as a useful standard for screening prophets, even though like all other criteria it was in itself inadequate. Thus, when Hananiah is described in the book of Jeremiah as "the prophet who was from Gibeon" (Jer 28:1) who gives oracles from Yahweh to Judaeans gathered in the temple precincts, the presumption is that, in the eyes of the community, he somehow has earned a hearing based upon a perceived reputation. He is, after all, called a prophet, and even the book of Jeremiah does not deny him this status. Jeremiah himself is willing to give him a hearing, even as Jeremiah walks away perplexed by, but not yet outright condemning, the oracle Hananiah gives (Jer 28:5-11). A later revelation to Jeremiah moves Jeremiah eventually to indict Hanaiah as one who "made this people trust in a lie" (Jer 28:15), and Jeremiah would as a result likely not find it objectionable to apply to Hananiah the epithet "false prophet." But since the people and opinion leaders of Jerusalem believed Hananiah and not Jeremiah, one of the influential factors that gave Hananiah his credibility was his already established status as a prophet, if not the message of good news that was tempting to believe.

SUMMARY

We close this chapter as we began with the observation that there is no single criterion by which an ancient Israelite could isolate prophets who might, or might not, be deserving of trust. Likewise, there is not even a cluster of criteria that together make the identification secure. Rather, as in all human endeavors, not only do those who are trustworthy often fail, but counterfeits and facades readily make their appearance when there is profit to be made, status to achieve, power to wield, influence to peddle, or prestige to flaunt.

It is therefore not an indictment of the prophetic phenomenon that it does not provide a means of separating out the charlatans. One does not immediately throw all one's money away simply because currency forgers often succeed in passing off their wares to the untrained eye. Nevertheless, a crisis in discernment does encourage the public to increased caution when the counterfeits become increasingly hard to detect and more widespread. We have discussed above emphatic guides that the Bible repeatedly returns to as marks of prophets who deserve a hearing: the means by which prophets were supported, the type of message they relayed, their reception by the community and their accuracy in predicting the future. These guides would be difficult to counterfeit, for in most cases their very nature undermined any gain that one might expect to achieve: poverty-level subsistence, a message that emphasized criticism and likely rejection.

It is true that one may not discard all one's currency immediately in the face of counterfeit money, but Gresham's Law has been repeatedly vindicated: bad money does characteristically drive good money out. It is possible that the diminishing profile of prophecy after the destruction of the temple in 586 B.C. was assisted by an increasing presence of misleading prophets in the heightened crisis at the beginning of the sixth century B.C., as witnessed by the prominence of prophets of peace who frustrate Jeremiah and Ezekiel in the books that bear their names.[39] Those who exploited prophecy for their own ends seemed to have flourished. Such prophets, whose messages of peace and vindication for Judah failed to materialize, may have profited in a variety of ways in the short term. In the long view, however, their failure to foresee Judah's fate added fuel to the ancient perception of prophets as those who spin out tales from their own imaginations (Jer 14:14; 23:16). In spite of this, and even as prophecy metamorphosed after the fall of Jerusalem, the guiding principles remained stable that helped ancient Israelites navigate the competing voices that claimed divine authorization.

---

[39]Jer 5:12-13; 6:13-15; 8:10-12; 14:13-15; 23:16-17; Ezek 13:10, 16.

# 16

# Summation

We began this study with a fourth-century Babylonian rabbi's attempt to explain a curious variation in the prophetic visions of Isaiah and Ezekiel. Isaiah's description of an encounter with God seemed merely allusive and laconic beside Ezekiel's detailed and finely brushed portrait, a contrast that Rabba compared to responses that one might expect from individuals coming from diverse social backgrounds. We come full circle now to recognize Rabba's great insight, for, as the preceding chapters demonstrate, there is a real divide between the recorded experiences of earlier prophets and those of later prophets.

A dramatic historical and social disjuncture separates Isaiah and Ezekiel. Isaiah lived in Judah during the days of the kingdom's independence when a king sat on the throne in close proximity to Yahweh's temple in Jerusalem. Ezekiel lived in Babylon as part of an enforced exile when Jerusalem and its temple were threatened and eventually destroyed. Is this social and historical diversity sufficient to account for the metamorphoses that prophecy exhibits? That is a speculative subject for another investigation, for discerning causes and effects with the minimal material that remains is a precarious undertaking. Regardless of the causes, the changes that took place in the presentation of the prophet's message are striking, and the contrasting historical contexts are inextricably linked as a part of these changes.

We have been able to go beyond that single contrast between Isaiah's and Ezekiel's vision of God. We have investigated a substantial number of features in Israelite prophecy that cumulatively affirm that what distinguishes Isaiah from Ezekiel in this one area is only a part of a much larger picture. The themes that we have investigated together demonstrate a gradual transformation of prophecy over time in a number of areas, vacillating features that encompass a broad spectrum of concerns. So many modifications appear over so broad a span of texts that nevertheless converge in pointing to the sixth century as the approximate time when most of these transformations took place.[1] If these texts had originated at one time and place, the striking divergences would be difficult to account for. There has certainly been minimal homogenizing, for distinctions have been allowed to stand. This is even more remarkable in the case of those prophetic texts where the contrast does not reflect favorably upon the prophet in question: when angels and not God speak to the prophet, when the prophet no longer finds himself in the comfortable dialogue of the divine council but in an increasingly austere relationship with God, when the prophet's insightful gaze is compromised to a hazy incomprehension, when the quality of the communication modulates to the prosaic, when miracles become a thing of the past.

This awareness of change that is not necessarily for the better is a feature of other biblical texts that have not been a part of this investigation. Texts from the Pentateuch, for example, place Moses on a pedestal that is shared by no other when he is contrasted with all subsequent prophets:

> If there is a prophet among you, I will make myself known to him in a vision, I will speak with him in a dream. It is not this way with my servant Moses. He is the most faithful in all my household. I speak with him mouth to mouth, even a vision, and not in riddles, and he looks upon the form of Yahweh. (Num 12:6-8)

---

[1]Modifications but marked continuities in the physical culture and literary productions of the period between the two temples in the sixth century B.C. and the earlier pre-exilic data form the thesis of Jill Middlemas's *The Templeless Age* (Louisville: Westminster-John Knox, 2007).

Moses' unparalleled encounter with Yahweh at Mt. Sinai (Ex 33:18–34:9) also endorses his eulogy: "No other prophet arose in Israel like Moses whom Yahweh knew face to face" (Deut 34:10). This affirmation that not all prophets are alike underscores that the best came first and that later generations do not measure up to the stature of their predecessors.

Other biblical texts speak of a dramatic diminution of the prophetic gift in the period after the exile. A postexilic psalmist who laments the destruction of the temple (Ps 74:3-8) also observes that "there is no prophet any more, nor is there anyone among us who knows how long" (Ps 74:9). An apparent eyewitness to the temple's demolition similarly mourns that Jerusalem's "prophets find no vision from Yahweh" (Lam 2:9). The Deuteronomistic history itself affirms a fluctuating availability of the gift of prophecy even during Israel's preexilic history, for at one point the comment is made, "Yahweh's word was rare in those days, there was no frequent vision" (1 Sam 3:1). The variability of prophecy over time thus appears as a fundamental fact that biblical texts make no effort to disguise. One hears in the book of Zechariah that individuals at some point will be reluctant to be identified as prophets:

> And it will be in that day . . . I will also remove the prophets and the unclean spirit from the land. And it will be that if someone should still prophesy, his father and mother who bore him will say to him, "You will not live because you spoke falsely in the name of Yahweh." When he prophesies, his father and mother who gave birth to him will stab him. It will be in that day that the prophets will each be ashamed of his vision when he prophesies, and they will not put on a hairy mantle in order to deceive, but he will say, "I am not a prophet. I am one who works the land." (Zech 13:2-5)

Indications from within the Bible that prophecy was in some sense declining as a prominent force in postexilic Israel is reinforced by later texts. The first to second century B.C. book of 1 Maccabees affirms that in the second century commonwealth, certain cultic decisions were deferred "until a prophet should arise to render a decision about them" (1 Macc 4:46; cf. 1 Macc 14:41), for long had been the "days when a prophet had not appeared to them" (1 Macc 9:27). Rabbinic tradition ratified this perspective in declaring that "since the days of the last prophets, Haggai,

Malachi and Zechariah, the Holy Spirit departed from Israel."[2] Because Judaism during the Persian period is such a sketchy subject with periodic incidental information available at best, analyzing the status of prophecy in the postexilic period is a complicated and speculative matter with a variety of defensible positions.[3] The material that we have looked at, however, identifies an unequivocal trajectory of decline that easily correlates with this tradition of the loss of prophecy. The gradual transitions that we have observed, transitions that accelerate in the sixth century B.C., therefore become an important element in discussing the status of prophecy in the postexilic period. It appears that prophecy had already in the century of the exile exhibited the seeds of what many witnesses testify to as its diminution and even disappearance. It remains remarkable that such a variety of texts from so many different individuals in so many distinct locales and times converge in a number of themes that unite in presenting a panorama of at least a part of the history of ancient Israelite prophecy.

---

[2]*b. Sanhedrin* 11a. This passage later insists that God still continued to reveal himself in another manner, specifically an echo *(bat qôl)* of a divine voice from heaven. According to *b. Bava Batra* 12a-b, some rabbis claimed that although prophecy was taken from the prophets when the temple was destroyed, it was still accessible to other individuals in Judaean society such as the wise, fools and children.

[3]For an introduction to a broad discussion, see Schniedewind, *Word of God in Transition*; Eric M. Meyers, "The Crisis of the Mid-Fifth Century B.C.E. Second Zechariah and the 'End' of Prophecy," in *Pomegranates and Golden Bells: Studies in Biblical, Jewish, and Near Eastern Ritual, Law, and Literature in Honor of Jacob Milgrom*, ed. David P. Wright, David Noel Freedman and Avi Hurvitz (Winona Lake, Ind.: Eisenbrauns, 1995), pp. 713-23; and Michael H. Floyd and Robert D. Haak, eds., *Prophets, Prophecy, and Prophetic Texts in Second Temple Judaism*, LBH/OTS 427 (New York: T & T Clark, 2006).

# Appendix

Although most Bibles format the text of Malachi as prose, NKJV and NAB are recent attempts to present the book as poetry. Petersen (1995) also presents a poetically-formatted translation accompanying his commentary. The problem with a poetic understanding of Malachi, however, is evident in the following list of contrasts between these three translations. In the first chapter of Malachi, there is not a single verse where there is agreement among these three as to how to versify the material, resulting in more than two dozen disagreements in thirteen verses. Half of these represent disagreement on the placement of direct discourse markers that identify speakers (Mal 1:2a, 2b, 4, 5, 6, 7, 8, 12, 13, 14). Although this is a common and debatable issue even within clearly poetic passages, the inconsistent treatment among the translations is troubling: (1) Petersen and NKJV present as a separate line what NAB does not (vv. 2b, 7, 8, 13, 14), (2) NKJV presents as a separate line what Petersen and NAB do not (vv. 4, 5, 12, 13), (3) Petersen presents as a separate line what NAB and NKJV do not (vv. 2a, 6). The remaining disagreements are even more troubling, when Petersen & NKJV present as a separate line what NAB does not (vv. 3, 9, 12), and when Petersen presents as a separate line what NAB and NKJV do not (vv. 10, 13). The considerable disagreement in versification in v. 6, 8, 14 underscores the lack of clarity that this is even poetry at all.

1:2a  "says the Lord." Petersen presents as a separate line; NAB and NKJV do not.

1:2b  "says the Lord." Petersen and NKJV present as a separate line; NAB does not.

1:3  "I hate Esau." Petersen and NKJV present as a separate line; NAB does not.

1:3  "His heritage/inheritance." NKJV connects with preceding line unlike Petersen and NAB.

1:4  "Even though Edom has said." NKJV presents as a separate line; Petersen and NAB do not.

1:5  "you will say." NKJV presents as a separate line; Petersen and NAB do not.

1:6  "hosts /A/ to you /B/ priests /C/ who despise my name." NKJV alone divides the line at A, Petersen alone divides the line at B, NAB alone divides the lines at C.

1:6  "You say." Petersen presents as a separate line; NAB and NKJV do not.

1:7  "You ask." Petersen and NKJV present as a separate line; NAB does not.

1:7  "by saying." Petersen and NKJV present as a separate line; NAB does not.

1:8  "governor /A/ would he be pleased with you /B/ would he accept you favorably." NAB alone makes no line break at A, Petersen alone makes no line break at B.

1:8  "says the Lord of hosts." Petersen and NKJV present as a separate line; NAB does not.

1:9  "that he may be gracious to us." Petersen and NKJV present as a separate line; NAB does not.

1:10  "who would shut the doors." Petersen presents as a separate line; NAB and NKJV do not.

1:10  "on my altar in vain." Petersen presents as a separate line; NAB and NKJV do not.

1:10  "from your hand." Petersen presents as a separate line; NAB and NKJV do not.

1:11 "incense/sacrifice offered to my name // and a pure offering" (NKJV and NAB); "incense and a pure offering // are presented to my name" (Petersen, which violates the Hebrew word order).

1:12 "in that you say." NKJV presents as a separate line; Petersen and NAB do not.

1:12 "its offering may be polluted." Petersen and NKJV present as a separate line; NAB does not.

1:13 "You also say." NKJV presents as a separate line; Petersen and NAB do not.

1:13 "says the Lord of Hosts." Petersen and NKJV present as a separate line; NAB does not.

1:13 "the lame and the diseased." Petersen presents as a separate line; NAB and NKJV do not.

1:14 "deceiver /A/ who has in his flock a male /B/ but under his vow /C/ sacrifices to the LORD what is blemished." NAB alone has no line break at A; Petersen alone has no break at B; NAB alone has no break at C.

# BIBLIOGRAPHY OF CITED WORKS

Ahlström, Gösta. *History of Ancient Palestine*. Minneapolis: Fortress, 1993.

Albertz, Rainer. *A History of Israelite Religion in the Old Testament Period. Volume One: From the Beginnings to the End of the Monarchy*. Louisville, Ky.: Westminster John Knox, 1994.

Alter, Robert. *The Art of Biblical Poetry*. New York: Basic Books, 1985.

Andersen, Francis I., and David Noel Freedman. *Micah*. New York: Doubleday, 2000.

Aucker, W. Brian. "A Prophet in King's Clothes: Kingly and Divine Re-Presentation in 2 Kings 4 and 5." pp. 1-25. In *Reflection and Refraction: Studies in Biblical Historiography in Honour of A. Graeme Auld*, edited by Robert Rezetko, Timothy H. Lim and W. Brian Aucker. VTS 113. Leiden: Brill, 2007.

Auld, Graeme, "Word of God and Word of Man: Prophets and Canon," pp. 237-51. In *Ascribe to the Lord: Biblical and Other Studies in Memory of Peter C. Craigie*, edited by Lyle Eslinger and Glen Taylor. JSOTSS 67. Sheffield, U.K.: JSOT Press, 1988.

Betz, Hans Dieter. *The Greek Magical Papyri in Translation*. 2nd ed. Chicago: University of Chicago Press, 1992.

Brown, Donald E. *Human Universals*. Philadelphia: Temple University, 1996.

Brueggemann, Walter. *Like Fire in the Bones: Listening for the Prophetic Word in Jeremiah*. Minneapolis: Fortress, 2006.

———. *Theology of the Old Testament: Testimony, Dispute, Advocacy*. Minneapolis: Fortress, 1997.

————. "Revelation and Violence: A Study in Contextualization," pp. 285-318. In *A Social Reading of the Old Testament: Prophetic Approaches to Israel's Communal Life,* edited by Patrick D. Miller. Minneapolis: Fortress, 1994.

Butterworth, Mike. *Structure and the Book of Zechariah.* JSOTSS 130. Sheffield, U.K.: Sheffield Academic, 1992.

Campbell, A. F. *Of Prophets and Kings: A Late Ninth-Century Document (1 Samuel 1—2 Kings 10).* CBQMS 17. Washington, D.C.: Catholic Biblical Association of America, 1986.

Charlesworth, James H., ed. *The Old Testament Pseudepigrapha.* 2 vols. Garden City, N.Y.: Doubleday, 1983-1985.

Chazan, Robert, William W. Hallo, and Lawrence H. Schiffman, eds. *Ki Baruch Hu: Ancient Near Eastern, Biblical, and Judaic Studies in Honor of Baruch A. Levine.* Winona Lake, Ind.: Eisenbrauns, 1999.

Christensen, Duane L. *Transformations of the War Oracle in Old Testament Prophecy.* Missoula, Mont.: Scholars, 1975.

Clampitt, Amy. "Robert Frost and the Better Half of Poetry," pp. 11-16. In *Written in Water, Written in Stone: Twenty Years of Poets on Poetry,* edited by Martin Lammon. Ann Arbor: University of Michigan Press, 1996.

Cogan, Mordechai, and Hayim Tadmor. *II Kings.* Garden City, N.Y.: Doubleday, 1988.

Collins, John J. "Response: The Apocalyptic Worldview of Daniel," pp. 59-66. In *Enoch and Qumran Origins: New Light on a Forgotten Connection,* edited by Gabriele Boccaccini. Grand Rapids: Eerdmans, 2005.

Coogan, Michael D. *The Old Testament: A Historical and Literary Introduction to the Hebrew Scriptures.* Oxford: Oxford University Press, 2005.

Coote, Robert B. "Yahweh Recalls Elijah," pp. 115-20. In *Traditions in Transformation,* edited by B. Halpern and J. Levenson. Winona Lake, Ind.: Eisenbrauns, 1981.

Crenshaw, James L. *Prophetic Conflict: Its Effect upon Israelite Religion.* BZAW 124. Berlin: de Gruyter, 1977.

Cross, Frank Moore, Jr. "Toward a History of Hebrew Prosody," pp. 298-309. In *Fortunate the Eyes That See: Essays in Honor of David Noel Freedman in Celebration of His Seventieth Birthday,* edited by Astrid B. Beck, Andrew H. Bartelt, Paul R. Raabe and Chris A. Franke. Grand Rapids: Eerdmans, 1995.

————. *Canaanite Myth and Hebrew Epic: Essays in the History of the Religion of Israel.* Cambridge, Mass.: Harvard University Press, 1973.

Cryer, Frederick H. *Divination in Ancient Israel and Its Near Eastern Environment: *A Socio-Historical Investigation.* JSOTSS 142. Sheffield, U.K.: Sheffield Academic, 1994.

Dalley, Stephanie. "Foreign Chariotry and Cavalry in the Armies of Tiglath-Pileser III and Sargon II." *Iraq* 47 (1985): 31-48.

Davis, Ellen F. *Swallowing the Scroll: Textuality and the Dynamics of Discourse in Ezekiel's Prophecy.* JSOTSS 78. Sheffield, U.K.: Almond, 1989.

Day, John. *God's Conflict with the Dragon and the Sea: Echoes of a Canaanite Myth in the Old Testament.* Cambridge: Cambridge University Press, 1985.

Duhm, B. *Das Buch Jesaia.* HKAT 3/1. Göttingen: Vandenhoek & Ruprecht, 1892 (5th ed. 1968).

Ehrensvärd, Martin. "An Unusual Use of the Definite Article in Biblical and Post-Biblical Hebrew," pp. 68-76. In *Sirach, Scrolls, and Sages: Proceedings of a Second International Symposium on the Hebrew of the Dead Sea Scrolls, Ben Sira, and the Mishnah, held at Leiden University, 15-17 December 1977,* edited by T. Muraoka and J. F. Elwolde. STDJ 33. Leiden: Brill, 1999.

Erman, Adolph. *The Ancient Egyptians.* New York: Harper and Row, 1966.

Floyd, Michael H., and Robert D. Haak, eds. *Prophets, Prophecy, and Prophetic Texts in Second Temple Judaism.* LBH/OTS 427. New York: T & T Clark, 2006.

Freedman, David Noel, and Andrew Welch. "Amos's Earthquake and Israelite Prophecy," pp. 188-98. In *Scripture and Other Artifacts. Essays on the Bible and Archaeology in Honor of Philip J. King,* edited by Michael D. Coogan, J. Cheryl Exum and Lawrence E. Stager. Louisville, Ky.: Westminster John Knox, 1994.

Fretheim, Terence E. *The Suffering God: An Old Testament Perspective.* Philadelphia: Fortress, 1984.

Geller, Stephen A. "Were the Prophets Poets?" *Prooftexts* 3 (1983): 211-21.

Gordon, Robert P., ed. *"The Place Is Too Small for Us": The Israelite Prophets in Recent Scholarship.* Sources for Biblical and Theological Study 5. Winona Lake, Ind.: Eisenbrauns, 1995.

Gowan, Donald E. *Theology of the Prophetic Books: The Death and Resurrection of Israel.* Louisville, Ky.: Westminster John Knox, 1998.

Grabbe, Lester L. *Priests, Prophets, Diviners, Sages: A Socio-Historical Study of Religious Specialists in Ancient Israel.* Valley Forge, Penn.: Trinity Press International, 1995.

Greenberg, Moshe. "On Ezekiel's Dumbness." *JBL* 77 (1958): 101-5.

Gressman, Hugo. *Der Messias.* Göttingen: Vandenhoeck & Ruprecht, 1929.

Hare, D. R. A. "The Lives of the Prophets," pp. 379-99. In *The Old Testament Pseudepigrapha*. Vol. 2. Edited by James Charlesworth. Garden City, N.Y.: Doubleday, 1985.

Harris, J. Rendel. *The Rest of the Words of Baruch: A Christian Apocalypse of the Year 136 A.D.* London: C. J. Clay & Sons, 1889.

Hartman, Louis, and Alexander A. Di Lella. *The Book of Daniel*. Garden City, N.Y.: Doubleday, 1978.

Heschel, Abraham J. *The Prophets, Part II*. New York: Harper & Row, 1962.

Hiebert, Theodore. *The God of My Victory: The Ancient Hymn in Habakkuk 3*. Harvard Semitic Monographs 38. Atlanta: Scholars, 1986.

Hilber, John W. *Cultic Prophecy in the Psalms*. BZAW 352. Berlin: de Gruyter, 2005.

Hill, Andrew E. *Malachi*. New York: Doubleday, 1998.

Huffmon, Herbert. "Jeremiah of Anathoth: A Prophet for All Israel," pp. 261-72. In *Ki Baruch Hu: Ancient Near Eastern, Biblical, and Judaic Studies in Honor of Baruch A. Levine*, edited by Robert Chazan, William W. Hallo and Lawrence H. Schiffman. Winona Lake, Ind.: Eisenbrauns, 1999.

Hunger, Herman. *Astrological Reports to Assyrian Kings*. SAA 8. Helsinki: Helsinki University Press, 1992.

Husser, Jean-Marie. *Dreams and Dream Narratives in the Biblical World*. Biblical Seminar 63. Sheffield, U.K.: Sheffield Academic, 1999.

Japhet, Sara. *I & II Chronicles*. Louisville, Ky.: Westminster John Knox, 1993.

Johnson, Sarah. "Rising to the Occasion: Theurgic Ascent in its Cultural Milieu," pp. 165-195. In *Envisioning Magic: A Princeton Seminar and Symposium*, edited by Peter Schäfer and Hans G. Kippenberg. Studies in the History of Religions 75. Leiden: Brill, 1997.

Jong, Matthijs J. de. *Isaiah Among the Ancient Near Eastern Prophets: A Comparative Study of the Earliest Stages of the Isaiah Tradition and the Neo-Assyrian Prophecies*. VTS 117. Leiden: Brill, 2007.

Joyce, Paul. *Divine Initiative and Human Response in Ezekiel*. JSOTSS 51. Sheffield, U.K.: JSOT, 1989.

Kang, Sa-Moon. *Divine War in the Old Testament and in the Ancient Near East*. BZAW 177. Berlin: de Gruyter, 1989.

Kessler, John. "Haggai, Zerubbabel, and the Political Status of Yehud: the Signet Ring in Haggai 2:23," pp. 102-19. In *Prophets, Prophecy, and Prophetic Texts in Second Temple Judaism*, edited by Michael H. Floyd and Robert D. Haak. LBH/OTS 427. New York: T & T Clark, 2006.

Kingsbury, Edwin C. "The Prophets and the Council of Yahweh." *JBL* 83 (1964): 279-86.

Klingbeil, Martin. *Yahweh Fighting from Heaven: God As Warrior and As God of Heaven in the Hebrew Psalter and Ancient Near Eastern Iconography.* OBO 169. Göttingen: Vandenhoeck & Ruprecht, 1999.

Knibb, M. A. "Martyrdom and Ascension of Isaiah," pp. 143-76. In *The Old Testament Pseudepigrapha.* Vol. 2. Edited by James Charlesworth. Garden City, N.Y.: Doubleday, 1985.

Koch, Klaus. "Is Daniel Also Among the Prophets?" pp. 237-248. In *Interpreting the Prophets,* edited by James Luther Mays and Paul J. Achtemeier. Philadelphia: Fortress, 1987.

Kugel, James. *The Idea of Biblical Poetry: Parallelism and Its History.* New Haven, Conn.: Yale University Press, 1981.

———. "David the Prophet," pp. 45-55. In *Pottery and Prophecy: The Beginnings of a Literary Tradition,* edited by James Kugel. Ithaca, N.Y.: Cornell University Press, 1990.

Lammon, Martin, ed. *Written in Water, Written in Stone: Twenty Years of Poets on Poetry.* Ann Arbor: University of Michigan Press, 1996.

Lange, Armin. "Literary Prophecy and Oracle Collection: A Comparison Between Judah and Greece in Persian Times," pp. 248-75. In *Prophets, Prophecy, and Prophetic Texts in Second Temple Judaism,* edited by Michael H. Floyd and Robert D. Haak. LBH/OTS 427. New York: T & T Clark, 2006.

Lehman, David. "Notes on Poetic Form," pp. 46-49. In *Written in Water, Written in Stone: Twenty Years of Poets on Poetry,* edited by Martin Lammon. Ann Arbor: University of Michigan Press, 1996.

Lind, Millard C. *Ezekiel.* Scottdale, Penn.: Herald, 1996.

Loewenstamm, Samuel E. "The Trembling of Nature during the Theophany," pp. 173-89. In *Comparative Studies in Biblical and Ancient Oriental Literatures.* AOAT 204. Neukirchen-Vluyn: Neukirchener Verlag, 1980.

Longman, Tremper, III, and Daniel G. Reid. *God Is a Warrior: Studies in Old Testament Biblical Theology.* Grand Rapids: Zondervan, 1995.

Lowth, Robert. *Lectures on the Sacred Poetry of the Hebrews.* Vol. 2. Translated by G. Gregory. London: 1787 [Georg Olms reprint, 1969].

Mays, James Luther. *Amos.* OTL. Philadelphia: Westminster Press, 1969.

Meier, Sam. "The Sword from Saul to David," pp. 156-74. In *Saul in Story and Tradition,* edited by Carl S. Ehrlich. FAT 47. Tübingen: Mohr Siebeck, 2006.

————. "Angel of Yahweh," pp. 53-59. In *Dictionary of Deities and Demons in the Bible*, edited by Karel van der Toorn, Bob Becking and Pieter W. van der Horst. 2nd ed. Leiden: Brill, 1999.

————. *Speaking of Speaking: Marking Direct Discourse in the Hebrew Bible*. VTS 46; Leiden: Brill, 1992.

————. "The King as Warrior in Samuel-Kings." *Hebrew Annual Review* 13 (1991): 63-76.

Meyers, Eric M. "The Crisis of the Mid-Fifth Century B.C.E. Second Zechariah and the 'End' of Prophecy," pp. 713-23. In *Pomegranates and Golden Bells. Studies in Biblical, Jewish, and Near Eastern Ritual, Law, and Literature in Honor of Jacob Milgrom*, edited by David P. Wright, David Noel Freedman and Avi Hurvitz. Winona Lake, Ind.: Eisenbrauns, 1995.

Meyers, Carol L., and Eric M. Meyers. *Zechariah 9-14*. Garden City, N.Y.: Doubleday, 1993.

Middlemas, Jill. *The Templeless Age: An Introduction to the History, Literature, and Theology of the "Exile."* Louisville, Ky.: Westminster John Knox, 2007.

Milavec, Aaron. "Distinguishing True and False Prophets." *Journal of Early Christian Studies* 2 (1994): 117-36.

Miller, Patrick D., Jr. *The Divine Warrior in Early Israel*. Cambridge, Mass.: Harvard University Press, 1973.

Montgomery, James. *A Critical and Exegetical Commentary on the Book of Kings*. ICC. Edinburgh: T & T Clark, 1951.

Motyer, J. Alec. *The Prophecy of Isaiah: An Introduction and Commentary*. Downers Grove, Ill.: InterVarsity Press, 1993.

Mowinckel, Sigmund. "The 'Spirit' and the 'Word' in the Pre-exilic Reforming Prophets." *JBL* 53 (1934): 199-227.

Mullen, E. Theodore. *The Assembly of the Gods: The Divine Council in Canaanite and Early Hebrew Literature*. Chico, Calif.: Scholars, 1980.

Müller, Karl F. *Das Assyrische Ritual*. MVAG 41.3. Leipzig: J. C. Hinrichs, 1937.

Mursil, Alois. *The Manners and Customs of the Rwala Bedouins*. Oriental Explorations and Studies 6. New York: American Geographical Society, 1928.

Naveh, Joseph. "Epigraphic Miscellanea." *Israel Exploration Journal* 52 (2002): 240-52.

Nissinen, Martti. "The Dubious Image of Prophecy," pp. 26-41. In *Prophets, Prophecy, and Prophetic Texts in Second Temple Judaism*, edited by Michael H. Floyd and Robert D. Haak. LBH/OTS 427. New York:T & T Clark, 2006.

Nock, Albert Jay. "Isaiah's Job," pp. 248-65. In *Free Speech and Plain Language*. New York: William Morrow, 1937.

Nogalski, James D. "The Day(s) of YHWH in the Book of the Twelve," pp. 617-42. In *SBL Seminar Papers 1999*. Atlanta: Society of Biblical Literature, 1999.

O'Brien, D. P. "'Is This the Time to Accept . . . ?' (2 Kings V 26b): Simply Moralizing (LXX) or an Ominous Foreboding of Yahweh's Rejection of Israel (MT)?" *VT* 46 (1996): 448-57.

Orlinsky, Harry M. *Ancient Israel*. 2nd ed. Ithaca, N.Y.: Cornell University Press, 1960.

Pardee, Dennis. "A New Ugaritic Letter." *Bibliotheca Orientalis* 34 (1977): 3-20.

Parke-Taylor, Geoffrey H. *Formation of the Book of Jeremiah: Doublets and Recurring Phrases*. SBLMS 51. Atlanta: Society of Biblical Literature, 2000.

Parpola, Simo. *Letters from Assyrian Scholars to the Kings Esarhaddon and Ashurbanipal*. 2 vols. AOAT 5/1-2. Neukirchen: Neukirchener-Vluyn, 1970-1983.

Parunak, H. Van Dyke. "Some Discourse Functions of Prophetic Quotation Formulas in Jeremiah," pp. 489-519. In *Biblical Hebrew and Discourse Linguistics*, edited by Robert D. Bergen. Winona Lake, Ind.: Eisenbrauns, 1994.

Paul, Shalom. *Amos*. Philadelphia: Fortress, 1991.

Petersen, David. *Zechariah 9–14 and Malachi*. Louisville, Ky.: Westminster John Knox, 1995.

Pinnock, Clark H. *Most Moved Mover*. Grand Rapids: Baker Academic, 2001.

Pratt, Richard L., Jr. "Historical Contingencies and Biblical Predictions," pp. 180-203. In *The Way of Wisdom: Essays in Honor of Bruce K. Waltke*, edited by J. I. Packer and Sven K. Soderlund. Grand Rapids: Zondervan, 2000.

Preuss, Horst Dietrich. *Old Testament Theology*. Vol. 2. Translated by Leo G. Perdue. Edinburgh: T & T Clark, 1992.

Rad, Gerhard von. "The Deuteronomic Theology of History in 1 and 2 Kings," pp. 154-66. In *From Genesis to Chronicles: Explorations in Old Testament Theology*, edited by K. C. Hanson. Fortress: Minneapolis, 2005.

Rendtorff, Rolf. "The Book of Isaiah—A Complex Unity: Synchronic and Diachronic Reading," pp. 109-28. In *Prophecy and Prophets: The Diversity of Contemporary Issues in Scholarship*, edited by Yehoshua Gitay. SBL Semeia Studies. Atlanta: Scholars, 1997.

Ricoeur, Paul. *Figuring the Sacred: Religion, Narrative, and Imagination*. Minneapolis: Fortress, 1995.

Roberts, J. J. M. "Prophets and Kings: A New Look at the Royal Persecution of

Prophets Against Its Near Eastern Background," pp. 341-54. In *A God So Near: Essays on Old Testament Theology in Honor of Patrick D. Miller,* edited by Brent A. Strawn and Nancy R. Bowen. Winona Lake, Ind.: Eisenbrauns, 2003.

Rofé, Alexander. *The Prophetical Stories: The Narratives About the Prophets in the Hebrew Bible, Their Literary Types, and History.* Jerusalem: Magnes, 1988.

———. *Israelite Belief in Angels in the Pre-Exilic Period as Evidenced by Biblical Traditions.* Ph.D. Dissertation, Hebrew University in Jerusalem, 1969.

———. *Introduction to Prophetic Literature,* translated by Judith H. Seeligmann. The Biblical Seminar 21. Sheffield, U.K.: Sheffield Academic, 1997.

Rowland, Christopher C. *The Open Heaven: A Study of Apocalyptic in Judaism and Early Christianity.* New York: Crossroad, 1982.

Rowley, H. H. "The Nature of Prophecy in the Light of Recent Study." *HTR* 38 (1945): 1-38.

Russell, D. S. *The Method and Message of Jewish Apocalyptic.* Philadelphia: Westminster Press, 1964.

Russell, Jeffrey Burton. *A History of Heaven: The Singing Silence.* Princeton, N.J.: Princeton University Press, 1997.

Sasson, Jack M. *Jonah.* AB. New York: Doubleday, 1990.

Savran, George W. *Encountering the Divine: Theophany in Biblical Narrative.* JSOTSS 420. London: T & T Clark, 2005.

Schaper, Joachim. "The Death of the Prophet: The Transition from the Spoken to the Written Word of God in the Book of Ezekiel," pp. 63-79. In *Prophets, Prophecy, and Prophetic Texts in Second Temple Judaism,* edited by Michael H. Floyd and Robert D. Haak. LBH/OTS 427. New York: T & T Clark, 2006.

Schniedewind, William M. *The Word of God in Transition: From Prophet to Exegete in the Second Temple Period.* JSOTSS 197. Sheffield, U.K.: Sheffield Academic, 1995.

Scholem, Gershom G. *Major Trends in Jewish Mysticism.* New York: Schocken, 1946.

Scott, R. B. Y. *The Relevance of the Prophets.* New York: Macmillan, 1944.

Siegman, Edward F. *The False Prophets of the Old Testament.* Washington, D.C.: Catholic University of America, 1939.

Stern, Ephraim. *Archaeology of the Land of the Bible: The Assyrian, Babylonian, and Persian Periods (732-332 B.C.E.).* New York: Doubleday, 2001.

Taylor, Joan. *The Immerser: John the Baptist within Second Temple Judaism.* Grand Rapids: Eerdmans, 1997.

Tov, Emanuel. *Textual Criticism of the Hebrew Bible.* 2nd ed. Minneapolis: Fortress, 2001.

Van Rooy, Harry V. "Prophet and Society in the Persian Period According to Chronicles," pp. 163-79. In *Second Temple Studies. 2. Temple and Community in the Persian Period,* edited by Tamara C. Eskenazi and Kent H. Richards. JSOTSS 175; Sheffield: JSOT, 1994.

Vawter, Bruce. "Were the Prophets *nābî's?*" *Biblica* 66 (1985): 206-20.

Ward, James M. *Thus Says the Lord: The Message of the Prophets.* Nashville: Abingdon, 1991.

Watson, Wilfred G. E. *Classical Hebrew Poetry: A Guide to Its Techniques.* Sheffield, U.K.: JSOT, 1984.

Wehrle, Josef. *Prophetie und Textanalyse—Die Komposition Obadja 1-21 interpretiert auf der Basis textlinguistischer und semiotischer Konzeptionen.* Arbeiten zu Text und Sprache im Alten Testament 28. St. Ottilien: Eos, 1987.

Williamson, H. G. M. "Hezekiah and the Temple," pp. 47-52. In *Texts, Temples, and Traditions: A Tribute to Menahem Haran,* edited by Michael V. Fox, Victor Avigdor Hurowitz, Avi Hurvitz, Michael L. Klein, Baruch J. Schwartz and Nili Shupak. Winona Lake, Ind.: Eisenbrauns, 1996.

Wilson, Robert R. *Prophecy and Society in Ancient Israel.* Philadelphia: Fortress, 1980.

————. "Interpreting Israel's Religion: An Anthropological Perspective on the Problem of False Prophecy," pp. 333-44. In *"The Place is Too Small for Us": The Israelite Prophets in Recent Scholarship,* edited by Robert P. Gordon. Sources for Biblical and Theological Study 5. Winona Lake, Ind.: Eisenbrauns, 1995.

————. "Poetry and Prose in the Book of Jeremiah," pp. 413-28. In *Ki Baruch Hu: Ancient Near Eastern, Biblical, and Judaic Studies in Honor of Baruch A. Levine,* edited by Robert Chazan, William W. Hallo and Lawrence H. Schiffman. Winona Lake, Ind.: Eisenbrauns, 1999.

Wolff, Hans Walter. *Joel and Amos.* Philadelphia: Fortress, 1977.

Wright, Charles. "Improvisations on Form and Measure," pp. 27-29. In *Written in Water, Written in Stone: Twenty Years of Poets on Poetry,* edited by Martin Lammon. Ann Arbor: University of Michigan Press, 1996.

Zimmerli, Walther. *Ezekiel I,* translated by Ronald E. Clements. Philadelphia: Fortress, 1979.

Zwettler, Michael. *The Oral Tradition of Classical Arabic Poetry: Its Character and Implications.* Columbus: Ohio State University Press, 1978.

# Author Index